WINNIPEG MODERN
ARCHITECTURE 1945–1975

EDITOR **SERENA KESHAVJEE**

DESIGN **HERBERT ENNS**

Churchill Secondary School (1955)
Moody, Moore, and Partners
D. Wookey principal design
Photograph: Henry Kalen (c. 1961)
285D2.1-2

UNIVERSITY OF MANITOBA PRESS

WINNIPEG MODERN
ARCHITECTURE 1945–1975

© The Authors, 2006

University of Manitoba Press
Winnipeg, Manitoba R3T 2N2 Canada
www.umanitoba.ca/uofmpress
Printed in Canada on acid-free paper by Friesens.

Book and cover design: Herbert Enns, OS 1 Design Inc.

Front Cover: Winnipeg International Airport (1964)
Green, Blankstein, Russell, and Associates
Bernard Brown and David Thordarson principal design
Photograph: Henry Kalen (1964)
217K3.2–57

Back Cover: Donahue Residence (1955)
Hosmer Boulevard
James Donahue principal design
Photograph: Henry Kalen (1961)
222 B1-16

Inside Cover Flaps: Photographs from series A25183-A25185,
1979, courtesy Province of
Manitoba Conservation

Library and Archives Canada Cataloguing in Publication

Winnipeg modern : architecture, 1945-1975 / edited by Serena Keshavjee.

Includes bibliographical references.
ISBN 0-88755-181-5 (bound).--ISBN 0-88755-691-4 (pbk.)

1. Architecture--Manitoba--Winnipeg--History--20th century.
I. Keshavjee, Serena, 1961-

NA747.W5W46 2006   720'.9712743
C2006-903350-1

Publication of this book has been made possible by the generous support provided by Allan Waisman and by the Promotion of Architecture Program of the Canada Council for the Arts.

Support for this book has also been provided by Stantec Architecture/GBR Architects; Smith Carter Architects and Engineers Incorporated; LM Architectural Group; MMP Architects, Incorporated; Number Ten Architectural Group; EQ3; KGS Group; Faculty of Architecture, University of Manitoba; Manitoba Hydro; Gerald A. Libling; and Mel P. Michener.

The University of Manitoba Press gratefully acknowledges the financial support for its publication program provided by the Government of Canada through the Book Publishing Industry Development Program (BPIDP); the Canada Council for the Arts; the Manitoba Arts Council; and the Manitoba Department of Culture, Heritage and Tourism.

This book is dedicated to my parents Fatehalli and Lucy Keshavjee,
and to the memory of Henry Kalen (1928–2004)

Permissions

We are grateful to the following people, organizations, and institutions for permission to reproduce images in this book.

We have reproduced material with permission from the collections of Gloria Kalen, Gustavo da Roza II, Stantec Architecture/GBR, Allan Waisman, Glenn Tinley, Gerald Macdonald, Ernest Mayer, Neil Minuk, Étienne Gaboury, James Christie, Oliver Botar, Herbert Enns, and the Province of Manitoba.

We have reproduced or adapted material with permission from: Archigram Archives (Shelley Power Literary Agency, Ltd.); *Étienne Gaboury* (Les Editions du Blé, Winnipeg); *Seed Catalogue* (Robert Kroetsch and Turnstone Press, Winnipeg); *Journal, Royal Architectural Institute of Canada; Architectural Design; Canadian Architect*; National Gallery of Art, Washington, DC, Gallery Archives; National Gallery of Canada; Winnipeg Art Gallery; National Archives of Canada, Canadian Architectural Archives, Panda Fonds; Archives of Manitoba; Province of Manitoba Conservation; Provincial Archives of Alberta; University of Winnipeg Archives; University of Winnipeg Library; University of Manitoba, Department of Archives & Special Collections, Winnipeg Tribune Collection (all images by Henry Kalen, unless otherwise attributed, are from the University of Manitoba, Department of Archives & Special Collections, Henry Kalen Collection); University of Manitoba, Architecture and Fine Arts Library; City of Winnipeg Archives and Records Control; Western Aviation Museum. All images are copyright, and may not be reproduced without permission.

CONTENTS

Acknowledgements

When I moved from Toronto to Winnipeg during the summer of 1996, I was prepared for the splendour of the Exchange district, which was to be declared a National Historic Site by Sheila Copps soon after I arrived. I was not expecting to find, however, the fine stock of Mid-Century Modernist buildings throughout the city. I grew up in Don Mills, the paradigmatic, planned North American Modernist neighbourhood, a suburban-style Garden City, with local parks, schools, and shops. Don Mills is well known for its Modernist buildings and gets lots of attention for it. No one ever mentions Winnipeg Modernism.

The idea for an anthology on Winnipeg Modern architecture came together when Phyllis Lambert, Director for the Canadian Centre for Architecture, heard my boasting about Winnipeg's Modern buildings and suggested I give her a tour on her next visit to Winnipeg (summer 2002). I asked Herbert Enns, professor at the Faculty of Architecture at the University of Manitoba, for help and he created a pamphlet representing some of the key Winnipeg Modernist structures, which became the basis of our related projects of an exhibition at the Winnipeg Art Gallery (WAG) and this book. Patricia Bovey and Donna McAlear, then respectively Director and Chief Curator at the Winnipeg Art Gallery, accepted my proposal for an exhibition in 2002. Curators Mary Jo Hughes and Helen Delacretaz at the WAG took on the project management during the long duration of the research. When Pierre Arpin was appointed Director of the WAG in 2005, he enthusiastically assisted with both the exhibition and the book. As the ideas for the book got bigger and loftier, David Carr, Director of University of Manitoba Press, stepped in to publish it. This anthology and the exhibition at the Winnipeg Art Gallery (August 2006) would not have happened without the support and help of these people at the initial stages.

I was able to research in the most important Canadian archives for architecture, the Canadian Centre for Architecture, the Canadian Architectural Archives, and the National Archives of Canada, but the most fertile ground was, of course, in Winnipeg. I was aided in my searches at the City of Winnipeg Archives and Records Control by Jody Baltessen, Senior Archivist, and Martin Comeau, Archivist. I was helped at the Archives of Manitoba by Christopher Kotecki, Reference Services Assistant, and at the University of Winnipeg Archives by Peter James, University Archivist. Krista Macdonald of Transportation and Government Services spent days digging up plans of provincially owned buildings. Mary Lochhead and Liv Valmestad of the Architecture and Fine Arts Library at the University of Manitoba were always gracious with their time. Librarian Kenlyn Collins from the WAG Archive must also be mentioned for her guidance. Shelley Bruce, Historical Buildings Officer, and John McNairnay, both of the Planning, Property and Development Department of the City of Winnipeg, introduced me to the Winnipeg Architecture Foundation Files and other treasures in that office. Shelley Sweeney, Head of Archives & Special Collections at the University of Manitoba, offered her support throughout the duration of the project, but especially when the Henry Kalen Archives moved from Gloria Kalen's house to the University of Manitoba in late 2005. Brian Hubner, Acting Head of the Special Collections during Sweeney's sabbatical, continued the work. Henry documented almost every important mid-century Modern building in the city, and it saddens me that he is not here to see the project to its fruition.

My research assistant at the University of Winnipeg, Aldona Dziedziejko, helped to gather accurate information regarding the illustrations included in this book. Dziedziejko also undertook the task of preparing biographies on the Winnipeg Modernist architects who were active during the mid-century. I thank Aldona for her great research skills, she has aided me in all aspects of the book. I am grateful to the University of Winnipeg Work Study Project and the Undergraduate Student Research Award in the Human Sciences for supporting her research over a period of three years. Another student from the University of Winnipeg, Jenny Western, now curator at the Art Gallery of Southwestern Manitoba, worked on the bibliography, which is the most extensive on Winnipeg Modernism to date. I thank the WAG for funding Western's work.

Some of the most active players in this project were the architects themselves, who gave of their time, their knowledge, and their archives. I thank Morley Blankstein, Bernard Brown, Gae Burns, James Christie, Étienne Gaboury, Douglas Gillmor, Gerald Macdonald, Lewis Morse, Mel Michener, Leslie Stechesen, and Allan Waisman for answering all my questions. I would also like to thank Neil Minuk for sharing his knowledge on James Donahue. Others who helped along the way include: Teyte Cottingham (National Film Board), Cynthia Coop, Gustavo da Roza, Linda Fraser (CAA), Alison Gillmor, Allan Hanna, Doug Hanna, Joan Harland, Grant Marshall, Gord McGarva, Lloyd and Marcia Sector, Kenneth Snider, Mavis Reimer. Bob Talbot and Ernest Mayer scanned images for the book. The Web site of John Martins-Manteiga, Director of Dominion Modern and Urbanism, documenting some of Winnipeg's Modern structures, was well used by my students. A special mention must be made of all the first-year students in the Environmental Design program at the Faculty of Architecture, who took the introductory architecture history course with me between 1999 and 2001, for their inspiring essays and photographs on Winnipeg Modern architecture.

This publication has been generously supported by two Canada Council Grants, the Assistance to Practitioners, Critics and Curators of Architecture Grant and the Assistance to the Promotion of Architecture Program. I thank Brigitte Desrochers, Architecture Officer, for directing me to these grants. It is a nice coincidence that John A. Russell, the Dean of the School of Architecture at the University of Manitoba (1946–1966) when many of these Modernist structures were being designed, was one of the founding members of the Canada Council in 1957. Allan Waisman was magnanimous in his contribution to the book. The funding raised by the WAG, led by the efforts of Herbert Enns, Cathy Collins, and during the final months, Vicki Klassen, was shared between the two institutions in a most cooperative manner. I thank Allan Waisman of Architectura, Smith Carter Architects, Stantec Architecture/Green Blankstein Russell Associates Architects Engineers, EQ3, Mel Michener, Gerald A. Libling, and KGS Group for their contributions to the exhibition and the book.

At the University of Manitoba Press, I was well supported by David Carr and Patricia Sanders, whose attention to detail was very much appreciated. Enns's design of both the book and the exhibition has made fundamental contributions to its intellectual content as well. Invaluable for me during this process were the advice and help of my partner Oliver Botar. Oliver not only read the essays, but has been a central part of this project since we drove into Winnipeg in 1996. My parents, Fred and Lucy, and my sons, Nadir and Devin, inspired me to keep up my motivation.

—Serena Keshavjee

I distinctly remember the colours, smells and light of the Modernist Princess Margaret Elementary School I attended in Winnipeg, with its shiny waxed corridor floors, glass block infill walls, and ultra-thin entrance canopies cantilevered above pipe columns. Across the playing fields on Rothesay Street, a modest Modernist shopping mall dispensed pharmaceuticals, travel advice, and groceries from behind slick and minimal aluminum and glass walls. I remember our strange 1959 Chevrolet Biscayne—a black beauty if there ever was one—looming large in our family's driveway: a stylish and spacious two-door sedan with wings. Playing basketball in high school included summer training camps at the University of Winnipeg. I remember carrying well-worn Chuck Taylor Converse sneakers in my gym bag as I ascended the escalators to the upper reaches of the super-graphic-lined Centennial Hall for the first time. Raised on CCM bicycles, *Hockey Night in Canada*, and the Guess Who—and the grandson of a suburban house builder and developer—I emerged from a subliminal Modernist cocoon on a steel-framed mezzanine high above the gymnasium inspired to study architecture.

At the University of Manitoba Faculty of Architecture I was taught by a cadre of gifted professors. I am indebted to professors Peter Forster, Carl Nelson, and Rory Fonseca. Their inspiring revelations of the cultural forces that shaped Modernist ideals have inspired my design of the publication and exhibition.

Upon my appointment as Head of the graduate Department of Architecture at the University of Manitoba in 1992, I was encouraged to explore the prospects for a Winnipeg Modernist Architecture retrospective by Diarmuid Nash, partner in the firm Moryiama Teshima Architects in Toronto, and Unversity of Manitoba alumnus. In March of 2001, I lectured for Dr. Keshavjee at the University of Winnipeg on Charles and Ray Eames, and a year later, we formalized plans for an exhibition and publication on Winnipeg's Modernist architecture.

David Carr of the University of Manitoba Press expertly managed the publication, Pat Sanders completed the exquisite text editing, and Cheryl Miki organized the publication's marketing and distribution. The high-quality image scans are by Friesens; The Lab Works; Ernest Mayer at the Winnipeg Art Gallery; Ken Borton; Brad Russell; and Bob Talbot at the University of Manitoba. The high quality of the press tests and printing set-up is a tribute to the expertise of Brad Schmidt and Donovan Bergman of Friesens. The typographic designer and professor David Cabianca gave me practical advice about modern fonts and their usage, and Daniel Melendez assisted with the titles and the exhibition text.

I am grateful to Jocelyn and David Laurence, children of Jean Margaret Laurence, for their enthusiastic permission to 'unravel' "North Main Car—Winnipeg" (1948), from the estate of Margaret Laurence, for presentation in the exhibition. The poem can be found in *The Winnipeg Connection: Writing Lives at Mid-Century*, Prairie Fire Press, Winnipeg. Robert Kroetsch and Turnstone Press generously gave permission to publish an excerpt from his *Seed Catalogue*.

Gloria Kalen deserves special acknowledgement for allowing Dr. Keshavjee and me to complete a detailed image-by-image search through Henry Kalen's vast archive of exceptional negatives and contact prints over many visits. Professor Grant Marshall and Professor Peter Forster accompanied me on the key initial architectural tours of Winnipeg. Professor Marshall also assisted me in colour selection for the exhibition and gave me many insights into the interior design history of the period.

The University of Manitoba Archives & Special Collections; the University of Manitoba Architecture and Fine Arts Library (and its Director, Mary Lochhead); the Faculty of Architecture Archives; the Archives of Manitoba; the Hudson's Bay Company Archives; the James Richardson Family Archives; and my good friend Louise Sloane, Reference Librarian at the Legislative Library, made contributions of inestimable value to my research.

For the exhibition at the Winnipeg Art Gallery, directors Patricia Bovey and Pierre Arpin supported the project from its inception through completion. Helen Delacretaz, Cathy Collins, Mary Jo Hughes, and Vicki Klassen provided excellent logistical and management support. The prep team of Carey Archibald, Steve Colley, Dan Dell'Agnese, Head of Museum Services Jasmina Jovanovic-Vlaovic, and Joy Stewart in Matting and Framing provided enthusiastic and inventive technical assistance.

Our high ambitions were enthusiastically supported by Brigitte Desrochers, the energetic and visionary Architecture Officer for the Canada Council, and I am exceedingly grateful for the Council's generous financial support. I would like to extend a personal note of appreciation to Peter Tielmann (EQ3); Scott Stirton and Alan Coppinger (Smith Carter Architects); Verne Reimer, John Petersmeyer, and Richard Derksen (Stantec Architecture Inc., formerly Green, Blankstein, Russell, and Associates); Allan Waisman (Waisman Architecture & Planning/Architectura); Terry Cristall (Number Ten Architectural Group); Judy Pestrak (Executive Director, Manitoba Association of Architects); and Dr. David Witty (Dean of the University of Manitoba Faculty of Architecture).

 Nancy LeBlond, daughter of John A. Russell, and her husband, Ted LeBlond, Principal at Stantec Architecture, generously shared their personal archival information and recollections.

My family has patiently persevered through this project's long gestation period with good humour. Jamie Enns, Sara Wray Enns, and Maem Slater-Enns have contributed great moral support.

I would like to convey—to the extent possible in text—my sincere appreciation to Dr. Serena Keshavjee, who contributed her vast energy, her great powers of concentration, and her extraordinary research skills to the project. She was able to manage the quite unexpected deluge of information, coordinate the contributions of authors, write an intense article on Centennial Hall, and gather up the loose ends of the project in her extensive, over-arching introduction. Her gifts of research, documentation, and intelligent criticism have given the publication a strong sense of intellectual coherence.

I have tried to invoke a sense of spatial and material depth in my design, applying principles of proportion, colour, spatial arrangement, and material selection normally associated with a work of architecture to this publication: the book has been designed like a building.

—Herbert Enns

WINNIPEG MODERN
ARCHITECTURE 1945–1975

INTRODUCTION

MODIFIED MODERNISM

Serena Keshavjee

Winnipeg's late nineteenth- and early twentieth-century economic boom, among other contributions, established a high standard for architecture in the city for the rest of the century. The quality of the bank architecture on Main Street alone demonstrates Winnipeg's prosperity during this period. (fig. 1.1, 1.2) However, Winnipeg's rich architectural legacy does not stop with heritage buildings in the Exchange district. Indeed, Winnipeg has been rightly seen as a kind of crucible of Canadian Modernist architecture. Under the leadership of John A. Russell (1946 to 1966), the School of Architecture of the University of Manitoba graduated some of the most important representatives of Canadian Modernism, such as John C. Parkin, Harry Seidler, and Douglas C. Simpson. Some graduates went on to important careers elsewhere, but others remained in Winnipeg, producing one of the richest stocks of Modernist architecture in Canada, a legacy of International Style buildings modified to suit Manitoba's regional demands. Other than Toronto, Vancouver, and Montreal, Winnipeg maintains more high-quality Modern buildings than any other Canadian city. Despite the relative lack of redevelopment pressure in Winnipeg, one cannot be complacent about these buildings. Most people are not aware that we are in the midst of a crisis of historical preservation. While heritage societies still put nearly all their efforts into protecting late nineteenth- and early twentieth-century buildings, in fact, it is Modernist and proto-Modernist structures that are the most endangered.[1] (fig. 1.3, 1.4, 1.5, 1.6) This anthology intends to draw attention to Winnipeg's outstanding Modernist buildings designed between 1945 and 1975, and is published to coincide with an exhibition held at the Winnipeg Art Gallery in 2006.

fig. 1.9
Royal Bank Building (1965)
Smith, Carter, Searle, and Associates
Valdis Alers principal design
Photograph: Henry Kalen (1965)
669F1 series

fig. 1.1
Main Street
South from Portage Avenue
Winnipeg Streets (1938)
Archives of Manitoba

fig. 1.2
"A Holiday on Main Street"
North from Portage Avenue
Winnipeg Streets, Main (c. 1910)
Archives of Manitoba N10923

fig. 1.3
Canadian Red Cross Building
(with redevelopment sign, 2004)
Moody, Moore, and Partners
Photograph: Ernest Mayer (2004)

fig. 1.4
Stevens and Sons Ltd.
(destroyed)
Photograph: Henry Kalen (1961)
269U3–8

fig. 1.5
Polo Park Shopping Centre (1959)
From *Winnipeg, Manitoba: The City of Unlimited Industrial and Commercial Opportunities* (1974)
City of Winnipeg Archives and Records Control

fig. 1.6
Postcard (1906)
T. Eaton Building (1904)
John Woodman
Oliver Botar Collection

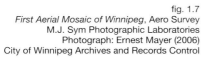

Besides its downtown department stores, Winnipeg has many shopping centres. The covered arcade at left permits all-weather shopping in comfort.

fig. 1.7
First Aerial Mosaic of Winnipeg, Aero Survey
M.J. Sym Photographic Laboratories
Photograph: Ernest Mayer (2006)
City of Winnipeg Archives and Records Control

fig. 1.8
Great West Life Building under Construction
Green, Blankstein, Russell, and Associates, and Morani Morri
Photograph: Henry Kalen (c. 1959)
269U3-13

fig. 1.10
"Looking North from the Fort Garry Hotel"
(27 June 1962)
City of Winnipeg Archives and Records Control
Mu 163, Box P2, File 80

Early twentieth-century events, including a recession in 1913, the advent of World War I, the opening of the Panama Canal in 1914, and the Winnipeg General Strike of 1919, followed by the depression of the 1930s, brought the city's expansion to a halt, a state of affairs that lasted until the late 1940s. Historian Alan Artibise has noted that because of this economic situation, "The period from 1914 to 1945 [was] the most difficult in Winnipeg's history."[2] There was very little significant growth of population from the 1920s to the 1950s, and, as a result, the built environment did not develop, either. (fig. 1.7) By the end of World War II, the urban landscape of Winnipeg had barely changed since 1913.[3]

In the period following WWII, all of North America enjoyed an economic boom and the International Modernist Style of architecture became the dominant style of this optimism. According to historian Edward Whitcomb, the 1950s and 1960s represented Winnipeg's cultural revival after a long stagnant period, and this is evident in the quality and quantity of the structures built during this time.[4] (fig. 1.8, 1.9 [p. 2], 1.10) In his essay, David Burley describes the political and social background to Winnipeg Modernism: "The forces of modernity profoundly transformed Winnipeg's urban landscape in the post-second world war era. . . ." As in the rest of Canada, Winnipeg's post-World War II economic boom was partly fuelled by returning soldiers, who finally able to go to university, marry, and have children.[5] This meant that there was a need for, and the resources to build, new homes (fig. 1.11, 1.12, 1.13, 1.14), new hospitals, new libraries (fig. 1.15, 1.16), new synagogues and churches (fig. 1.17, 1.18, 1.19), and new shopping centres. Winnipeg also needed a more elaborate infrastructure to support this mostly suburban expansion around the city. It was during these years that the transportation system, the Winnipeg floodway, and the hydroelectrical dams such as those in Pinawa were developed. As Martin Tessler's photographic essay on "Living Modernism" documents, many of these Modernist structures are still in good use, although not all are in good repair.

fig. 1.11
Perspectival Drawing (1959)
Gerald and Joan Macdonald Residence
Ward and Macdonald
Gerald Macdonald principal design
Photograph: Ernest Mayer (2006)
Gerald Macdonald Collection

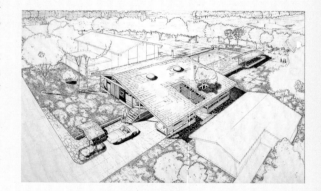

fig. 1.12
Gerald and Joan Macdonald Residence (1960)
Ward and Macdonald
Gerald Macdonald principal design
Photograph: Henry Kalen (1965)
710 B1 series
Gerald Macdonald Collection

fig. 1.13
Gerald and Joan Macdonald Residence (1960)
Ward and Macdonald
Gerald Macdonald principal design
Photograph: Henry Kalen (1965)
710 B1 series
Gerald Macdonald Collection

fig. 1.14
Donahue Residence Rendering (1955)
Print of original pencil on vellum perspective drawing
Hosmer Boulevard
James Donahue
City of Winnipeg Archives and
Records Control

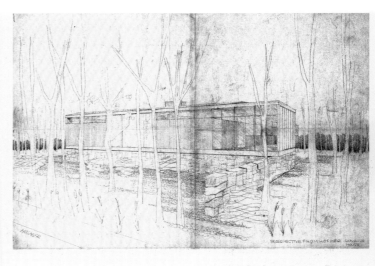

fig. 1.15
St. James Public Library (1957)
Smith, Carter, and Katelnikoff
Photograph: Henry Kalen (c. 1960)
136D5.1–4

fig. 1.16
St Vital Public Library (1963)
George A. Stewart
Photograph: Henry Kalen (1963)
466D5.1–1

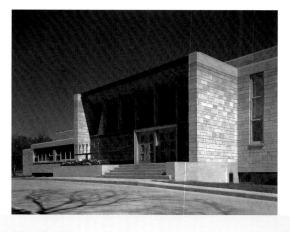

As the children from the post-war marriages grew up, the demand for schools and universities was unprecedented. Mel Michener, for example, has described a point in his career when the architectural firm Libling, Michener, and Associates had contracts for 100 schools in Manitoba.[6] President Wilfred C. Lockhart, of the newly formed University of Winnipeg, stated, "with every addition to the physical plant students came to crowd the available space."[7] In the late 1940s and the 1950s, the University of Manitoba moved its graduate program, its Arts and Science division, and many of its colleges to Fort Garry (including the School of Art, which joined that campus in 1965), developing a spacious riverside campus. (fig. 1.20, 1.21, 1.22) Brandon College and United College (University of Winnipeg) acquired their university status during this period, as well.[8]

An expansive building period due to prosperous economic times does not necessarily ensure architecturally interesting production, however. One of the reasons for the high quality of Manitoban Modernist architecture is the School of Architecture at the University of Manitoba. When architecture was first taught at the university in 1913, it was only the third such school to do so in Canada, and the only school in the Western provinces until 1946, when the University of British Columbia opened its doors.[9] John A. Russell, an American trained at the Massachusetts Institute of Technology, who became head of the School of Architecture in 1946, was central to the advent of Modernist architecture in Manitoba through his teaching, engagement with the arts community, and his publishing record. In an article in *Queens Quarterly* in 1955, he described the formal characteristics of Modernist architecture:

> the best architecture today is characterized by clarity and order in its design, by sound structural expression, by simplicity of inner spaces (the fundamental architectural commodity), by dignity of proportion and by a unity of the whole. It no longer has to struggle to free itself from the curious academicism of the early years of our century when much of the art on this continent was suffering from an eclectic "hangover" induced by too many stylistic revivals in the nineteenth century.[10]

fig. 1.17
Shaarey Zedek Synagogue (1949)
Green, Blankstein, Russell, and Associates
Cecil Blankstein and Charles Faurer principal design
Photograph: Henry Kalen
206N1.4–6

fig. 1.18
Westridge United Church (Donnelly United Church) (1964)
Moody, Moore, and Partners
Peter Holtshousen principal design
Photograph: Henry Kalen (1962)
338N1.2–5

fig. 1.19
Holy Family Ukrainian Catholic Church (1963)
Zunic and Sobkowich
Radoslav Zuk principal design
Photograph: Henry Kalen (1963)
454N1.1–4

fig. 1.20
St John's College Residence and Chapel (1958)
University of Manitoba
Moody, Moore, and Partners
Photograph: Henry Kalen (c. 1962)
283D3.1–12

fig. 1.21
University of Manitoba Residence Cafeteria (1964)
University of Manitoba
Waisman, Ross, and Associates
Photograph: Henry Kalen
535D3.2–23A

Russell felt strongly that the creation of contemporary architecture should not be based on traditional values and aesthetics. Modernist architecture, he suggested, was a reaction against Historicism or revival architecture, which appropriated historical styles, such as the Greek and Roman styles that dominate Winnipeg's Exchange district and its environs; for example, the 1912 Bank of Montreal. "Modern" architects held that historical styles did not reflect local experience and conditions. A building created in a past style was not, according to Russell, "an expression of the period in which it is built and of the civilization surrounding it."[11] By the late nineteenth and early twentieth centuries in Europe and North America, artists, architects, and designers who considered themselves avant-garde were rejecting historical styles and searching for an up-to-date style that would reflect the changes of their own period.[12]

The search for a Modern style led architects to experiment with the latest technologies that developed out of the Industrial Revolution, including the production of steel, large panes of plate glass, and newer industrial building types, such as railway stations and grain storage bins. Early Modernist architects were also imbued with a social consciousness that proposed to make the world a better place by improving living conditions. They tended to view industry and technology as progressive forces. Some of the most famous practitioners of Modernism came out of the German Bauhaus school. With Hitler's rise to power, by the early 1930s, these artists and architects emigrated to America and began teaching in universities, widely disseminating both the style and philosophy of Modernism throughout North America.

Russell's description of Modernist architecture as being clear and orderly in its design, simple in its interior spaces, and unified in its look, sums up the main formal characteristics of this Bauhaus or International Style. Most Modernist buildings share a common vocabulary of abstracted forms, transparency, and spatial flow. These common tropes developed from an interest in using functional design combined with technology that separated the skeleton of

fig. 1.22
Animal Sciences Building (1962)
University of Manitoba
Smith, Carter, Searle, and Associates
James Donahue principal design
Photograph: Henry Kalen (1962)
367D31–8

9

Serena Keshavjee

the structure from its encasing walls.[13] Sarah Williams Goldhagen's efforts to broaden this often repeated, reductive formalist definition of Modernist architecture has refocussed the debate on the importance of regional elements of site, topography, and local materials, elements that have always been important in Winnipeg because of the severe climatic conditions.

The flat roofs, non-load-bearing walls skinned with glass or masonry, the lack of decoration, and the simple symmetrical proportions of the Bauhausian-International Style are perfectly embodied in Winnipeg's early government buildings such as the Norquay Building (1959) (fig. 1.23), Libling, Michener, and Associates' (with Gaboury) Manitoba Health Service Building (1959), the International Airport (1962–65), City Hall (1964) (fig. 1.35), and adventurous corporate structures such as the Northern Sales Building (1953) (fig. 1.24). But, as Kelly Crossman points out in his essay in this anthology, "Manitoba Modernists sought out the possibilities inherent in Winnipeg's morphology and topography." Even the paradigmatic International Style structures such as the Manitoba Health Service Building and the Norquay Building reflect regional adaptations like the aluminum *brises soleil* and the use of Tyndall stone.[14] The biomorphic lines of a Modernism considered more organic are seen predominantly in Winnipeg churches, such as St. John Brebeuf (1965) (fig. 1.25), and most consistently in the 1960s work of Étienne Gaboury, including Precious Blood (1968) (fig. 1.26), Holy Family Roman Catholic Church (fig. 1.27), and, beyond his ecclesiastical architecture, in the Lower Fort Garry Interpretive Centre (1979). Gaboury's writings express an emphasis on identity, both personal and regional, in his buildings: "My definition of architecture as being 'space structured to serve human needs' implies a polarity between space and humans. Indeed, although space is the essential matter of architecture, human beings are its object and raison d'être. Architecture is of necessity anthropocentric."[15]

Manitoba's particular Modernist ethos developed along several creative fronts. The School of Architecture was not the only cultural institution to hire a

fig. 1.24
Northern Sales Building (1953)
Waisman, Ross, and Associates
Charles Faurer and Allan Waisman principal design
Photograph: Herbert Enns (2006)

director from outside Canada: others, including the School of Art (founded in 1913), and the Winnipeg Art Gallery (founded in 1912), followed suit and hired internationally, creating a fertile artistic and architectural environment in Manitoba that inspired the production of Modern art and architecture that rivalled bigger North American cities. William McCloy was recruited from the University of Iowa in 1950 to head the School of Art, after it joined the University of Manitoba as the country's second Fine Arts department within a university.[16] Steeped in the tradition of German Modernism, Ferdinand Eckhardt had worked as the Director of Education and Development at the Austrian State Art Galleries in Vienna before joining the Winnipeg Art Gallery in 1953.[17] The efforts of these people working at these institutions helped introduce the international avant-garde in both the art and architectural fields to Winnipeg.

In addition to his emphasis on Modernism in architecture, J.A. Russell was also very committed to building up Winnipeg's local avant-garde community. For example, he refused a prestigious job as director of the Faculty of Architecture at the University of Toronto in order to remain in Winnipeg.[18] As head of the School of Architecture, he encouraged students to study in the United States and the United Kingdom, giving them the opportunity to meet some of the most important architects of the twentieth century. As a result of this encouragement, two Winnipeggers, Morley Blankstein and Isadore Coop, worked directly with Mies van der Rohe in Chicago.[19] In Blankstein's Winnipeg General Post Office (fig. 1.28, 1.29) and Coop's Pharmacy Building (fig. 1.30) at the University of Manitoba, the simplicity and honesty to material and purity of forms reflect the highest formal ideals of the International Modernist movement. Ernie Smith went to the Massachusetts Institute of Technology (MIT), followed by Douglas Gillmor, who graduated with his Master's degree in 1955, having had contact with Eero Saarinen and Buckminster Fuller. Alan Hanna met the Modernist architect Louis Kahn when he studied at MIT in 1956. Lewis Morse travelled to London in 1968 and joined forces with Arup and Associates. According to a number of architects, Manitoba's School of Architecture was "the only school that mattered during this period."[20]

11

Serena Keshavjee

Nor was it only students who had international connections. Faculty member James Donahue, who designed the elegant Faculty of Architecture building in 1959, with Smith, Carter, and Katelnikoff (fig. 1.31), studied directly under Walter Gropius, the founder of the Bauhaus, and his colleague Marcel Breuer, at Harvard. During the summer of 1959, Gustavo da Roza II (hereafter da Roza) also worked for Gropius at the Architect's Collaborative in Cambridge. Another faculty member, Wolfgang Gerson, graduated from the West of England Academy in 1936 and then from the Architectural Association in London.[21] Russell also worked to counteract Winnipeg's isolation by bringing in a first-class roster of lecturers and exhibitions. From the Walter Gropius exhibition (1954) to the Le Corbusier exhibition (1959) (fig. 1.32), and speakers, including Sibyl Moholy-Nagy, Alan Watts, Ralph Erskine, and Buckminster Fuller, Winnipeggers had little trouble keeping up with current intellectual and design trends.[22] Russell was also instrumental in initiating a number of high-powered architectural competitions in Winnipeg, including the competition for the WAG building and for the new City Hall.

Another factor in the Winnipeg mid-century architectural scene was the connection between the fine arts and architecture, a link enthusiastically championed by Russell. He was closely involved in the arts in general, designing sets for the theatre and ballet, and serving on the boards of the Royal Winnipeg Ballet and of the Winnipeg Art Gallery. At the WAG, he took on the role of president from 1964 until 1966, when he died unexpectedly. It was Russell and Ferdinand Eckhardt who were instrumental in garnering support to build a new structure to house the WAG's growing collection.[23] Russell's interest in art was well known and he was entrusted by the Deputy Minister of Transport, John R. Baldwin, to organize the competitions for the art to be placed at the Winnipeg International Airport. According to Bernard Flaman, the art programs for the new Edmonton, Toronto, and Winnipeg airports built in the early 1960s had to promote Canada as a modern country in preparation for the centenary celebrations. For the most part, abstract art was chosen.

fig. 1.33
Buckminster Fuller Lecture Announcement
From John Russell's scrapbook
(c. 1950s–1960s)
Photograph: Herbert Enns (2006)

fig. 1.31
School of Architecture (1959)
(John A. Russell Building)
University of Manitoba
Smith, Carter, and Katelnikoff
James Donahue principal design with Doug Gilmor
Grant Marshall interior design
Photograph: Henry Kalen (1962)
249D4.2–6

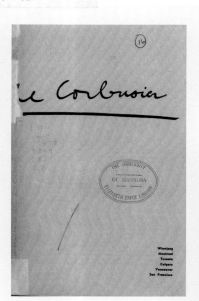

fig. 1.32
Le Corbusier Exhibition Catalogue Cover
School of Architecture, University of Manitoba (1959)
Architecture and Fine Arts Library
University of Manitoba

fig. 1.34
Northern Lights, Relief Sculpture (1964)
John Graham
Winnipeg International Airport
Green, Blankstein, Russell, and Associates
David Thordarson and Bernard Brown principal design
Photograph: Henry Kalen (c. 1964)
217K3.2–40

fig. 1.36
Winnipeg Centennial Stationery (1974)
City of Winnipeg Archives and
Records Control Mu–2

fig. 1.35
Mayor's Message (1967)
From *Winnipeg: Your Celebration City for "67"*
City of Winnipeg Archives and Records Control

Winnipeg, Your Celebration City for "67"

Winnipeg's new Civic Centre showing the Administration Building and part of the Council Chamber Building in the foreground.

STEPHEN JUBA
MAYOR

MEMBERS OF
CITY COUNCIL

Aldermen

L. H. CLAYDON
J. CROPO
M. H. DANZKER
E. J. ENNS
L. HALLONQUIST (MRS.)
J. GURSON HARVEY, Q.C.
WM. McGARVA
G. McLEOD
R. E. MOFFAT
D. A. MULLIGAN
P. PARASHIN
S. REBCHUK
B. SWAILES
L. STINSON
E. I. TENNANT (MRS.)
A. C. WADE
I. WOLCH
J. ZUKEN

MAYOR'S MESSAGE

Winnipeg, standing as it deems at the Gateway to the Golden West, has probably more reasons to give thanks in the Centennial year of our great country than almost any other part of Canada.

As Mayor of Winnipeg, I extend a personal invitation to you to come to the greatest sports spectacle ever held in Canada from July 22nd to August 7th, 1967. The Pan-American Games bring to Winnipeg and for the first time to Canada the largest assembly of amateur athletes ever brought together.

You can also thrill to the sport of Kings at Assiniboia Downs, Western Canada's finest track. The Downs features a modern grandstand, with pari-mutuel betting wickets on all three levels.

Great changes are being effected in Winnipeg, a handsome Civic Centre and across the street is rising the Manitoba Centennial project. Centennial year in Winnipeg will be filled with activities having a wide appeal for every visitor.

Come to the glorious West in 1967 and get your share of Western hospitality, Winnipeg style, equaled no where in the world.

MAYOR.

The Winnipeg Art Gallery

PRESIDENT: GEORGE AIKEN, F.C.A.
DIRECTOR: FERDINAND ECKHARDT, Ph.D.

May 13, 1971.

The Director,
Public Archives of Canada,
395 Wellington Street,
Ottawa,
Ontario.

Dear Sir,

The Winnipeg Art Gallery is in the happy position to announce that we will move very soon into our new building, a $5 million project. An unpleasant situation in temporary quarters, seeming almost indefinite, will be over and we hope to have in the future a gallery which, through its modern facilities for humidity and light control and by its outstanding architectural design, will be one of the most impressive museum buildings on this continent.

The opening formalities, for which we expect many museum people, collectors, dealers and art friends from all over the world, will take place between September 24th and 26th with the actual opening Saturday, September 25th at 11.00 a.m. The programme will include two official dinners, a folk festival performance to show the rich ethnic background of this community, social events, parties at the different private collections, a full programme in and around the gallery; above all, a remarkable exhibition called "CANADA - THE WORLD - YESTERDAY AND TODAY" which will include works of art taken from our collection, leading museums and private owners.

Before we can send formal invitations to professionals and art friends, we would like to know the number of people interested in coming to Winnipeg for this unique occasion. May we ask you to send us a list of such people in your museum so that we may send them a personal invitation.

I am looking forward to hearing from you at your earliest convenience.

Yours sincerely,

Ferdinand Eckhardt
Director

200 VAUGHAN STREET WINNIPEG 2 MANITOBA 942-2483

fig. 1.37
Winnipeg Art Gallery Stationery
Invitation to the Opening
May 13, 1971

fig. 1.38
Cover, *Canadian Architect* (January 1960)
Elevation for Winnipeg's New City Hall
Winning Competition Entry
Green, Blankstein, Russell, and Associates
David Thordarson and Bernard Brown principal design

fig. 1.39
City Hall Model
Photograph: Bill Rose
City of Winnipeg Archives and Records Control

fig. 1.40
Empty Site of City Hall from Main Street
Photograph: Henry Kalen (1962)
369V5–1

Prominent Saskatoon Modernist Eli Bornstein's and Winnipeg Modernist John Graham's spectacular reliefs on the south and north walls of the terminal, respectively (fig. 1.34), as well as veteran Quebec Modernist artist Alfred Pellan's semi-circular painting entitled *The Prairie*, each abstracted some aspect of nature, a theme they considered vital to life in Manitoba.[24]

Several other factors beyond the School of Architecture helped disseminate the idealism of Modernism within Manitoba. The confluence of the Canadian, Manitoban, and Winnipeg centenary celebrations in 1967, 1970, and 1974, respectively (fig. 1.35, 1.36), and Dufferin Roblin and Steven Juba's plans to revitalize "beleaguered" downtown Winnipeg meant that politicians at all levels of governance were keen to see Manitoba's built environment given more prominence. The new Winnipeg Art Gallery was supported, for example, by the Manitoba Centennial Citizens Campaign in 1967 and 1970, a Government of Canada Centennial Grant, and Province of Manitoba Centennial grants.[25] (fig. 1.37) As with the competition for the Winnipeg Art Gallery, the competition for City Hall, at a site between Memorial Boulevard and Osborne Street north, was national in scope, with close to 100 entries. Like the WAG competition, it too was won by a local firm, Green, Blankstein, and Russell, and was presided over by John Russell. (fig. 1.38) The competition was modelled somewhat on Toronto's City Hall (1958-1965) competition, with a view to building an equally astonishing structure in Winnipeg that would boost civic pride and rejuvenate the declining core of the city.[26]

fig. 1.41
Main and Market (c. 1962)
Photograph: Henry Kalen
369V5–8

The late decision to change the site of the new City Hall to Main Street from Memorial Boulevard, after the competition had been awarded, had significant consequences for the city. It meant demolishing the old City Hall and the Market Building, and entirely reworking the design for the new building.[27] (fig. 1.39, 1.40, 1.41) These changes upset the architects involved and others who did not support the demolition of Winnipeg's Victorian-style City Hall. However, the placement of City Hall on Main Street did indeed begin the redevelopment of the immediate area, with the Manitoba Centennial Arts

fig. 1.42
Manitoba Museum of Man and Nature (1970) and Planetarium (1968)
Associated Architects for Manitoba Cultural Centre
Green, Blankstein, Russell, and Associates,
Moody, Moore, and Partners (with James Christie),
Smith, Carter, Searle, and Partners
Photograph: Henry Kalen
1282E–14

15

Serena Keshavjee

fig. 1.43
Winnipeg City Hall and
Administration Building (1964)
Green, Blankstein, Russell, and Associates
David Thordarson and Bernard Brown
principal design
Photograph: Henry Kalen
1602A2–4

Centre (fig. 1.42, 1.43, 1.44) and the addition of a large public housing project for Lord Selkirk Park, north of City Hall on Dufferin Avenue.[28] (fig. 1.45, 1.46) Mayor Steven Juba's hope for the new City Hall was that "the proposed beautiful building should contribute to the revitalization of this historical area in Winnipeg. . . . It is our sincere hope . . . that this area will have been redeveloped as a significant example of urban renewal in a Canadian City and will be a source of pride for the citizens of Winnipeg."[29] Despite the efforts of mid-century politicians, at least on paper, to bring back Winnipeg, the fear that the downtown was losing out to the suburbs was well founded. As David Burley's essay elucidates, in the 1960s and 1970s, numerous schemes and publicity campaigns commissioned by civic administrators attempted to reverse Winnipeg's declining downtown. (fig. 1.47, 1.48) Unfortunately, most of these schemes were unrealized and Winnipeg finds itself today in a much worse situation than Juba or Roblin would have imagined in the 1950s, with thriving, unattractive suburban shopping areas such as the St. James-Polo Park area, and an under-utilized core area.

Throughout Canada during the 1960s, efforts were made to promote the country as a modern nation, particularly in view of the impending centenary celebrations. The federal *Massey Report*, commissioned in 1951 to investigate the state of Canadian architecture and arts, pointed to a number of problems, including the imitative Historicist style of architecture and "characterless" pre-war public buildings throughout Canada. As Eric Arthur put it:

> Our town halls . . . are for the most part dreary monuments where people would not go except for the payment of taxes or fines; our older post offices can only be described as sordid; our prewar public libraries give the appearance of being gloomy strongholds for the preservation of precious incunabula; and our smaller railway stations, in V-jointed varnished lumber, have not changed in design since the track was cut out of the prairie or primeval forest.[30]

fig. 1.44
Manitoba Museum of Man and Nature (1970) and
Planetarium (1968)
Associated Architects for Manitoba Cultural Centre
Green, Blankstein, Russell, and Associates,
Moody, Moore, and Partners (with James Christie),
Smith, Carter, Searle, and Partners
Photograph: Henry Kalen
851E5–49

fig. 1.47
Centennial Gardens
Libling, Michener, and Associates
Photograph: Henry Kalen (1970)
532B2–4

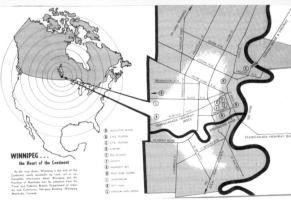

fig. 1.48
"Winnipeg ... the Heart of the Continent"
Mayor's Office, City Council
From *Winnipeg: The City of Unlimited Industrial and Commercial Opportunities* (1974)
City of Winnipeg Archives and Records Control

fig. 1. 45
"Slum Area, Dufferin Ave" (1964)
Winnipeg Views 115
Archives of Manitoba

fig. 1.46
Lord Selkirk Park (1967)
Libling, Michener, and Associates
Photograph: Henry Kalen (1970)
1356B4–13

Winnipeg is making great strides industrially. Here are some plants recently built in the new Inkster Industrial Park. At right is the new Mall Centre, with the Bus Depot and the Mall Hotel.

fig. 1.49
Inkster Industrial Park
From *Winnipeg: The City of Unlimited Industrial and Commercial Opportunities* (1974)
City of Winnipeg Archives and Records Control

The timing of the *Massey Report* was impeccable, and it had a major influence on encouraging Canadian architecture, art, and design to modernize. During the last third of the twentieth century, Canada was presented as a "progressive" country through the production and promotion of astonishing Modernist architecture such as that displayed at Montreal's Expo '67, the Centennial Centre for Science and Technology in Toronto (Raymond Moriyama, architect, 1969), and the Manitoba Centennial Arts Centre (1967). In the City of Winnipeg's 1967 Centennial brochure, page after page of modern-style factories, shops, and schools are prominently displayed. (fig. 1.49) The underlying message is that the Modernist style represents an up-to-date, thriving city. (fig. 1.50, 1.51, 1.52) As is evident with their support for buildings such as City Hall, the Manitoba Centennial Arts Centre, and the WAG, governments at the civic, provincial, and federal levels used Modern architecture as a promotional tool. The enthusiasm generated about new buildings in the press during the mid-century is surprising for a contemporary reader. However, as the authors in this anthology demonstrate, the powerful symbolic value of architecture was well understood during this period by governments and the public alike.

This anthology contains eight articles on Winnipeg Modernist architecture, written by a diverse group of scholars, architects, and art and architectural historians. Included are biographies of some of the most important architects and designers and a bibliography complied by research students at the University of Winnipeg, Aldona Dziedziejko and Jenny Western.[31] Since there is little published material on this body of architecture, all the principal authors have conducted original research on these little-known buildings.[32] This anthology is not, by any means, a comprehensive examination of Winnipeg Modernism. Many areas remain to be researched.

While some of the most important architects of the period are discussed to some degree, including James Donahue, David Thordarson, Bernard Brown, Wolfgang Gerson, John A. Russell, Gustavo da Roza II, Lewis Morse, and Étienne Gaboury, other major players are not. This uneven coverage is due to

17

Serena Keshavjee

fig. 1.50
"From the Old to the New"
City of Winnipeg Official Opening of the New City Hall, October 5, 1964
City of Winnipeg Archives and Records Control

the fact that only a handful of scholars are working in the field of Winnipeg architecture, and finding documentation from this period remains a challenge. Much of it lies uncatalogued in the off-storage sites of the local architectural firms, making it virtually impossible to use. Most of us relied on the help of senior architects and their private documentation, on period journals, on government archives from all three levels, and archives from the universities of Winnipeg and Manitoba. I carried out research in the National Archives in Ottawa, the Canadian Centre for Architecture, and the Canadian Architecture Archives.[33] In Manitoba, we are singularly privileged in having an intact and organized archive of first-rate Modernist architectural photography by Henry Kalen, a trained architect and one of the Canadian masters of architectural photography. Kalen generously gave me full access to his archive, which documents with an image and minimal information almost every Modern structure built in this city from the late 1950s until the 1990s. Some of the basic research for this book and a majority of the images come from Kalen's archive. Sadly, Henry died before this project was complete and I have dedicated this book to him.[34] (fig. 1.53)

Despite the lack of recent analysis on this period of Manitoba's architectural history, we did have models to follow: a series of publications on Canadian Modernist architecture has appeared since 1987 on Toronto, Vancouver, Calgary, Lethbridge, and Montreal.[35] One of our chief goals was to contribute to this growing scholarship on Modern Canadian architecture.

The first essay in the anthology, by social historian David Burley, examines the economic and social factors that led to the second and equally significant building boom in Winnipeg after 1945. What he has established is that after almost a generation of stagnation, the end of World War II, a progressive government, and a strong architectural school profoundly transformed Winnipeg's urban landscape; between 1945 and 1975 Winnipeg physically became a different city, one with skyscrapers, a built-up downtown, suburban sprawl, and housing projects. (fig. 1.54, 1.55) Burley documents the expansive

fig. 1.53
Self-Portrait (c. 1960s)
Henry Kalen
Gloria Kalen Collection

WINNIPEG MODERN
Architecture: 1945–1975

From the Old.

....to the NEW

fig. 1.51
"From the Old to the New"
City of Winnipeg Official Opening of the New City Hall,
October 5, 1964
City of Winnipeg Archives and
Records Control

fig. 1.52
"From the Old to the New"
City of Winnipeg Official Opening of the New City Hall,
October 5, 1964
City of Winnipeg Archives and
Records Control

fig. 1.54
East Kildonan Suburbs and Rossmere Golf Course
Photographer unknown (c. 1962)
Gerald Macdonald Collection

and optimistic building that occurred in the years of 1948 and 1969, leading to what he sees as Modernism's demise in Winnipeg: the closing off of the famous Portage and Main intersection to pedestrians with the construction of the Trizec Building in 1974. By filling in the gap regarding the socio-economic history of post-World War II architecture in Winnipeg, Burley's critique of Modernism, based on early sources, especially from the *Winnipeg Tribune*, contributes significantly to our understanding of this culturally vital period in Canada's recent history.

Burley sees Modernist architecture as having failed the general public, but as Martin Tessler's photographic essay, selected by Herbert Enns, indicates, Winnipeggers have accommodated themselves to Modernist buildings, and, indeed, some of these buildings are well-loved and well-used structures. Arriving during the height of the summer in 2005, Tessler frequented Winnipeg's pools, ice cream parlours, and shopping centres to capture "Living Modernism," the title of his essay. Because Henry Kalen's photographs, which appear throughout this book, presented Modern buildings as—typical for the time—stark, unpeopled ideals of architectural perfection, Tessler was commissioned to produce colour images of the way Modernist structures were adapted for actual use. His lively images of the St. Vital pool and the Bridge Drive-in, filled with children, demonstrate the importance of these buildings to Winnipeg summer culture.

My essay continues the contextual approach taken by Burley. I examine the University of Winnipeg's decision to remain a downtown-based university, rather than move to the suburbs to join the other colleges at the University of Manitoba. Its successful integration into the downtown environment was realized by the construction of Centennial Hall (1970-72), a stylish mega-structure built over the existing university buildings. Designed by Lewis Morse for Moody, Moore, Duncan, Rattray, Peters, Searle, and Christie, it represented the University of Winnipeg's efforts to be an accesible urban education centre. Centennial Hall anticipates both in style and symbolism the Centre Georges

19

Serena Keshavjee

Pompidou (1971–77, Renzo Piano and Richard Rogers) in Paris. These two inner-city megastructures expose their internal workings and highlight them with primary colours. Both buildings reflect the liberationist ideals of the late 1960s; the architects made efforts to produce plans and design elements that would facilitate an accessible, non-hierarchical educational experience.

The authors in this anthology do not always agree about Modernism's legacy. Burley is critical of Modernism's centralized, hierarchical, and totalizing approach, which, he believes, paid no heed to the needs of its users. Architectural historian Kelly Crossman challenges the definition of Modernism as a monolithic architectural practice, perceiving it instead as responsive to its environment. Like Sarah Goldhagen, he proposes that the International Style was not one fixed formula for building. International Style structures in Winnipeg reflect the local architects' response to the 1960s debates regarding regional adjustments to that dominant style.[36] Focussing on two of Winnipeg's most successful practitioners, James Donahue and David Thordarson, who are usually understood as epitomizing the International Style of Modernist architecture, Crossman examines their interest in Manitoba's natural environment, their response to its severe climate, and their use of local materials such as Tyndall stone. He concludes that Winnipeg's Modernist architects, despite their proximity to iconic figures such as Mies and Gropius, were not generically copying the International Style, but modifying it to fit regional requirements. Manitoba Modernists, he maintains, sought out the possibilities inherent in Winnipeg's landscape and strove to make their buildings habitable and enjoyable for their clients.

Herbert Enns's contribution is also wide-ranging in its scope and ideas. Enns looks at the role of western prairie settlement patterns in shaping the city's infrastructure during the mid-century. He focusses on three of Winnipeg's most important International Style structures, the John A. Russell Building, the Manitoba Health Service Building, and the Winnipeg International Airport. Enns concludes that land settlement patterns, prairie light, and vast space

20

fig. 1.55
Portage Avenue (1966)
Photograph: Henry Kalen (1966)
1602A2–4 c

forced Manitoba architects to modify their Modernism. Like Crossman, he sees Winnipeg architecture as being profoundly affected by the region.

Bernard Flaman has researched the policy of the Canadian Department of Transport, which in the early 1960s commissioned local firms to build international airports in Toronto, Edmonton, and Winnipeg. He has written a series of articles on the art and architectural program of Canadian airports, the "largest public art project ever realized in Canada."[37] In Winnipeg's case, Green, Blankstein, and Russell were hired to design the International Airport. The promotional material for these airports boasted state-of-the-art equipment and "modern" design. As Flaman explains, the coordinated program for the airports and the decision to furnish them with salient examples of Canadian abstract art and Modernist furniture reflect the government's attempt to fulfill the directive of the 1951 *Massey Report* to forge a Canadian identity. With these airports, including the Miesian terminal at Winnipeg, the government was hoping to create an up-to-date, modern Canadian identity.

Terri Fuglem has extensively examined the work of Gustavo da Roza II, who won the national competition for his groundbreaking design for the Winnipeg Art Gallery in 1971. (fig. 1.56, 1.57) John Russell outlined the requirements for the new art gallery building in 1966, deciding against a building that would dominate the art:

> On the aesthetic side the building should be dignified and impressive, yet inviting; it should not be a tour-de-force or overpowering, nor should it be dull and pedantic; it should be dynamic and alive, avoiding the cliches of modern or historic styles; it should be neither a "box" nor a "Guggenheim"; yet it should have the simple elegance of the former and might have the sculptural quality such as the latter has. . . . Above all, the building should have a character, an architectural expression, which immediately conveys the impression that it is an art gallery—one designed especially for its location and, therefore, in harmony with as well as complementary to its neighbors and immediate environment.[38]

21

Serena Keshavjee

THE WINNIPEG ART GALLERY, WINNIPEG, CANADA

fig. 1.57
Winnipeg Art Gallery (c. 1970)
Gustavo da Roza
Perspectival drawing
Photograph: Ernest Mayer (2006)
Winnipeg Art Gallery Archive

Although Russell did not live to see it, Gustavo da Roza's triangular design was described by the judges as a "building that combines the shapes of the jet-age future with the arrow-shape pattern that has links with Manitoba's past."[39] Architectural historian Harold Kalman has convincingly argued that the WAG building anticipated the more famous National Gallery in Washington, DC (1974) by I.M. Pei.[40] Fuglem advances this comparison and also looks at another important contribution to Winnipeg architecture by da Roza, the numerous houses he designed throughout the city for a range of clients. Fuglem sees this series of dwellings, with their mannered and exaggerated elements, as rejecting the purity of Modernism; that is, as a move towards Post-Modernism. It is interesting to note that both Crossman and Fuglem point out the symbolic importance to architects of the colour white in Winnipeg, a city that is blanketed in snow for almost four months of every year.

As Crossman points out, by the late 1960s the Winnipeg architecture scene became more diffuse. Faye Hellner outlines the sources of Étienne Gaboury's organic style, in particular his introduction to Corbusier's work as a student in France, his exposure to Catholicism in his childhood, and his response to living on the prairies. Gaboury dismisses the notion of an "international" Modernism: "The ideology of the International style advocates a borderless architecture and rejects all organic or regional expression." Instead, he understands that humanity is part of the environment, and architecture, to be successful, must respond and relate to that environment.[41]

What becomes evident in Hellner's article, and almost all the other articles in the anthology, is that regional adaptations were fundamental to Manitoban architectural practice, and that one may begin to talk of a localized architectural movement based around the University of Manitoba. The plea in the 1951 *Massey Report* for the development of a regional Canadian architecture adapted to the land-area, climate, and local materials was clearly heeded in Winnipeg; here we find a modified Modernism.[42] Russell gave priority to regionalism in his pedagogy at the University of Manitoba. He firmly believed

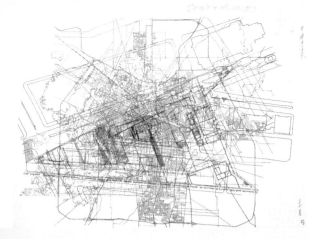

that "Architecture is closely related both to the geographic locality for which it is designed and the people for which it is designed."[43] He was attracted to faculty members who had a similar approach, as in the case of da Roza and Donahue, and they in turn influenced their students, such as Gaboury and Thordarson. As with the artistic reliefs and murals commissioned for the Winnipeg International Airport, which highlight nature as a fundamental theme for Manitobans, the role of nature in the urban environment of the city was part of the building philosophy of mid-century Winnipeg architects.

Gaboury's structures grow from the ground, da Roza's houses frame intimate views of forested yards, and even a consummate Miesian such as Thordarson skinned his buildings in Manitoba fossilized limestone—a golden-hued stone imprinted with the evidence of ancient local life. The forces of nature are strongly felt in Winnipeg. From the extremely cold winters, to the plagues of summer insects, to the city's establishment on a lake basin, to the organic development pattern because of the confluence of two major rivers, the Red and the Assiniboine, to the frequent flooding of these rivers—this city fights every season against being taken back to its "natural" state. As Gaboury argues, "We inevitably become swept up by the major dynamics of nature and we ignore it at our peril."[44] At a time when Canadians were trying to define essential Canadian qualities, Russell, living with the extremes of Winnipeg as long as he did, understood there could be no such thing, at least in terms of architecture. He believed that "Canadian Architecture" had to be created to suit each of the individual regions. It had to develop like "subsoil" from the local climatic conditions.[45] If the optimism felt in Canada during 1967 has waned somewhat, we are now more aware of our regional differences and strengths than ever before. Like the Canadian cultural mosaic, Manitoba Modernist architecture succeeds because it adapts to and celebrates the local natural and built environments.

Serena Keshavjee

ENDNOTES

1   These points were made by Oliver Botar in a presentation to the Winnipeg City Council on 20 June 2001, as they were deciding on the fate of John Woodman's c. 1904 proto-modernist, Chicago-style Eaton Building. The Eaton Building was destroyed in 2003.

2   Alan Artibise, *Winnipeg: An Illustrated History* (Toronto: James Lorimer and National Museum of Manitoba, 1977), 109–10. Winnipeg historians are now challenging the oft-repeated story that the completion of the Panama Canal was detrimental to Winnipeg's prosperous economic situation. See Jim Blanchard, *Winnipeg 1912: Diary of a City* (Winnipeg: University of Manitoba Press, 2005); also conversations with David Burley (February 2006); and J.M. Bumsted (22 March 2006).

3   Artibise, *Winnipeg*, 133, 163.

4   Edward A. Whitcomb, "Hope Revived 1955–1970," in *A Short History of Manitoba* (Stittsville, ON: Canada's Wings, 1982), 53–60.

5   Robert Bothwell, Ian Drummond, and John English, *Canada since 1945: Power, Politics and Provincialism* (Toronto: University of Toronto Press, 1989), 82–84.

6   Mel Michener in conversation with the author, 2005.

7   W.C. Lockhard, "Sixteen Years," text of his retirement speech at the University of Winnipeg, 1970; and Bothwell, Drummond, and English, *Canada since 1945*, 106–11.

8   Whitcomb, "Hope Revived," 55.

9   Adele Freedman, "West Coast Modernism and Points East," in *The New Spirit: Modern Architecture in Vancouver 1938–1963*, ed. Rhodri Windsor-Liscombe (Montreal: Canadian Centre for Architecture/Vancouver: Douglas and McIntyre, 1997), 10. Architecture was taught within the Faculty of Arts at the University of Manitoba beginning in 1913. In 1920 a Faculty of Engineering and Architecture was set up. It offered a post-graduate Master of Architecture degree by 1935. The School of Architecture was set up by 1945 and a Faculty of Architecture was in place by 1963. See the Web page for the Department of Architecture at the University of Manitoba, www.umanitoba.ca/architecture/arch/index.htm. (accessed 2 November 2005)

10 John Russell, "Our Lively Arts: Canadian Architecture," *Queens Quarterly* LXII, 2 (Summer 1955): 236.

11 Ibid., 237.

12 For a good, standard definition of Modernist architecture, see, for example, William J.R. Curtis, *Modern Architecture since 1900* (Upper Saddle River, NJ: Prentice Hall, 1996), 21.

13 For an excellent discussion about Modernist architecture that goes beyond the standard formalist definition, see Sarah Williams Goldhagen and Réjean Legault, eds., *Anxious Modernisms: Experimentation in Postwar Architectural Culture* (Cambridge: MIT Press, 2001), especially Goldhagen's article "Coda: Reconceptualizing the Modern," in particular regarding architecture embodying an era, 305–07. Also see Sarah Williams Goldhagen, "Something to Talk about: Modernism, Discourse, Style," *Journal of the Society of Architectural Historians* 64, 2 (June 2005): 144–67. Here Goldhagen states that the reliance on formalist tropes to define Modernism is reductionist and unsatisfactory.

14 Goldhagen points out that the International Style and organic style in the end have more in common than not, something evident in the work of the Manitoba Modernist Étienne Gaboury. See her "Something to Talk about," 151. She suggests moving away from simplistic, formalist definition and proposes a socio-political categorization instead. "If the critical

literature of the last several decades has made one thing clear, it is that neither a definition of the new architecture after the First World War nor a framework of analysis for modernism can be founded on style.... Only when the interlocking cultural, political and social dimensions that together constitute the foundation of modernism in architecture are identified and analyzed can we properly make sense of modernism's initial complexity and its evolution over time." Goldhagen, "Coda: Reconceptualizing the Modern," 302–03.

15 Étienne J. Gaboury, "Métaphores et métamorphoses en architecture," *Cahiers franco-canadiens de l'Ouest 3*, 2 (Autome 1991): 184. Translated in Faye Hellner, *Étienne Gaboury* (Winnipeg: Editions du Blé, 2005), 23–34. Also see Goldhagen's definition of Situated Modernism, which suits Gaboury very well, in "Coda: Reconceptualizing the Modern," 312ff. In light of Goldhagen's reconceptualizing of Modernity, it is interesting to note that Gaboury counts as the beginning of his foray into Organicism and regionalism one of the most perfect International Style buildings in Canada, his Manitoba Health Service Building of 1959.

16 Thank you to Oliver Botar for this information.

17 For more information on Ferdinand Eckhardt, see the Eckhardt-Gramatte Foundation. www.egre.mb.ca (accessed May 2005). See also Ferdinand Eckhardt, "21 Years of the Winnipeg Art Gallery," unpublished manuscript, 1986. My thanks to Ernest Mayer for this document.

18 Freedman, "West Coast Modernism and Points East," 18.

19 Ibid., 18–19. Morley Blankstein in conversation with the author, summer 2002.

20 Allan Waisman in conversation with the author, June 2005. Charles Dankzer, Étienne Gaboury, Gae Burns, and Leslie Stechesen made similar statements about the architecture program at the University of Manitoba.

21 Information for the above architects comes from numerous sources, including interviews by Aldona Dziedziejko for the biographies (2004 and 2005). On da Roza, see Terri Fuglem's essay in this volume. Regarding Wolfgang Gerson, see Windsor-Liscombe, ed., *The New Spirit: Modern Architecture in Vancouver 1938–1963*, especially 203.

22 This list comes from various sources including Russell's scrapbook at the Faculty of Architecture, University of Manitoba, Étienne Gaboury, Winston Leathers, and an e-mail to the author from Charles Danzker, 15 March 2005.

23 According to Professor Grant Marshall, Russell was instrumental in the success of the Royal Winnipeg Ballet and the Winnipeg Art Gallery. Marshall notes that Russell gave generously of his time, advice, and skills, even to the extent of designing sets for the ballet and the local theatre. He was beneficent with funding, as well, even out of his own pocket. Regarding Russell's role in the new WAG building, see Eckhardt, "21 Years of the Winnipeg Art Gallery." Also see J. Siemens, "John A. Russell," *Warehouse* 14 (2005): 45–74.

24 Russell organized a major conference held in Winnipeg in 1963 that celebrated the Department of Transport's art program for the new international airports across Canada and the fiftieth anniversary of both the School of Architecture and the Winnipeg School of Art. See "The Arts in Architecture: the Festival of Arts," pamphlet, 1963, no page. My thanks to Eli Bornstein for this information and pamphlet.

25 See "Winnipeg Art Gallery Building," Clara Lander Library, WAG Archives, file A176.4. My thanks to Kenlyn Collins for her help with these archives. The quotation "beleaguered" comes from Bernard Peter Brown, "City Hall Introduction: Brief History" (Winnipeg: Winnipeg Architecture Foundation, 2001).

Serena Keshavjee

26   The site of the new City Hall was meant to reflect the "government district of Winnipeg" and create an impressive vista from downtown Memorial Boulevard, past a low-lying City Hall, and to the Legislative Building. See the description in "Winnipeg City Hall Competition," *Canadian Architect* (January 1960): 36. The startling Niemeyer-esque building, designed by David Thordarson and Bernard Brown, that won the competition was never built, however. As Bernard Brown explains, with the election of Dufferin Roblin's government in 1958, the emphasis was placed on revitalizing one of Winnipeg's most "beleaguered" areas—that of Main Street, which was described by F.A. Rahkin in 1957 as needing "$50 million in slum clearance." See Brown, "City Hall Introduction," and "Do We Need a New City Hall?" speech delivered by F.A. Rahkin (4 October 1957), City of Winnipeg Archives and Records Control, City Hall, Old and New File. Everyone seems to agree that Main Street was a very depressed area. It was described as "slum" by Gordon Chown in a letter to Eric Thrift, Winnipeg Town Planning Commission, on 17 May 1954 (City of Winnipeg Archives and Records Control, City Hall Old and New File, 4195 [2]), and "greatly in need of urban renewal," see, "Winnipeg City Hall," *Canadian Architect* (January 1965): 53. Duff Roblin had already begun to question the Broadway site in favour of the Main Street site in a letter to Steven Juba dated 4 May 1960; see City of Winnipeg Archives and Records Control, City Hall, Old and New File. According to Ed Whitcomb, Roblin was active in introducing reforms to help Winnipeg's core area; see "Hope Revived," 56.

27   Brown, "City Hall Introduction." Also see the letters between Duff Roblin and Steven Juba dating from 4 May 1960 and 30 May 1960, in which Roblin exerts subtle pressure to change the site for the new City Hall away from the Broadway-Osborne site; City of Winnipeg Archives and Records Control, City Hall, Old and New File. The Broadway-Osborne site had been given to the city by the province in 1957. See John A. Russell, "The Saga of City Hall," *The Journal, Royal Architectural Institute of Canada* (January 1960): 35–38; and Russell, "A Modern City Hall," *The Saturday Review* (23 and 30 December 1933).

28   E.G. Simpson, "Winnipeg's New City Hall and Urban Renewal," p. 11, source unmarked, City of Winnipeg Archives and Records Control, City Hall, Old and New File. Also see the Aronovitch and Leipsic Limited greeting card, "A City's Despair," which advocated to "clear the slum areas, erecting in their place new accommodation at a reasonable cost for families and individuals on low incomes" (Archives of Manitoba, Winnipeg Views, 115, "Slum area, Dufferin Ave," 1964).

29   "The Sod Turning Ceremony for the New City Hall," speech by Mayor Steven Juba (12 June 1962), City of Winnipeg Archives and Records Control, City Hall, Old and New File, 4195. Also see letter from Nathan Phillips to Steven Juba, 12 November 1957, City of Winnipeg Archives and Records Control, City Hall, Old and New File.

30   Geoffrey Simmins, ed., "The Massey Report: Architecture and Town Planning: The Royal Commission on the National Development in the Arts, Letters, and Sciences (Ottawa 1951)," in *Documents in Canadian Architecture* (Peterborough, ON: Broadview Press, 1992), 185–86, and see full quotation in the same volume in Eric Arthur, "Architecture," 203.

31   I am grateful to the University of Winnipeg Work Study Project and the Undergraduate Student Research Award in the Human Sciences for supporting the research of Aldona Dziedziejko, who was able to work on this project over a period of three years. Jennifer Western was supported by funding from the WAG and the Young Canada Works in Heritage Organization internship.

32   There is a rich bibliography of contemporary secondary source material from *Canadian Architect* and *The Journal, Royal Architectural Institute of Canada*. For more recent analysis, see William Thompson, *Winnipeg Architecture* (1975,

Winnipeg: Faculty of Architecture, University of Manitoba, 2002); Kelly Crossman, "North by Northwest: Manitoba Modernism, c. 1950," in *Journal of the Society for the Study of Architecture in Canada* 24, 2 (1999): 61–69; and Hellner, *Étienne Gaboury*. For excellent unpublished documentation on Winnipeg Modernist buildings, see the Winnipeg Architecture Foundation's building files, Historical Buildings Committee, the City of Winnipeg, 2001. I thank Shelly Bruce for her help with these files.

33 I thank the WAG for funding these research trips.

34 I would like to thank Gloria Kalen for kindly allowing me to continue my research after Henry Kalen passed away. The Henry Kalen Archive is now being housed at the University of Manitoba, Archives & Special Collections. I thank Shelley Sweeney and Brian Hubner for their help.

35 See Marc Baraness et al., *Toronto Modern Architecture 1945–1965* (Toronto: Coach House Press, The Bureau of Architecture and Urbanism, 1987); Graham Livesey et al., *Twelve Modern Homes, 1945–1985* (Calgary: Aris Press and University of Calgary Press, 1995); Windsor-Liscombe, ed., *The New Spirit: Modern Architecture in Vancouver 1938–1963*; Geoffrey Simmins, ed., *Calgary Modern: 1947–1967* (Calgary: The Nickle Arts Museum, 2000); Christopher Thomas and Kim Reinhardt, "Victoria Moderna (1945–1975): Of Civic Myth and Difference in Modern Architecture," *Journal of the Society for the Study of Architecture in Canada* 26, 3, 4 (2001): 3–14; Gerald Forseth et al., *Lethbridge Modern* (Lethbridge, AB: Southern Alberta Art Gallery, 2002); Andre Lortie, ed., *The 60s: Montreal Thinks Big* (Montreal: Canadian Centre for Architecture, Douglas and McIntyre, 2004).

36 Crossman, "North by Northwest: Manitoba Modernism."

37 On Canadian airports, see Rhodri Windsor-Liscombe, "Grounding the New Perspectives of Modernism: Canadian Airports and the Reconfiguration of Cultural and Political Territory," *Journal of the Society for the Study of Architecture in Canada* 28, 1, 2 (2003): 3–14; and Bernard Flaman, "When 'la Dolce Vita' met 'True Canadianism': Canadian Airports in the Sixties," in *Made in Canada: Craft and Design in the Sixties*, ed. Alan C. Elder (Montreal: McGill-Queen's University Press, 2005), 17.

38 John A. Russell, *The Concept of the New Winnipeg Art Gallery Building* (Winnipeg: Winnipeg Art Gallery, 1967), n.p.

39 Robin Taylor, "Unique Arrowhead a Winner," *Winnipeg Tribune*, 19 December 1967, pp. 1–2; in "Culture Recreation Sports and Exhibition Buildings in Manitoba to 1990," compiled by Carol Steer, Winnipeg, Manitoba, 1992.

40 Harold Kalman, *A Concise History of Canadian Architecture* (Toronto: Oxford University Press, 2000), 578.

41 Gaboury, "Métaphores et métamorphoses en architecture," 192. Translated in Hellner, 23–34.

42 Simmins, "Massey Report," 187.

43 Russell, "Our Lively Arts," 237.

44 Gaboury, "Métaphores et métamorphoses en architecture," 193.

45 Russell, "Our Lively Arts," 241.

Serena Keshavjee

WINNIPEG'S LANDSCAPE OF MODERNITY
1945–1975

David Burley

After almost a generation of stagnation, Winnipeg's urban landscape was profoundly transformed by the forces of Modernism in the post-Second World War era. Nothing so dramatic had affected the built environment since the boom of the early twentieth century had convinced enthusiasts that Winnipeg would be the Chicago of the North. That dream had failed by 1914. But the optimistic recovery of capitalism after a decade and a half of depression and a second war, the pursuit of normal family life after years of postponing marriage and children, and the state's new willingness to intervene and plan social and economic development unleashed forces of creative destruction within the city and its suburbs. From the late 1940s through the early 1970s, metropolitan Winnipeg took on an ever-changing look, stretching upwards and spreading outwards. New buildings, new sub-divisions, new roads, and new plans each year replaced and displaced more and more of the decaying core, smoothed the flow of people around the city, sheltered families in sprawling residential enclaves, removed low-income families to new social housing projects, and almost every day promised a more rational urban environment. (fig. 2.1)

fig. 2.1
Parkade
Photograph: Henry Kalen (1961)

Despite the design of buildings that self-consciously rejected the past and despite the self-confident planning for totalizing change, the landscape of modernity in Winnipeg embodied profound contradictions that ultimately generated criticism, conflict, and its own qualification and change. The upward thrust of vertical capitalism downtown and the horizontal sprawl of continually replicating, nucleated single-family households in the suburbs tore up the city, and greater Winnipeg was left an urban landscape of pluralistic incongruities. The stark contrast between the new offices and old warehouses, between planned suburbs and degraded slums, between cultural centres and empty streets provoked a reassessment of the spatial reorganization—as if the centrifugal forces that drove middle- and lower-middle-income families to the suburbs clarified in the new-old city centre the imbalances of power among financial wealth, state power, and the core-area poor. By the early 1970s community activists and neighbourhood groups challenged planning and building from the top by politicians, developers, planners, and architects. The need for urban renewal—the driving force of Winnipeg Mid-Century Modernism—remained manifest, but the process of renewal, citizens now demanded, must become participatory.

The forces, experiences, and expressions of Modernism and its articulation in the Mid-Century Modernist style in architecture and design are, by their nature, slippery and subject to changing senses of meaning. Modernism, the self-conscious pursuit of the new—which becomes old at its moment of realization—expresses dissatisfaction with the imperfect past and harbours a conviction that willed and rational planning can control human affairs and human nature in ways that will progressively improve the human condition and liberate the human potential. As Marshall Berman has described it, "To be modern is to find ourselves in an environment that promises us adventure, power, joy, growth, transformation of ourselves and the world—and at the same time threatens to destroy everything we have, everything we know, everything we are."[1] From the eighteenth century, perhaps, modernity has been a series of displacements, each one a change in what had been just previously the much-desired object of human longing and effort. Modernism as a style in art, architecture, and design has been both an aesthetic response to those changes—celebrating and promoting change—and also, dialectically, contributed to the most recent condition of modernity that itself becomes the target for change. But in pursuit of "the better," seeking human freedom and social creativity, theorists Adorno and Horkheimer warned, the totalizing grasp of the project, the plan, threatens to control, dominate, and oppress those whose individuality and peculiarities do not seem to fit in or to move with the same speed in the same direction as the goal.[2]

As Berman reflected on Modernism in New York City, "The innate dynamism of the modern economy, and of the culture that grows from this economy, annihilates everything that it creates—physical environments, social institutions, metaphysical ideas, artistic visions, moral values—in order to create more, to go on endlessly creating the world anew."[3] The landscape of modernity that has resulted has been a quest for the embodiment of principles of freedom, justice, and human celebration, values in tension not always compatible with one another. In the built environment, that tension, as David Ward and Olivier Zunz have argued, reduces to that between the centripetal and centrifugal forces of rationality and pluralism, respectively, held together by recognition that to function well and justly, the city requires a design for the rational allocation of space, but also that to plan is to constrain free action.[4]

The architectural expression of Modernism, the Modernist style, "is the will of the age conceived in spatial form," as Mies van der Rohe asserted in the 1920s.[5] To be challenging and to upset what exists, the Modernist style assumed a disengagement from its present that required a view from above and outside, and that frequently strained its affinities for the people it sought to serve but whom it occasionally conceived of as being in need of instruction and not yet ready to understand. The Modernist style, Harold Kalman claims, reached Canada in the 1930s and was firmly grounded by the 1950s. Inspired by Le Corbusier, Ludwig Mies van der Rohe, and Walter Gropius, to name the

31

major proponents, architects sought to build function in form, to enclose volume and space rather than impress with mass, to rise and spread with regularity and proportion rather than symmetry and balance, and to achieve elegance with simple, undecorated materials.[6] Beyond such generalities, however, the Modernist style, even in its temporally more limited Mid-Century expression, remains open to debate. Fortunately, architectural historian Sarah Williams Goldhagen has maintained that rather than as a set of forms and stylistic principles, Mid-Century Modernism can better be understood as an architectural culture. As a culture within which architects studied and worked, Modernism was grounded in a rejection of the authority of tradition, though not necessarily a rejection of the past; a commitment to the utility of architecture in achieving political goals, though objectives ranged from advancing, through reforming, to replacing liberal democratic capitalism; and a desire to express the spirit of the times, either embracing the technological future or trying to situate buildings on a humane scale, sensitive to users and location.[7]

Such differences of directions within common understandings of purpose necessarily promoted professional debate, as architects energetically advanced their own positions and willingly turned on the works of those who adopted different perspectives. So was Mid-Century Modernism experienced in Winnipeg. In Manitoba, the School of Architecture—reorganized as a faculty in 1963—at the University of Manitoba not only trained some of the leading Canadian Modernist architects but also, as Kelly Crossman argues, developed a distinctive regionalist expression of that style.[8] Their works marked Winnipeg's modern landscape.

I.

A decade and a half of depression and war had left much of Winnipeg's urban landscape drab and dreary, and the city in 1945 looked not greatly different from in 1914, only much more worn. With the completion of the Legislative Building on Broadway in 1921 and the construction of the impressive Hudson's

32

Bay Company department store on Portage in 1926, only a few more large public and commercial buildings had been put up between the wars, certainly nothing to compare with the boom of the early twentieth century. In the absence of economic growth, the extensive warehouse district, the row of banks along Main Street, and the conspicuous residences of the wealthy off Broadway, on Armstrong's Point, and across the Assiniboine River in Crescentwood remained fading reminders of the city's former prosperity. Through the 1930s, businesses failed, buildings were deserted, and the city acquired many formerly valuable properties. While apartment blocks and detached housing filled in some vacant lots within the city in the 1920s, and while many families, working families especially, moved to the suburbs for cheaper accommodation, new housing construction in the interwar era was insufficient to provide shelter for new families, and the consequent overcrowding of older residences contributed to the wear and tear that degraded many formerly comfortable homes. Only 2303 dwelling units had been constructed in the five years to 1943, while 13,429 couples had married. Where were they to live?[9]

After the war, to this pent-up demand was added the need to accommodate the growing number of new families formed by returning soldiers and by men and women who had been unable to marry during the Depression. And the parents who conceived the "baby boom" wanted to own their own homes. In 1952 the Winnipeg Housebuilders' Association conducted a survey to discover "the most important aspect of the modern home." Families living in cramped rooming houses and apartment suites wanted kitchens with labour-saving conveniences "to make it easy for the girls"; they wanted room and picture-window views, but, as one woman declared, most just wanted "Possession."[10] Their demand for housing stimulated real-estate development within Winnipeg and even more throughout its suburban municipalities. Through the postwar period, metropolitan Winnipeg's population grew steadily from 297,739 in 1941 to 535,480 in 1971. (fig. 2.2) In the half-decade after the war, metropolitan Winnipeg experienced a higher per capita rate of new house construction than any other major Canadian city, and the number of households increased

33

David Burley

Many fine apartment buildings are continually being erected in central Winnipeg as well as in neighbouring residential districts.

Here are two of the new apartment buildings in Winnipeg. The one at right overlooking Central Park, is 20 storeys high and has four hundred suites.

fig. 2.4
Regency Tower
Cumberland Street
From *Winnipeg, the Capital City of Manitoba*
City of Winnipeg Archives and
Records Control

fig. 2.3
"In the Distance, Regency Tower on Central Park" (1964)
University of Manitoba Archives & Special Collections
Winnipeg Tribune Collection
PC 18/256/18–256–057

fig. 2.2
"Fall 1971"
Aerial view of the University of Winnipeg
University of Winnipeg Library
SC–4–1, 84–107–1

from approximately 70,000 to 90,000.[11] The pace of development provoked exaggerated comments in the press that Winnipeg had become "filled up."[12] But by 1950 the supply of building lots within the city proper, at least those that could be assembled for tract development, was dwindling and developers' attention turned to the suburban municipalities. Residential construction in the suburbs had always exceeded that in the city, but the difference between the two grew rapidly. In 1949 and 1950 Winnipeg issued building permits for 43 percent of the value of new housing construction in the metropolitan area; by 1959 and 1960 it accounted for just 13 percent.[13] Unable to fill in much more, from the 1960s the city of Winnipeg grew upwards as new high-rise apartment towers downtown promised an exciting new urban lifestyle for those who wanted to stay close to the centre of things. (fig. 2.3, 2.4) But the suburbs lost little of their draw and, as a result, the city of Winnipeg's population dropped in the 1960s and at the end of the decade the population of the suburban municipalities, which remained politically autonomous from the city until 1972, exceeded that of the city.

Suburban development dynamically altered the city during the third quarter of the century and itself changed in character. New, integrated, development companies assembled land, hired architects and planners, built or subcontracted construction, marketed suburban homes and lifestyles, and arranged mortgage financing with national financial corporations, guaranteed by the federal government's Central Mortgage and Housing Corporation. Mass production, mass marketing, and mass consumption of housing now caused some people to worry about the quality of accommodation, the amenities of life, and the aesthetics of the suburbs.

Others argued that providing decent housing for a democratic society necessarily required a check on excessive individualism, about which the public, especially women, must be educated. Delivering a lecture at the University of Manitoba in 1949, noted Modernist architect Serge Chermayeff of Chicago's Institute of Design criticized consumer ambitions. "Do we want shelter . . . or

David Burley

fig. 2.5
Wildwood Park (1950)
University of Manitoba Archives & Special Collections
Winnipeg Tribune Collection
PC18/7243/18–6475–004

monuments? . . . Do we want housing units as instruments in the business of living or do we want them as memorials and symbols of ancestral fumbling and unformulated hopes?" Acknowledging that years of deprivation had repressed self-expression, he nonetheless lamented contemporary self-indulgence in housing, especially that of women. "Man embraces woman, who demands architectural millinery if not actual monuments. The bed, for example, is a monument and a space hog. Storing things under the bed is regarded as bad practice: it impinges on ideas of self-respect. But do we want the bed to be a 'climate pocket' for sleeping purposes, or do we want it there in all its glory as a memento and promise?" So long as such aspirations interfered with design, Chermayeff expected little innovation and little progress in dealing with the shortage of decent housing.[14]

Without referring to it, Chermayeff may have been hoping for suburbs like Wildwood, which was then under development. (fig. 2.5) Winnipeg's first major post-war suburban project, Wildwood Park, was one of North America's few experiments in "reversed" suburban design, which oriented houses towards pedestrian movement through park-life landscapes rather than facing streets. Its developer, J. Hubert Bird, had been inspired by Clarence Stein's and Henry Wright's innovative plan for Radburn in New Jersey in the late 1920s.[15] In 1945, with financial backing from Great West Life Assurance Company, Bird hired local architects Green, Blankstein, and Russell as planning and architectural design consultants to adapt the concept to the Fort Garry site. Experience with wartime military construction persuaded Bird to use prefabricated components that permitted the erection of houses already roughed-in for fixtures and finishing within a few hours. As the *Tribune* explained in 1945, "The project is big enough to allow the company to retain special work crews, trained to do some particular job of building. . . . By this method company officials say that more efficient workmanship may be obtained. . . . The scheme is really a mass production housing project, but designed to break away from the disadvantages which might attend mass production of homes. Special care will be taken to avoid monotony of uniform architectural design."[16] Or, rather,

monotony was concealed. Only five or six floor plans were designed for the 286 lots, but each offered half a dozen exterior variations in trim in "delicate house colors [that] look well in this green setting: rust, turquoise, lemon yellow, chocolate, eggshell, dove grey, deep green, french blue, apricot," all selected by a female designer.[17] No two houses with the same exterior were placed adjacent or in sight of one another. The development neared completion just in time for the 1950 flood.

Another feature of the new suburb was the shopping centre, welcomed for its convenience, but portentous for its effects on older commercial districts. Opened in 1947, "Wildwood's ultra modern community store" advertised itself as "the first of its type in the Dominion to offer attractively to shoppers everything they need—under one roof." (fig. 2.6) The 14,000-square-foot "modern fire proof brick building . . . gives its fortunate residents the unique and thrilling experience of first class city shopping in their own community." Its clothing departments offered items "carefully selected . . . for the discriminating class of residents in Wildwood": small wares, toiletries, and cosmetics; kitchen and electrical appliances; and laundry and dry cleaning services. Other facilities included a post office, a place to pay telephone bills, a pharmacy with bicycle delivery service, a beauty salon, a gas station with overnight repair service, a snack bar, restrooms, and a bowling alley, which, the public was assured, provided "a wholesome environment for the young people." The focal point, however, was the "gigantic food division that offers everything from groceries to fruit, meat, and fish" with over 2000 different items of "select groceries" including a "mammoth array of fresh fruits and vegetables" of "dewy freshness. . . ." "The latest in shopping carts" and "a huge parking area" assured convenience.[18]

Perhaps the shopping centre was the most important local precedent set by Wildwood. As other subdivisions were developed, developers, planners, and politicians assumed that suburban residents appreciated and wanted the convenience of shopping close to home and not having to take extra time off

David Burley

work to buy the complete range of products needed by "to-day's modern 'on-the-go' family."[19] Proximity and free parking encouraged "a 'family' approach to buying,"[20] as parents and children drove to the "plaza." And housewives "can bring their children along and dress quite informally without looking out of place."[21] Complaints from suburbanites when commercial developments lagged behind housing construction were taken as confirmation of these attitudes.[22]

The shopping centre, as new concept, reached its full articulation in Winnipeg with Polo Park. (fig. 2.7, 2.8) Retail chain Simpsons-Sears and local developers announced their joint venture in 1954, although financing arrangements delayed construction of the modern department store and the shopping centre until 1956. Money concerns also forced architects Green, Blankstein, Russell, and Associates to modify their design, which originally had called for a completely enclosed space. Their sensitivity to the western environment was vindicated just four years after the centre's 1959 opening when they were asked to draw up plans to enclose the mall, the first such change in Canada to a shopping centre.[23] The architects' concern with the quality of the space, however, had convinced the developers to commission public art, and invitations went out to George Swinton (fig. 2.9), Richard Williams (fig. 2.10), and Duane Eichhold of the University of Manitoba's School of Art, and to commercial artist James Willer (fig. 2.11), a specialist in fountains, to submit designs for "art the man in the street will appreciate."[24] Its unique amenities, its location, and its novelty attracted commercial tenants, making it the second largest centre in Canada by 1966.[25] As well, it attracted major finance capitalists: Cemp Investments, headed by Charles Bronfman, had contributed half the original financing (excluding the Simpsons-Sears store) and in 1961 bought out its Winnipeg partners.[26] By 1968 management estimated that eight million shoppers would visit the centre that year.[27]

Across Winnipeg, architects designed more and more shopping centres. To mention just a few projects, Green, Blankstein, Russell, and Associates

fig. 2.7
Simpsons-Sears Building, Polo Park (1959)
Green, Blankstein, Russell, and Associates
Mosaic by George Swinton (1959)
Photograph: Henry Kalen (1961)
185G9–1

fig. 2.8
Interior of Polo Park (1963)
Green, Blankstein, Russell, and Associates
Photograph: Henry Kalen (1968)
1024G–9–1

fig. 2.9
Simpsons-Sears Building (1959)
Mosaic by George Swinton
Photograph: Henry Kalen (1961)
185G9–2

fig. 2.10
Mock Wall (1959)
Richard Williams
Precast concrete
Polo Park
Photograph: Henry Kalen (1961)
185G9 series

fig. 2.11
Cocks and Sun Screen (1959)
James Willer
Precast concrete and metal
Polo Park
Photograph: Henry Kalen (1961)
185G9 series

fig. 2.12
Northgate Plaza (c. 1960)
Green, Blankstein, Russell, and Associates
Photograph: Henry Kalen (1960)
154G9–1

fig. 2.13
Northgate Bowl (c. 1962)
Waisman, Ross, and Associates
Allan Waisman Collection

fig. 2.14
Westwood Village Shopping Centre
Waisman, Ross, Blankstein, Coop, Gillmore, Hanna, and Associates
Watercolour rendering
Photograph: Henry Kalen
646G–9

designed Northgate Plaza (fig. 2.12, 2.13), described in 1964 as offering "the ultimate in comfort." Smith, Carter, and Searle undertook the Northdale Shopping Centre, one in Tuxedo, another in Transcona, and the Co-op Shopping Centre at Ellice Avenue and Wall Street. Blankstein, Coop, Gillmor, and Hanna were architects for the Westwood Shopping Centre in St. James. (fig. 2.14, 2.15) Waisman, Ross received the contract for Grant Park Plaza (fig. 2.16), while its successor firm, Number Ten Architectural Group (formed in 1964 when Waisman, Ross merged with Blankstein, Coop, Gillmor, and Hanna), designed Crossroads Centre.[28] Shopping centres became an integral part of "the 'community'-home development—scores of houses laid out on a master plan with a central shopping area."[29] First demonstrated in Wildwood, subsequent examples broke with the intimate scale of Wildwood and did not often replicate Wildwood's unique survey.[30]

fig. 2.15
Westwood Village Shopping Centre (c. 1964)
Waisman, Ross, Blankstein, Coop, Gillmore, Hanna, and Associates
Photograph: Henry Kalen (1965)
646G9–2

fig. 2.16
Dominion Store, Grant Park Plaza (c. 1963)
Waisman, Ross, and Associates
Photograph: Henry Kalen (1963)
453G9–1

When first promoted in 1952, the suburb Garden City in West Kildonan raised speculation about another Wildwood, perhaps because of its allusion to early twentieth-century housing innovations. However, its proposed scale—1250 houses built over a fifteen-year project at a cost of $16,000,000—precluded that model. Instead, its inspiration was a similarly named suburb of Minneapolis. Great West Development Company hired Wildwood's architects, Green, Blankstein, Russell, and Associates, to plan an even larger project, a $50 million, 4000-home development to be built over five years in St. James.[31] That project, like Garden City and the 3000 homes in Windsor Park in St. Boniface, did replace rectangular street grids with crescents and bays off limited arterial routes, but, with houses and garages facing the street, they also restored the association of automobile and suburb.[32] (fig. 2.17)

By the end of the 1950s, when huge developments seemed commonplace, mass-produced suburbs increasingly came under criticism for their homogeneity. A meeting of the housing committee of Metropolitan Council of Greater Winnipeg in August 1961, for example, felt frustrated in recommending policies to improve suburban housing design. Councillor Bernie Wolfe's statement

fig. 2.17
Cherry Crescent
Windsor Park (1957)
University of Manitoba
Archives & Special Collections
Winnipeg Tribune Collection
PC18/3578/18–2800–150

that "housing setbacks are so standardised on some streets that you could fire a shot down the building line without obstruction" provoked Councillor Jack Blumberg to criticize "developments . . . so stereotyped that the houses looked like chicken coops. . . . There are certain streets in River Heights where it looks as if builders all used the same plan." (fig. 2.18) However, George Rich, Metro housing commissioner, thought good design incompatible with "the housing developer's rights." As he explained, "a man understandably could feel his rights have been violated if he is told he must do this and may not do that." Rich hoped that "enlightened developers" would adopt good design as a way of increasing property values.[33] For him, market self-interest conveniently limited the need for planning interventions.

Informing these deliberations was a 1960 report on Canadian suburbs by the Royal Architectural Institute of Canada.[34] In September 1959, fearing that "exploding suburbs could become a cancer," the institute had launched a national inquiry into the "sick spots in suburban growth." Heading the inquiry were two graduates of the University of Manitoba's School of Architecture, Peter Dobush of Montreal and John C. Parkin of Toronto, along with Vancouver architect C.E. (Ned) Pratt. At the outset, Dobush declared his conviction that "we feel that architects should participate more" in planning suburbs.[35]

fig. 2.18
River Heights (1949)
University of Manitoba, Archives & Special Collections
Winnipeg Tribune Collection
PC18/7243/18–6475–023

During the inquiry's Winnipeg hearings, architects complained that city planners were uninterested in housing design. Morley Blankstein of Blankstein, Coop, Gillmor, and Hanna complained that Winnipeg's planners were more interested in freeways, bridges, and sewers than the "architectural elements that lead to human happiness." His partner, Alan H. Hanna, added that people did not always find in the suburbs the basic design elements—enclosed heated space, completely private outdoor space, and accessible public space—necessary for an enjoyable living environment.[36]

The result of this inattention to aesthetics, the inquiry reported, was a dreary and "drab life in suburbia," with an undistinguished sameness to the houses

David Burley

fig. 2.19
Executive House (1959)
Libling, Michener, and Associates
Mel Michener principal architect and partner-in-charge
Leslie Stechesen principal design
Terry Tergesen revisions
Photograph: Henry Kalen (1961)
232B2.1–4

and streets; "you can set a man down blindfolded in any given suburb and he won't be able even to approximate his location in Canada." While a uniform national building code and easily obtained housing plans, especially from American sources, explained some of the homogeneity, the root cause was suburbanites who, strangely, were happy in their homes—the reason: "a desire to keep up with the Joneses. Public opinion seems to require that the average man live in a private, one family unit in the suburbs."[37] During the inquiry's public hearings in Winnipeg, A.B. Stovel, an architect with Frank R. Lount and Sons, had concurred with these sentiments and had admitted the thousand houses built by the firm in greater Winnipeg since 1946 did reveal that, "like most builders, we tend to mimic a bit." But that was what house buyers wanted: "They are attracted by what they see." They did not want to buy in older parts of the city where, in any case, the costs of land assembly and the dispersal of crews priced new construction beyond prevailing values in the neighbourhood. He felt that the firm was forced to build what "we don't want to build." He would have preferred row housing: "It is far more practical to have a nice row of homes than a bunch of little boxes." But planners did not like row houses and, in Winnipeg, buyers associated them with the dilapidated slum terraces in the core area.[38] Suburban families may have been "excited by home ownership" and serious about their family responsibilities, as sociologist S.D. Clark lectured the inquiry,[39] but they occasionally expressed their frustration with their daily monotony. "Housewives complained that present-day houses have a boring dull, rubber-stamp similarity . . . [that] looked like slums almost before they were occupied. . . . The same plan [was] used for every exposure . . . [with] garish colours shouting for attention."[40]

The only bright spots the inquiry found were in publicly owned rental housing. Their report optimistically encouraged the cultivation of "great new city areas" that combined social diversity in "blends of efficient flats for working couples, houses with space on the ground floor for those who are raising young children, and simple central cottages" for the elderly.[41] Peter Dobush had a special warning to his hometown, pointing out that blight in the city's centre

fig. 2.20
Grosvenor House Apartments (1961)
Libling, Michener, and Associates
Photograph: Henry Kalen (1961)
200B2.1–57

42

fig. 2.21
Waisman Cottage (1961)
Husavik, Manitoba
Waisman, Ross, and Associates
Allan Waisman principal design
Photograph: Henry Kalen (c. 1964)

fig. 2.22
Waisman Cottage (1961)
Husavik, Manitoba
Waisman, Ross, and Associates
Allan Waisman principal design
Photograph: Henry Kalen (c. 1964)

was the price of suburban sprawl and that "there appears to be no attempt to rehabilitate the core of the city."[42] When the Royal Architectural Institute of Canada received the report, it exhorted its members to take greater responsibility for planned residential environments.[43]

Some Winnipeg architects took up the challenge. Libling, Michener, and Associates in 1961 won a Massey Silver Medal for the Executive House (fig. 2.19), a luxury apartment block on Wellington Crescent, and the next year won a Canadian Housing Design Award for 449 Ralph Avenue in Transcona and a Certificate of Merit for a single housing project at 232 Morgan Crescent in Assiniboia. Again they were honoured in 1963 for their design for Village West, a townhouse development in Westwood, and also for Grosvenor House, an apartment building. (fig. 2.20) Their design for townhouses in Southwood Glen in Fort Garry drew favourable press notice for offering the "discriminating resident" unique rental accommodation. Other Winnipeg architects earned their own accolades. Waisman, Ross also received a 1961 Massey Silver Medal for a summer residence at Husavik. (fig. 2.21, 2.22) Blankstein, Coop, Gillmor, and Hanna won an award in the multiple housing project category for their project on Grant Avenue and Centennial: "The project is interesting because it introduces row housing into a neighbourhood of single and semi-detached houses. It proves that row housing if sensibly handled, can be an asset to many urban residential areas by relieving their visual and social monotony." Étienne Gaboury and Gustavo da Roza too were acknowledged for their affordable single-family house designs. Notable as these achievements were, a more sobering comment was made in 1968 when provincial Minister of Industry Sidney Spivak regretted the lack of entries in the housing category for a provincial architectural competition. In any case, architects could only change the urban landscape if developers could profit from their designs and if buyers could afford them. Alexander Cross, in contrasting E.P. Taylor's development of Don Mills near Toronto with the Campeau Builders Ltd. projects in Ottawa, demonstrated that different

43

capitalist profit strategies—one stressing long-term market appeal and the other a quick turnover of operating capital—either enhanced or diminished the opportunities for Modernist architectural design. Too often, in Winnipeg, their works were unique examples, rather than models for replication.[44]

II.

A healthy urban and national economy, which, during the 1960s, confronted no serious setbacks to its record expansion, fed Winnipeg's growth. After the war, no longer the "gateway to the west" or western Canada's largest city, Winnipeg nonetheless benefited as the supply and service centre for the recovering agricultural and resource economies of Manitoba, most of Saskatchewan, and northwestern Ontario. Its diversified manufacturing sector—too easily overlooked because of its many small and medium-sized firms—provided a foundation for employment in the quarter century after the war, as the factory payroll rose by 45 percent in real dollars over the period. Winnipeg's importance as a transportation centre remained secure, as was its prominence as a financial, administrative, and distributional metropolis. New to the urban economy was the stimulus of big provincial and federal government employment and expenditure. Not only did the new programs of the welfare state inject money into the economy, they also employed a growing number of public service workers, and metropolitan Winnipeg, with 54 percent of the province's population in 1970, benefited disproportionately from the presence of 68 percent of provincial employees. Solid, perhaps stolid, as the city's growth was, its future prospects, by the end of the sixties, were appreciated more by insiders than by national developers, who preferred more dynamic centres of growth.[45]

Through the 1950s and 1960s, the urban economy demanded space. It grew outward into suburbs and upwards with office towers and high-rise apartment buildings. Height marked the increasing cost of centrally located space not just for offices and stores, but also for automobile parking. Height also

44

Assiniboine below Maryland Br.

fig. 2.23
Shaarey Zedek Synagogue (1948–49)
Green, Blankstein, Russell, and Associates
Photograph: Henry Kalen (1951)
206N1.4–2

fig. 2.24
Assiniboine River below Maryland Bridge (1950)
Photograph: Harold K. White Studio
City of Winnipeg Archives and Records
Control Box 4 file 63

fig. 2.25
Canadian Red Cross Building (1948)
Moody, Moore, and Partners
Photograph: Henry Kalen (1961)
269U3–4

captured the imagination, symbolizing thrusting financial power and a new "cliff-dwelling" lifestyle of work and residence in the city, but also above it.[46]

Non-residential construction accounted for just 40 percent of the value of building permits issued in the metropolitan area in 1949 and in 1950. By 1959 and 1960, that had risen to 60 percent, two thirds of which was within the City of Winnipeg.[47] Large projects left the most noticeable imprints on the landscape. Regularly, month after month, year after year from the late 1940s through 1960s, the press reported significant public and private investment, millions of dollars, for hospitals, churches, schools, universities, office buildings, shopping complexes, cultural centres, and more—too many projects to list. Added to the category of big projects in the 1960s were high-rise apartment buildings.

Two years, 1948 and 1969, show the variety of projects planned and undertaken in modern Winnipeg. Nineteen forty-eight, with building permits for $18.6 million in the city and another $10.9 million in the suburban municipalities, was the best year for the construction industry since 1912. Among the largest non-residential permits were the Winnipeg Technical Vocational School ($2 million), Winnipeg General Hospital's maternity facility ($1,090,000), Winnipeg Winter Club ($483,000), Manitoba Telephone System's Fort Rouge exchange ($357,000), Inkster Avenue public school ($354,000), Shaarey Zedek Synagogue ($350,000) (fig. 2.23, 2.24), Imperial Oil office ($300,000), the Canadian Red Cross Building on Osborne Street ($250,000) (fig. 2.25), City Dairy addition ($190,000), Winnipeg Electric garage ($150,000), Empire Brass office and showrooms ($150,000), Canadian National Institute for the Blind ($175,000), Aberdeen School addition ($175,000), Ukrainian National Federation clubrooms ($125,000), Misericordia Hospital additions ($131,500), Ogilvie Flour Mills warehouse ($110,000), and Inman Motors garage ($100,000).

From that level, building activity steadily increased. So many projects came on-stream that developers in the 1960s sounded blasé when giving interviews.

45

David Burley

In 1960 R.B. Golsof, managing director of the Winnipeg and Vancouver development firm Lease Hold Investments, remarked about a $2 million, eleven-storey office building at Hargrave and York, "It's just another thing going up. We're beyond the stage of making announcements. We're building everywhere"—also in Winnipeg, the Confederation Life Association building at Edmonton Street and York Avenue, and the City Centre Motor Hotel on Carlton Street.[48]

New office buildings clustered in the core area. Broadway was transformed from a fading residential street of formerly elegant apartments into the financial district. Investors Syndicate (fig. 2.26), Monarch Life, and Sovereign Life built modern offices there, while Great West Life's head office on Osborne Street, built for $7.3 million in 1957, anchored the street. The City, too, contemplated a new City Hall on Broadway after the provincial government gave it land opposite the Legislative Building in 1956. (fig. 2.27) But two years later, the new government of Duff Roblin pledged to support large-scale renewal in the South Point Douglas area if the City built on Main Street. With some hesitation, Council agreed and moved into the new $9.2 million City Hall in 1965. (fig. 2.28) But the City balked at larger redevelopment, believing that the one project would be sufficient to encourage private investment. As proof, Mayor Stephen Juba welcomed the Canadian Wheat Board Building on Main Street, completed in 1963 at a cost of $3.2 million, as one force changing the "sagging downtown" into a "revitalized city heart."[49] In response to the City's hesitation, Roblin took the initiative and proclaimed that the Province would commemorate the nation's centennial with a new arts centre across from City Hall. Like others, he worried that "Winnipeg was well on its way to becoming a 'donut' with a fleshy body of industry, business, and commerce ringing a corroded city centre."[50]

City construction in the quarter century after the war peaked in 1969, and every week, it seemed, press conferences brought Mayor Juba and developers to trumpet another large project.[51] In May 1969 the *Winnipeg Tribune* reported

fig. 2.26
Investors Syndicate Building
University of Manitoba, Archives & Special Collections
Winnipeg Tribune Collection
PC18/7243/18–6475–81

fig. 2.27
Model for City Hall on Broadway Avenue (c. 1960)
Competition Winning Scheme
Green, Blankstein, Russell, and Associates
Photograph: Herbert Enns (2006)

fig. 2.28
City Hall (1964)
Green, Blankstein, Russell, and Associates
David Thordarson and Bernard Brown principal design
Photograph: Henry Kalen (c. 1963)
460L2.1–12

an impressive list of projects valued at $136 million under construction or on the drawing board:[52] St. Stephen's Broadway United Church and apartment and commercial complex ($3.9 million); Place Louis Riel, a twenty-five-storey apartment building ($6 million); Chateau 100, a twenty-six-storey apartment and office complex ($5.3 million); Evergreen Place, a thirty-eight-storey apartment tower ($5 million); Cumberland House, sixteen floors of apartment suites above three parking levels and ground-floor commercial space ($4.5 million); a thirty-five-storey convention centre, auditorium, hotel, and recreational complex south of the Hotel Fort Garry ($15 million); an eighteen-storey apartment and twenty-five-storey office complex on Graham Avenue ($15 million); skywalks on Graham Avenue ($4.8 million) (fig. 2.29); the Manitoba Theatre Centre ($2.2 million) (fig. 2.30); the eighteen-storey Board of Grain Commissioners office building ($5 million); the twenty-four-storey North Star Inn; two twenty-storey hotel towers on Graham Avenue ($8 million each); the Manitoba Museum of Man and Nature ($3.5 million) (fig. 2.31, 2.32); the University of Winnipeg's Lockhart Hall ($3.2 million) and later Centennial Hall; the Winnipeg Art Gallery ($4 million) (fig. 2.33); an eight-year urban renewal project behind the Centennial Arts Centre, with office tower ($5.5 million), apartment hotel ($4.5 million), and other commercial buildings, parks, and a marina; and what was praised as the catalyst for downtown business redevelopment, Lombard Place (fig. 2.34), the thirty-two-storey Richardson Building, eighteen-storey Winnipeg Inn (fig. 2.35), the Bank of Canada Building, and underground shopping concourse at Portage and Main ($28 to $35 million).[53]

One financial executive doubted whether 40 percent of the projects would be funded.[54] But what did it matter? In such booming times, others would surely replace them! Later that year, rumours were heard that Libling, Michener, and Associates would be the architects for a Graham Avenue complex of nine apartment towers, of twenty-five to thirty storeys each, totalling 2250 units.[55] But the big news in 1969 was the completion of the Metropolitan Winnipeg Downtown Plan, unveiled on 5 June.[56] (fig. 2.36, 2.37, 2.38) The Downtown Plan, years in the making, expressed the optimism and boosterism

fig. 2.29
Winnipeg Skywalk System
Photograph: Henry Kalen
1507W

fig. 2.30
Manitoba Theatre Centre (1970)
Number Ten Architectural Group
Allan Waisman principal design with Michael Kirby
Photograph: Henry Kalen (1968)
1103E6

fig. 2.31
"Center of Cultural Activities"
Manitoba Centennial Arts Centre
From *Winnipeg, Manitoba,
the City of Unlimited Industrial and
Commercial Opportunities* (1974)
City of Winnipeg
Archives and Records Control

LEFT. Front entrance to the Concert Hall.

BELOW: A view of the entire Centennial Arts Center.

center of CULTURAL activities

There is good reason why Winnipeg has become recognized as one of the outstanding cultural centers on the continent. Its theatre is among the top five in North America and has staged world and Canadian premieres. The Royal Winnipeg Ballet is one of four ballet companies in the world to receive royal patronage. The Winnipeg Symphony Orchestra performs around sixty concerts during the year. The Celebrity Concert series bring many of the world's leading artists to the city. Summer theatre provides four musicals a year for Winnipeg's large theatre-going public. The many ethnic groups in the city also excel in cultural events.

Manitoba's Centennial Arts Center is a joint Municipal and Provincial multi-million-dollar Centennial project. A complex of four buildings, it features a Concert Hall, Planetarium, Museum, Research Center, and parkade.

BELOW: The sweeping interior of the Concert Hall.

BOTTOM: The Museum Exhibition area.

fig. 2.32
Manitoba Centennial Arts Centre, Steinkopf Gardens (1967)
Museum of Man and Nature (1970)
Associated Architects:
Green, Blankstein, Russell, and Associates,
Moody, Moore, and Partners (with James Christie),
Smith, Carter, Searle, and Associates
Photograph: Henry Kalen (1969)
1282E–16

fig. 2.33
Winnipeg Art Gallery
under construction (1969–71)
Associated Architects:
Number Ten Architectural Group and
Gustavo da Roza
Isadore Coop principal-in-charge
Gustavo da Roza principal design
Photograph: Henry Kalen (c. 1971)
1449–E1–13

fig. 2.34
Richardson Building, Lombard Place (1969)
University of Manitoba, Archives &
Special Collections
Winnipeg Tribune Collection
PC18/7128/18–6191–018

fig. 2.35
Lombard Place Development (1967–69)
(Richardson Building and Winnipeg Inn)
Smith, Carter, and Searle, and
Skidmore, Owings, and Merrill
with Valdis Alers
Photograph: Henry Kalen (1967)
863F–108

fig. 2.36
Sketch of Downtown Winnipeg
Metropolitan Winnipeg Downtown Plan (1969)
Photograph: Ernest Mayer (2005)

fig. 2.38
Model
Metropolitan Winnipeg Downtown Plan (1969)
Photograph: Ernest Mayer (2006)

fig. 2.37
Sketch of Central Park (1969)
Metropolitan Winnipeg Downtown Plan (1969)
Photograph: Ernest Mayer (2006)

stirred by anticipation of Manitoba's 1970 Centennial. The plan proposed a huge redevelopment of the entire area south of Portage Avenue to the Assiniboine River between Main and Osborne streets and north of Portage to Ellice Avenue between Cumberland and Colony streets; the cost over twenty years was estimated at $173 million, with private enterprise picking up about two thirds of the cost. The intent was to serve the "best interests of the ordinary people" and to "encourage the return of people to live" downtown. High-density apartment buildings, an expanded University of Winnipeg, shopping and office facilities, hotels, multilevel parking structures, and a convention centre were to be balanced with a domed conservatory, a winter garden, recreational facilities that included a skating rink and swimming pool, and wide stretches of continuous green space along the river. (fig. 2.37) All would be linked together by "sidewalks in the sky."[57] Even before the plan received municipal and provincial government approval, which did not occur for nearly another year, private developers jumped on board with their own contributions to implement details in the grand design. In late June 1969, a $50 million private redevelopment project was announced for Eaton's parking lot on Graham Avenue: an Investors Group office tower higher than the Richardson Building; a three-storey, 300-room hotel atop seven storeys of parking; a 300-suite apartment tower; two theatres; 100,000 square feet of commercial space—all linked together and to existing complexes with skywalks, an aviary, and conservatory. Architect Allan H. Waisman enthused that it was "the largest project to hit this city, if not the Prairies. It's absolutely unique for the continent. It's the kind of thing that's extremely exciting and it's happening right here in Winnipeg." Mayor Juba marvelled, "We're now entering the space age. We are going to live in an artificial community . . . a climatically controlled downtown."[58]

The new built environment stimulated architects to claim a larger canvas for their creativity; architects, they argued, with their sensitivity to humane living and working environments, could, on a larger scale, transform the city, combining social conscience with technical innovation and businesslike efficiency. Looking at Winnipeg's core in 1970, Gerald A. Libling of Libling, Michener, and Associates complained that, despite the boom, more than a third of the buildings were in poor condition; a plan was needed to resolve "what we now have—unorganized chaos."[59] His partner, Mel P. Michener, saw the problem as organizational: "As our society becomes more complex and interrelated we must develop new administrative techniques to identify functional needs and relate those to one another."[60] To Peter Arnott of Regina, president of the Royal Architectural Institute of Canada, the answer was obvious: "Architects have a unique talent for organizing and making order out of confusion [to make] the city a better place to live."[61] Maitland Steinkopf, Manitoba's Minister of Public Works and Chairman of the Centennial Commission developing the arts centre complex, encouraged these ambitions: "Architects are indispensable to good government. . . . Sound development, as presented by the architects is not just the 'city beautiful', but an important adjunct to the production of our economic stability and the guidance of our future growth."[62]

Eager to advance the modern, architects were often their own most severe critics. Just as Modernism accepted the destruction of an old landscape to create the new landscape, so too architects hoped to change their profession for its Modernist calling. Some critics felt that architects' professional culture, proud of artistic creativity but insensitive to the larger landscape and lacking in business acumen, limited their contributions. Herbert H.G. Moody endorsed the biting criticism that planner Eric Thrift levelled at Winnipeg architects before the Royal Architectural Institute of Canada's inquiry on suburbs: "prima donnas regarding themselves as being touched by genius," many architects showed "disregard or ignorance of elementary principles of civic design and designed individual homes with little, if any thought given to the relationship of the house to its neighbours."[63] Later, Moody still lamented "the tendency of some architects to think of their work as the creation of individual masterpieces"; too many played "the egocentric designer" who desired "to erect a monument to himself."[64] In a similar vein, Vancouver's Arthur Erickson scolded architects at a meeting of their Manitoba association for being wedded to their profession's past. "We have a Renaissance point of view. . . . Somehow we are out of the mainstream of the great forces shaping our cities."[65] James Searle of Winnipeg's Carter, Smith, and Searle wanted to change the attitude of "the man-in-the-street [who] still holds the image of the architect as being an artist-designer rather than the rounded technological expert he must be today."[66]

Their artistic pretensions and disdain for financial details and their clients' practical interests cost architects influence and status. Minneapolis architect Robert Cerny upbraided the profession at a Winnipeg meeting in 1960. "There seems to be an arrogant disregard for the business side,"[67] he said, and, unfortunately, the respect and control architects had previously claimed on the basis of their aesthetic superiority no longer determined their clients' decisions. At a Manitoba Association of Architects seminar in 1965, John Lyon Reid of San Francisco observed, "It used to be that the architect was something of an artistic leader in the community . . . [and] could determine the sort of building he would design, consulting with only one or two persons—his clients. But now the individual client is slowly becoming a corporate client and the architect works with committees or commissions instead of individuals."[68] Gerald A. Libling expressed some sympathy for corporate concerns. Modern executives took good net earnings, not "ostentatious architectural embellishments," as marks of prestige. The architect's task was to "communicate" a building, to "relate it architecturally to its function," "combining function with beauty and economy."[69]

At a lecture in 1965, architect John C. Parkin of Toronto urged Winnipeg architects to direct their creative energies to new tasks. Architects must assume "a role of leadership in rebuilding cities. . . . Are not those architects who are working at the larger scale, with groups of buildings, the forerunners of the higher purpose of architecture—architecture as a social art? . . . Let us not be as slow in achieving mastery over the social forces at work as our immediate predecessors were in assuming mastery of the technical realities of

fig. 2.39
Demolition at Portage Avenue and Main Street for the Trizec Building (1974)
University of Manitoba, Archives & Special Collections
Winnipeg Tribune Collection
PC18/6558/18–5672–022

fig. 2.40
Trizec Building, Winnipeg Square (c. 1974)
Smith, Carter, and Partners
Photograph: Henry Kalen (1974)
16875A–15

the last century."[70] Ready for new challenges, in 1969 Parkin merged his firm with Smith, Carter, and Searle to form the country's largest architectural and engineering concern in the country and the tenth largest in the world. Ernest J. Smith explained that their ambition was "for a Canadian firm for the first time to compete in effectively expanding its operations on a truly international scale."[71]

The partnership did not last. Perhaps attesting to the stress of strong-willed creative architects working together, Parkin withdrew in early 1971 over "philosophical differences." After his departure, Smith, Carter Partners, with offices across Canada, continued the direction the partnership had charted, designing complex buildings and operational systems, complete packages in some contracts, for medical buildings and airports.[72] Smith, Carter was well positioned to undertake Winnipeg's last large project of the 1970s, the Trizec Building. (fig. 2.39, 2.40)

Even as these new projects were announced and as architects dreamed of designing on a larger scale, some observers doubted whether the boom could be sustained. Interest rates and labour costs were increasing, population growth was slowing, and no new industries were locating in Winnipeg. In 1969-70 the federal government, concerned with inflation, cut its construction budget, and the provincial government delayed its own projects, much to the displeasure of local business, which complained that Winnipeg and other "have-not" regions were paying the cost of cooling the overheated Toronto and Ontario economies. A Toronto developer thought high taxes and the newly elected New Democratic government of Edward Schreyer made Winnipeg too expensive for business; as well, "There's got to be a sense of excitement. . . . There is nothing drawing developers to Manitoba."[73] As a result, private construction dropped by more than a third in 1970 from the previous year and, at the beginning of 1971, observers predicted a drop of more than 50 percent in the coming season.[74] The downturn proved just an anticipation of the more structural difficulties that the Canadian economy would confront over the next

55

decade from rising energy costs, competition from new industrial powers, and global inflation. During the 1970s very few big projects were undertaken. Bits and pieces of the Downtown Plan were undertaken, most notably the Convention Centre, but nothing on the scale of the original dreams. And architectural firms let staff go.

Architect Allan Waisman, also partner in the development firm R.C. Baxter Ltd., warned in 1971 that Winnipeg had reached the "saturation point" for every category of building.[75] Office space was not being fully used in the postwar era. In the fifteen years through to 1962, for example, approximately two million square feet of office space were added to the downtown—much more than was needed. The pursuit of prestige, gratification of corporate egotism, or hopeful speculation resulted in overbuilding. But so too did corporate strategy. National or regional head offices of financial institutions required a lot of high-rent space and, in a growing economy, could anticipate needing even more. Investing in a building with more space than immediately necessary generated additional revenue from leasing until that space was required. But property managers in 1963 complained that 175,000 square feet of new space and 200,000 square feet in older buildings stood vacant and they feared that the competition had rendered older buildings so unprofitable that vacancies would increase even more. Older facilities suffered from their inability to offer parking to their tenants, whose employees were among the growing number of suburban commuters. One manager holding his own on Broadway observed, "It's tough competition for the downtown jungle."[76] Managers of older buildings felt constrained from raising rents, lest they drive out tenants. At the same time, they were compelled to improve building facilities and amenities, even though one manager lamented that investing in improvements is "like putting money in a hole" and another opined that he "would never recommend that a client invest in a building as a straight landlord."[77] In 1969, for example, $1 million in renovations to the Somerset Building on Portage Avenue, built before the first war, increased its rents by one third so that they were comparable to those for space in the new Richardson Building,

WINNIPEG MODERN
Architecture: 1945–1975

the city's prestige office location.[78] Even as new projects were announced, the vacancy rates in older buildings continued to increase and, by 1969, many blocks south of Portage Avenue and along Main Street were vacant.[79] One property manager estimated that in 1973, 250,000 square feet of medium to lower grade office space remained vacant.[80]

The Trizec project painfully demonstrated the problems, costs, and waste of overbuilt office space. In 1972, after more than a year of negotiations, Trizec Corporation of Montreal, in a joint venture with the Bank of Nova Scotia, reached an agreement with the City to develop the southwest corner of Portage and Main. Trizec promised a four-acre complex, designed by Smith, Carter Partners, with two, thirty-four-storey office towers, a department store and additional retail space, a hotel and theatre, and underground shopping concourse linked to Lombard Place—a development of about a million square feet. The City agreed to expropriate additional land, to build a large underground parking garage and to lease the "air rights" above it for office construction, to undertake necessary road improvements, and to close the corner of Portage and Main, thereby forcing pedestrians underground through the shopping concourse. In total the City invested about $28 million. But with a slowing economy and a surplus of office space, Trizec could not find tenants and delayed the project, cutting back building to 300,000 square feet and dragging its completion until 1980. A 1975 Tri-Level Task Force on Winnipeg's Downtown concluded that Winnipeg's politicians, impressed by grand designs and civic ambitions, had made an extravagant and wasteful bargain for a project well beyond the needs of the city's slow-growth economy. The Trizec Building became a symbol of the political influence of developers, the pliability of civic politicians, and the disregard for people and street life.[81]

Perhaps tongue-in-cheek—but perhaps not—architect Jonas Lehrman offered a solution to the problem of unused space. Why have we assumed, he wondered, that architecture should be permanent, when other commodities are not and are cast aside in favour of more fashionable and "even whimsical"

57

David Burley

items? Buildings only serve their functions for so long and then require continual change as needs change. Why not grant them a finite lifespan, like paper clothes and paper plates? Inspired by the malleable space of shopping centres in which commercial space was constantly reconfigured as businesses start, grow, and fail, he proposed that "a possible future therefore for the built part of our cities could be a large urban web or framework within which people live and work in inexpensive, technically-advanced, disposable and fashionable infill units." Such an organization of disposable space would require considerable and continual planning and design. Architects, of course, could provide guidance in such a plastic city.[82]

III.

Extensive as suburban housing and downtown high-rise office and apartment developments were, a *Winnipeg Tribune* editorial warned, "There is a danger that the prestige office buildings may turn out to be islands in . . . slums."[83] Private development, observed with excitement, could not achieve a more general renewal of Winnipeg's oldest areas. In 1960 W.T. Haxby, a research assistant with the Urban Renewal and Rehabilitation Board, explained, "Because urban deterioration is increasing faster than present correction methods can cope with it, those families who can afford it 'escape' to the suburbs. Downtown stores follow the family groups and soon other commerce and industry join the 'flight' to the suburbs."[84] In 1967 the planning committee of the Metropolitan Winnipeg Council painted a bleak picture: half the population of Greater Winnipeg lived in substandard housing and, it warned, "Unless downtown is cleaned up, it will continue to lose people and businesses."[85]

Urban renewal was contentious in Winnipeg because the issue elided responses to separate, and not necessarily compatible, problems. From one point of view, renewal was an aesthetic solution to the decay of buildings and neighbourhoods that hurt civic pride in the city as a dynamic place to live, work, and conduct business. Rundown buildings and neighbourhoods depressed property values and were simply ugly. Clearing space for private redevelopment could restore property markets and enlarge the supply of quality commercial and residential accommodation. From another perspective, degraded buildings demonstrated that residents could not afford shelter in private markets, and more unaffordable housing simply moved low-income families around. Renewal required subsidized housing. In Winnipeg's contentious and class-divided political environment, those who recognized the severity of one dimension of renewal frequently rejected arguments from the other concern.[86] Political divisions stalled action. Winnipeg voters turned down expenditures on public housing in 1953 and on redevelopment in the Point Douglas area in 1956.[87]

After these failures, and over the next decade and a half, architects and planners—working in municipal government, at the University of Manitoba, or in private practice—collaborated with social workers, some politicians, and a few socially conscious business figures to keep renewal on the public agenda. In 1972, for example, Mel P. Michener, chair of the Manitoba Architects Association committee on low-income housing, declared, "The architects' association believes Canada has sufficient economic strength to provide every citizen with housing which is safe, comfortable and sanitary."[88] (Of course, architects also sought contracts for the plans and projects.) Leading the renewal and low-income housing campaign was the Greater Winnipeg Social Welfare Council, chaired for a time during the 1950s by Elizabeth Lord, who was one of the city's few women architects.[89] In 1954 the Council persuaded the City to cosponsor a study of the area with "the largest concentration of blight," that from Princess to Sherbrook streets between Notre Dame Avenue and the Canadian Pacific Railway tracks.[90] (fig. 2.41) The report completed in 1957 by Wolfgang Gerson of the Planning Research Centre at the School of Architecture revealed appalling conditions and helped to fix the image of Winnipeg slums in the public mind. His renewal plan and designs for the area informed planning debates over the next decade.[91] (fig. 2.42, 2.43)

David Burley

fig. 2.41
Housing in the CPR-Notre Dame Area (1959)
University of Manitoba
Archives & Special Collections
Winnipeg Tribune Collection
PC18/3585/18–2814–008

Declaring his "full agreement with the Gerson report,"[92] in 1958 Mayor Juba won Council approval for a six-person Urban Renewal and Rehabilitation Board. With representatives from labour, business, the Welfare Council, and the professions—one of the latter being John Russell, director of the School of Architecture—the committee planned the step-by-step renewal of the inner city.[93] The next year the City announced a modest beginning, a collaborative federal/provincial/municipal project to build 165 subsidized units in the Burrows-Keewatin project on the northwest edge of the city. The project was intended to provide shelter for families relocated in a succession of slum clearances: as neighbourhoods were cleared, new housing projects would be built, and then more families relocated. When Burrows-Keewatin was finished in 1963, the City embarked upon its first slum clearance, a 108-acre tract between Sutherland and Selkirk avenues from Main to Salter streets. Beginning with eleven acres for a second low-income project, Lord Selkirk Park, the neighbourhood was to be renewed over twenty years. The Central Mortgage and Housing Corporation appointed Libling, Michener, and Associates consulting architects—the first time it had retained a local firm to design an entire project—for the 349 units in nineteen row-house units and seven-storey apartment block. By the time the project was ready for occupancy in 1967, its redevelopment had forced 2000 people to move.[94]

In the end, what had overcome the City's inertia was the Gerson report's contention—by no means original, since the Welfare Council had argued similarly for years—that degraded housing contributed to family breakdown, juvenile delinquency, and public health dangers. And Gerson and the Council reminded those who opposed public expenditure that taxpayers were already spending money, wasting money, on the slums in welfare payments, public health charges, and law enforcement, all without prospect of longer term amelioration. The only beneficiaries were the "slum lords."[95] Crucial in convincing civic leaders to take this argument seriously was the endorsement of Alex Robertson, president of building materials firm Winnipeg Supply and

David Burley

fig. 2.43
Perspective Drawing
Design for a Neighbourhood in the CPR-Notre Dame Area (1957)
Wolfgang Gerson
*An Urban Renewal Study for the City of Winnipeg:
The CPR-Notre Dame Area*

fig. 2.42
Design for a Neighbourhood in the
CPR-Notre Dame Area (1957)
Wolfgang Gerson
*An Urban Renewal Study for the City of Winnipeg:
The CPR-Notre Dame Area*

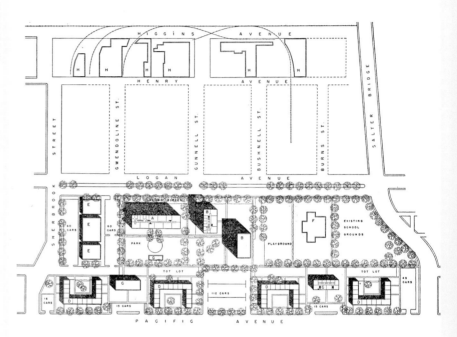

SCALE

A   8 STOREY APARTMENT BUILDING
B   9 STOREY APARTMENT BUILDING
C   3 STOREY WALK-UP APARTMENTS
D   ROWHOUSE COURTS
E   SHOPPING CENTRE
F   EXISTING DUFFERIN SCHOOL
G   EXISTING PARK BUILDING

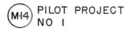 PILOT PROJECT
NO I

The area north of Logan
Ave is cleared for industrial development. South
of Logan Ave is cleared for residential redevelopment. Almost all families now living in the area can
be rehoused here. The first apartment block is built at
the north side of Dufferin Park. The park is extended
to the east and will form the centre of the neighbourhood. Proper plant screening is needed to provide
protection from the traffic and noises of Logan Avenue

Fuel and active Chamber of Commerce member. Public housing, businessmen concurred by 1960, was a good investment.[96]

Securing public support had required an argument that first equated slums with the social problems of people who lived there and then offered a cost-effective architectural solution to those problems, the housing project. The rhetoric on public housing pathologized both deteriorating neighbourhoods and the people who lived there. As historian Alan Mayne has contended, "Slums . . . are constructions of the imagination." To acknowledge their discursive dimension does not deny the impoverishment of daily life, but it does dissociate place and people, and questions how and why the character-istics of the former came to be attributed to the character of the latter.[97] Created imaginatively and discursively so modern urban planning and archi-tectural design could cure it, "the slum" held public attention.

But the term "slum" angered those homeowners in such neighbourhoods be-cause the label depreciated their property values; it frightened those who resented the building of housing projects in their neighbourhoods; and it insulted slum residents who were given little voice in the political process because they were presumed to be dysfunctional and uncaring. Among the quickest to protest from all three perspectives were women, deeply commit-ted to their families and homes and resentful of policy decisions that paid them little attention.

Discourse on the slum after the second war became generalized as "blight," as "disease." As Frances Russell wrote in the *Winnipeg Tribune* in 1966, "A city dies slowly and inevitably, neighbourhood by neighbourhood. Its mortal illness is slum development, a blight which spreads and engulfs like a cancer."[98] The discourse assumed that social maladjustment and parental incapacity of slum dwellers were contagious and a threat to those with whom they came into contact.[99] Landlords, trying to escape blame for renting decrepit accommoda-tion, vividly described tenants "smashing the toilets, smashing the doors. . . .

63

David Burley

The welfare gives them the rent, but they won't pay it. . . . They drink wine and have children—that's all."[100] Wolfgang Gerson summed up the association of people and place in his description of the CPR-Notre Dame area: "The general impression of the area is one of untidiness, spottiness, and haphazard growth. . . . The accretion [in backyards] of boxes, shacks, makeshift garages, and all sorts of debris is a demoralizing sign of 'I don't care any more' disorder."[101]

Homeowners moved to the suburbs to escape the decay and they resented any threat of its encroachment. Through the 1950s, residents of the modest suburbs in Winnipeg's north and east ends lobbied vigorously against subsidized housing, which, they expected, would quickly degrade into new slums and depreciate their property values.[102] The "furious housewives" of Troy and Chamberlain avenues in the North End, for example, opposed a project proposed for their area in 1957, "protesting what they [and their husbands] feared would become a 'shack town'—offering a front room vista of 'garbage dumps.'"[103] Similar concerns forced the City to move the Burrows-Keewatin project about a kilometre west from its proposed site. A band of "militant wives" had declared, "We're boiling mad. We don't want to be discriminating, but if they built low-rental houses across the street this area will become a slum district in no time flat."[104]

Even in older neighbourhoods, householders, often just getting by themselves, protested against the shifting of slums, as residents of blocks cleared for renewal moved into cheap accommodation nearby. In 1966, for example, residents on Magnus Avenue in the North End complained, "The city has allowed the slums to shift. . . . Our neighbourhood has had an influx of citizens who are not prepared to maintain desirable standards of property and moral conduct."[105]

Inner-city residents objected to having their neighbourhoods designated as slums and themselves as slum dwellers. Labels stuck. Owners knew that their properties would become less valuable and, anticipating expropriation at

fig. 2.44
Triangle Gardens (1957)
Waisman and Ross
Wolfgang Gerson principal design
Photograph: Henry Kalen
187B4–2

market value, they were reluctant to maintain buildings already old. A woman living on Stephen Street, for example, concluded, "Point Douglas is becoming a slum because everyone says it's a slum. . . . Up to a few years ago people round here took pride in their homes. Then there was all this talk of it being a slum" and so residents let their properties deteriorate.[106] The deterioration of their neighbourhoods—marks of the "I don't care any more" disorder—diminished the arguments of those who protested expropriation and made them just look greedy.[107]

The promoters of subsidized housing offered an architectural solution: good housing would overcome bad habits. In 1955 Alex Robertson gave Wolfgang Gerson an opportunity to demonstrate what public housing would look like and what it could do. He enlisted twenty-six businessmen to invest in a limited-dividend corporation to build Winnipeg's first low-income housing project. Gerson, assisted by architects Allan H. Waisman and Jack M. Ross, was hired to design Triangle Gardens, a thirty-unit project at Herbert Avenue and Eaton Street in Elmwood. (fig. 2.44) Working within a low budget, which provided little for landscaping, the architects tried to sustain visual interest by staggering the five row houses, of two- to four-bedroom units, at right angles to one another on the flat and featureless triangular site and by painting brightly coloured panels on white walls with grey outlining. Opened in March 1957, Triangle Gardens also expressed Gerson's conviction that low-income projects "should be kept small and distributed throughout the city, in suitable residential areas to help integrate the families housed within the project with the surrounding community."[108]

In 1959 the *Winnipeg Tribune* reported favourably on its first residents. One, a mother of seven whose husband had abandoned their family, had reluctantly placed five of her children in the care of the Children's Aid Society and, with the other two, had moved in with her parents. "The places that were suitable were far too expensive," she said; "the places I could afford were not fit for human beings." Moving into the Elmwood project, she had reunited her family. Thankful for her good fortune, she said, "I've been reading some of the stories about people living in the slums—people who are on welfare—and I can imagine what it must be like."[109] She was the ideal candidate for public housing. To ease public concerns about former slum dwellers' turning public housing into new slums, authorities promised a social triage. The Winnipeg Housing Authority restricted families on welfare to one-quarter of all households in the City's projects; thereby, "ghetto types"[110] could be limited and others rehabilitated. But "a slum is a state of mind," contended City Welfare Director G.G. Myers, and so, all former slum dwellers needed to learn about good living. Journalist Heather Robertson explained the approach: "If the city pays part of the rent, the city has the right to demand a family obey certain rules. Subsidized housing is, therefore, only the cornerstone for a massive program of assistance and rehabilitation aimed at the mental and social side of life."[111] Assessing the program at work in Burrows-Keewatin, Robertson wondered whether "the 'slum psychology' had been wiped out." Not a "poverty ghetto," she nonetheless concluded: "Burrows-Keewatin is not, however, a normal community. It is planned. It is controlled by strict rules. . . . Burrows-Keewatin is a goldfish bowl. The Big Brother of the Winnipeg Housing Authority is looking in everyone's window. . . . This lack of privacy has its benefits. Crime has been virtually wiped out because . . . there are no dark corners."[112]

In 1965, as families settled into Burrows-Keewatin and as the Lord Selkirk Park project was under construction, the City returned its attention to the core area, encouraged by a long-standing offer from the provincial government of Duff Roblin to contribute to redevelopment around the City Hall.[113] It commissioned a renewal study for the almost 700 acres of South Point Douglas and the CPR-Notre Dame area, home to 11,500 people.[114] Two consortia took on the consultancy contracts. To study South Point Douglas, Co-ordinating Architects and Planners brought together Green, Blankstein, and Russell Associates; Moody, Moore, and Partners; Smith, Carter, and Searle Associates; and a Toronto concern, Project Planning Associates. The second study went to Associated Architects and Planners, directed by local planner Earl Levin

David Burley

and including Waisman, Ross; Blankstein, Coop, Gillmor, and Hanna; Libling, Michener, and Associates; Murray V. Jones and Associates Ltd. of Toronto; and Urban and Regional Consultants Ltd. of Toronto.[115]

The release of the designs in 1967, coinciding with the self-confidence of Canada's Centennial, stirred great excitement. The first phase, estimated to cost $100 million, concentrated on the symbolic centre of the city: beginning from the City Hall and a new cultural centre with concert hall, museum, and planetarium, and theatre complex around an elevated open plaza above a parking garage, a covered pedestrian mall was to stretch eastward through an eight-acre park, down to the Red River and a marina. The park, modelled on Copenhagen's Tivoli Gardens, would offer small shops, restaurants, amusement places, and open-air theatre to Winnipeggers, including the workers in the office buildings and the residents of apartments and hotels to be built along the edges of the mall.[116]

The second report in 1968 focussed more on residential construction and proposed renewal of the 506-acre section of the core from Notre Dame Avenue to the Canadian Pacific Railway tracks from Main Street to Arlington Street. Associated Architects and Planners presented a vision that "holds out the promise that by 1986 every citizen in Greater Winnipeg can have a decent place to live." Anchoring the redevelopment would be expansion of the medical buildings on the west and, to the east, a large "government office precinct" around City Hall. Linking the two institutional complexes, William Avenue would be widened to become "the Broadway Ave. in this part of town complete with boulevards with trees." Prominent, north of this artery, would be a twenty-eight-acre educational park, with a high school, elementary schools, community centre with recreational facilities, and parks. Chinatown, for two blocks on King Street, was to become a pedestrian mall, "a mecca of continental eating places, sidewalk cafes and gift shops." New facilities were offered for the garment industry, which, since the Depression, had occupied cheap space in the warehouse district, all under one roof on land bounded by Main Street and Notre Dame Avenue. Manufacturers, wholesalers, and distributors would use ground-level space for display and loading, while upper floors would be for manufacturing and offices. Other industry was to be relocated to large hangar-like buildings north of new housing developments. New residential construction would greatly increase rental accommodation, which, planners assumed, was growing in popularity. Approximately 7500 new housing units on either side of William Avenue, mostly high-rise apartments with some low-income public housing, would replace the 4400 units in the area.[117]

A grand vision it was. But across North America, this sort of planning came under increasing attack from countless critics and neighbourhood activists, who, like Jane Jacobs, concluded that plans and urban renewal projects were "irrelevant to the workings of the city" and succeeded only in making cities "sacrificial victims" to the theories of planners and architects.[118] Vigorous neighbourhood protests, most impressively and successfully effected by the residents of Toronto's Trefann Court, resisting the clearance of their homes in 1966, finally caught politicians' attention.[119] Any prospect for the realization of Winnipeg's grand vision ended with the federal government's disenchantment with what its Task Force on Housing and Urban Development called in its 1969 report "the bulldozer technique" of urban redevelopment.[120] Unimpressed with the number of housing units that had been built, disillusioned by the stigmas attached to project residents, and disappointed that homeowners had been expropriated, Ottawa in 1969 cut its funding for mammoth projects, like Winnipeg's.[121]

Everything the task force addressed had occurred in Winnipeg. Burrows-Keewatin was segregated.[122] Many people who lived in rundown neighbourhoods resented their association with the slums and protested their exclusion from the decisions affecting their homes. They wanted action and, as early as 1958, formed "self-help" organizations to lobby government. And, in 1961, approximately a hundred women urged aldermen "to throw off [their] indifference to the plight of slum families."[123] Later, even though Council refused

David Burley

fig. 2.45
Lord Selkirk Park (1967)
University of Manitoba Archives & Special Collections
Winnipeg Tribune Collection
PC18/256/18–256–080

to appoint residents to its special committee considering the clearance of the Lord Selkirk Park area, inner-city residents kept pressing their concerns about neighbourhood conditions.[124]

Segregation and authoritarianism, of course, were consequences of the association of urban renewal with low-income housing condemned by the federal Task Force on Housing and Urban Development: the projects had become the new "ghettos of the poor," who now were "semi-wards of the state."[125] The Central Mortgage and Housing Corporation delivered that judgement sharply to the City in 1969 when it refused to fund an apartment building complex, designed by Libling, Michener, and Associates, that would add another 1000 suites to the existing 400 units in Lord Selkirk Park. (fig. 2.45, 2.46) Expansion on such a scale would bring "the spectre—and consequent virulent criticism from both tenants and public—of an enormous public housing ghetto." The proposal and its rejection moved journalist Val Werier to observe, "The language itself used to describe such ventures is symptomatic of the philosophy of planners. Never are the suites or apartments in a development referred to as suites or apartments. They are called 'dwelling units' or 'housing units'. It reflects the lack of warmth and individuality in such projects."[126]

IV.

The downturn in construction activity and the cutback in urban renewal projects muted boosterist noise in the 1970s, so that dissenting voices, growing louder through the previous decade, received more attention. The urban landscape had been treated as a disposable commodity, with insufficient appreciation for the people who lived and worked within its space. Lost in the modern design were the unique bits of the past that gave the city its individual character.

As the 1960s ended, architect Imre Halasz of MIT, visiting critic at the Faculty of Architecture, regretted Winnipeg's authoritarian public buildings. "It is

fig. 2.46
Lord Selkirk Park (1967)
Libling, Michener, and Associates
Photograph: Henry Kalen (1970)
1356B4–10

shameful," he opined, "to see [the new public safety building] more powerful than city hall." Elsewhere, he looked for more humane environments to offset the vulgar demonstrations of power, the "great phallic symbol sticking up in one corner"—perhaps in reference to the Richardson Building.[127] His sentiments, expressed near the close of the building boom, had been anticipated.

A few years earlier, Theodore Matoff, a controversial assistant professor of architecture at the University of Manitoba, had lamented the inability of Winnipeg's builders and architects to express freedom and democracy properly in their designs. In a series of articles in the *Winnipeg Tribune*, he offered mixed reviews of the city's Modernist buildings, especially the City Hall, which architects across the country had generally applauded.[128] On viewing the plans for City Hall, Nova Scotia architect John L. Darby thought it "ahead of its time. That's good because you can't look back." Paul Morency of the Montreal School of Architecture found it "very refined," while Thomas Howarth of the Toronto School of Architecture judged it favourably as "exotic." John C. Parkin was impressed that "the building pays an enormous amount of respect to the site . . . and will strengthen the heart of the city."[129] Less concerned with its innovative design, Matoff condemned its authoritarian spatial articulation of citizen and authority. "This city hall, this architecture of Democracy, has separated itself from the very way of life which gave its structure birth." Its facades were "repetitious, dull," and its windows were "lifeless" with views of automobile traffic. The walkways "were never intended for the citizen to walk upon." And if citizens intruded inside, they confronted barriers connoting authority's suspicion. Large bronze bars ran vertically across the entrance to Council chamber, "guarding" the openings on the southern ending of the building, and metal screens on opposing sides of the chamber were "stillbirths of fear." Those attending Council meetings experienced a spectator sport: "The citizen-participant-voter-spectator is placed remotely high above on either side of the council chamber, in two pews. He looks vaguely down on . . . the inner sanctum of officialdom." Instead of a building that celebrated "the aspirations, dreams, and goals of our Democratic way of life . . . the 'reflection' given by our City Hall is that of a Democracy that distrusts itself. In every architectural decision of this building, extreme prudence has replaced imaginative discipline."[130]

Without that imagination and discipline publicly to challenge and inspire, citizens were served meaningless and self-indulgent chances to express their individuality and freedom privately in their suburban homes. Matoff lamented that builders and architects had developed the "intensely humanistic scale" of Wildwood into the more recent "banality" of "the endless, shapeless form" of subdivisions like Tuxedo Park. An absence of communal identity produced pathetic built-expressions of individuality: "The little architectural status symbols of a piece of stone or brick wall, a band of wood veneer on the front façade, all found higgledy-piggledy side by side in the typical suburb are the vain voices of little children all shouting 'look at me, look at me!'"[131] But the carport overruled even these feeble declarations of individuality: "why should one's transportation machinery be placed in front of the entry to one's dwelling? . . . Perhaps the machine really is more enduring in our society."[132]

Increasingly, other voices, too, lamented the "bleakness" and "dreary" visual effect of the modern landscape, as *Tribune* reporter Val Werier described the newly completed Lombard complex at Portage and Main in 1970. Werier regretted, "It does not do much for the corner that symbolises the city. . . . Among certain builders there appears to be the view that Winnipeg is a conservative city and that the people are not interested in fun and games and stimulating surroundings." In a series of articles after the Trizec project and the underground concourse had been announced, he tried to drum up support for a more human scale with sculptures, benches, and a plaza. Why not ban the cars, instead of the people?[133] A few years later Werier similarly complained about the new Convention Centre, a project that was intended to revive downtown redevelopment. It had an "austere style, dreamed up by someone with a mole complex." How could architects ignore Winnipeg's most startling natural feature, its big, bright blue sky?[134] Why did the buildings and "packaged cities" designed by planners and architects leave so little place for the ordinary citizen and the simple pleasure of being in the street?[135]

Similar concerns over the lack of concern for people at Portage and Main provoked Winnipeg Pollution Probe, an environmentalist advocacy organization, to launch a court challenge in 1974 because no one had assessed the impact of the Trizec development on the environment. Construction was stalled for a time. Discounting the effect on the natural environment, the assessment report nonetheless recognized that crossing the street underground would inconvenience pedestrians, though it might give them some relief from the winds that the building would funnel and concentrate above ground. But, more significantly, as political scientist David Walker concluded, the challenge "opened up the question of the acceptability of large scale projects without at least a cursory glance at their consequences on the physical make-up of the city."[136]

That questioning also challenged the need to knock down so much of the old landscape, something described in one newspaper article as "the rape of our city's past."[137] Complaining about "the Trizecian nightmare," reporter Leonard Marcoe doubted whether Winnipeg, a small city with plenty of unused downtown space, ever really needed office towers. In building so many, "entrepreneurs of renewal projects have indiscriminately removed essentially good, often unique, buildings from our city scene—buildings which could have softened the impersonality, the numbing sameness of today's international look."[138] Val Werier likewise appreciated "old buildings [that] soften the environment and stand as a contrast to today's functional designs in concrete and glass."[139]

Winnipeg's heritage movement, which, in 1970, had succeeded in preventing the demolition of Dalnavert, home of former premier Hugh John Macdonald, was encouraged when author Pierre Berton addressed the Manitoba Historical Society in its 1975-76 season. Berton regretted "the cult of newness" and

74

he sadly missed the parts of old Winnipeg that had been demolished. He was staggered to think that, more than a heritage lost, human labour and time could be so thoughtlessly erased from the landscape; not just buildings, but traces of those who built and used them were gone. Where the old had been left, the new abused it: "I saw the most dreadful site I've seen in Canada in your City. . . . I saw a beautiful old classical building on one side of the road and on the other side of the road I saw a beautiful new modern building, and then! Joining one building to the other I see this glass tunnel. . . . They had poked this huge gargantuan phallic symbol right in the middle of this gorgeous classic edifice." He reminded his audience, "The city is our home. Until it has a lived-in look, a home has no texture."[140]

If buildings could be preserved, then less drastic rehabilitation measures, rather than clearances, could improve the landscape. For example, architect Elizabeth Lord, executive director of the Winnipeg Division of the Canadian Planning Association, promoted the "Norwich Plan," named after the English town. Under its provisions, local businessmen hired a board of architects and planners to design a block-by-block clean-up, so that, with minor repairs and fresh paint, a much more appealing commercial district would attract shoppers back downtown. The Downtown Business Association was convinced, as was the Manitoba Architects Association. Knowing that merchants, already losing business to the shopping centres, were reluctant to upgrade their premises if higher property taxes would be the first consequence, Mayor Juba hoped to find some way to exempt improvements from increased property assessments.[141]

In a similar vein, the Manitoba Architects Association came to recognize that small projects in large numbers could upgrade the landscape and, in the summer of 1972, introduced a "Storefront Architects" program. Operating out of its offices on Lombard Avenue, architects and students offered construction and design advice to people who could not afford the services of an architect. Marshall Haid, president of the association, admitted, "There's some justification in this feeling" that architects "only serve the wealthy, the government and big business." In particular, he hoped that self-help groups, the sort of organizations the federal government encouraged with its new approach to renewal through neighbourhood improvement programs, would avail themselves of the service. Haid wanted to involve the association in advocacy planning with neighbourhood associations.[142]

Haid's comments were a humbling admission that whatever architects might have built, and despite inquiries, warnings, and visions in the past for a better future, the profession had, in the end, served its corporate and governmental masters only too well. For too long, Haid confessed, "The architects as an organization have not really spoken up and challenged developments that are ugly and demeaning." Professor Edward Lindgren of the School of Architecture agreed and argued that the provincial architects act needed amendment that would permit architects to refuse a client's request to design something that was not in the community's interest.[143]

V.

By the early 1970s, Winnipeg scarcely resembled the city of 1945. The most obvious changes to the urban landscape were the spreading suburbs of single-family, mostly owner-occupied homes; downtown office buildings, high-rise hotels and apartment blocks amid parking lots and fringed with deteriorating neighbourhoods; and, too large to be hidden, but still segregated, the housing projects. All attested in their different ways to Winnipeg's optimistic recovery from depression and war. The clean lines of Modernist buildings, the almost modular suburban communities, and the visionary plans for the future proclaimed a rational clarity in organizing human activities within an urban landscape.

The Modernist enterprise, however, remained incomplete. Plans exceeded both the ability of the city's economy and resources to fulfil them—as demonstrated in the Trizec project—and the willingness of government to ignore the people whom development affected—as in urban renewal. Modernism generated the source of its own weakness; its accomplishments were its own critique. The mass development and mass production of detached housing gave families what they wanted—refuge in their own homes—but at a cost of uniformity and an appearance of a self-indulgence that promoted sprawl and ignored the decay left behind. Architecture concerned with giving form to function imposed spatial structure on activity with a mechanistic austerity that seemed to forget the individuals who lived, worked, and moved within that space. Planning to coordinate segmented the city and then exercised an expert authority to integrate its parts. But where in the master plan of the whole was there room for dissenting visions and diversity?

Ironically, dissent, criticism, and self-criticism arose among the architects of Modernism itself. Optimistic about the democratic promise of design to create a better world for people, they could not ignore the complaints of common people that a human scale and a humane sensibility were lost in the assertion of professional control. The logic of Modernism and the rejection of the past for a brighter future inevitably and necessarily produced the rejection of the most recent past, a Modernist past. Not all architects confronted their Modernist products critically, but some did.

In spite of itself, the modern landscape remained pluralistic, as the whole could not be transformed, and as some neighbourhoods escaped, resented, or resisted becoming new. The contrast between what had changed and what would not became more firmly drawn. Ironically, the past, which Modernism had assailed, seemed to many people in the seventies perhaps not a golden age, but a time of character and accomplishment on a human scale, with a built heritage to be preserved and a pace of life to be recovered. The new desire to preserve and cultivate roots rejected the ahistorical, astringent purity of Modernist forms, but, in so doing, it chose, like Modernism, to discard a part of the past, the Modernist past.

77

David Burley

ENDNOTES

The collection of *Winnipeg Tribune* newspaper clippings files held in the Archives & Special Collections at Elizabeth A. Dafoe Library at the University of Manitoba was the single most important source used in this study. In the notes below, the abbreviation *WT* indicates articles published in the *Tribune*. In some cases the dates stamped on the clippings had faded and were illegible. Citations in those cases include the article titles, as much of the date as can be read, and the number of the file in which they were found. File numbers are not cited for articles that can be dated.

1   Marshall Berman, *All That Is Solid Melts into Air: The Experience of Modernity*, 2nd ed. (Harmondsworth: Penguin, 1988), 15. Cf. Raymond Williams, "When Was Modernism?" *New Left Review* 175 (May–June 1989): 48–52.

2   Max Horkheimer and Theodor Adorno, *The Dialectic of Enlightenment*, trans. John Cumming (London: Allen Lane, 1973); Jürgen Habermas, *The Philosophical Discourse of Modernity: Twelve Lectures*, trans. Frederick G. Lawrence (Cambridge: MIT Press, 1990), 106–30.

3   Berman, *All That Is Solid*, 288.

4   David Ward and Olivier Zunz, "Between Rationalism and Pluralism: Creating the Modern City," in *The Landscape of Modernity: New York City, 1900–1940*, ed. Ward and Zunz (Baltimore: Johns Hopkins University Press, 1992), 3–15.

5   Cited in David Harvey, *The Condition of Postmodernity: An Inquiry in the Origins of Cultural Change* (London: Blackwell, 1989), 21.

6   Harold Kalman, *A History of Canadian Architecture, vol. 2* (Toronto: Oxford University Press, 1994), 779–81 ff.

7   Sarah Williams Goldhagen, "Coda: Reconceptualizing the Modern," in *Anxious Modernisms: Experimentation in Postwar Architectural Change*, ed. Goldhagen and Réjean Legault (Montreal: Canadian Centre for Architecture; Cambridge: MIT Press, 2000), 301–23. Also "Something to Talk about: Modernism, Discourse, Style," *Journal of the Society of Architectural Historians (JSSAC/JSÉAC)* 64 (June 2005): 144–66.

8   Kelly Crossman, "North by Northwest: Manitoba Modernism, c. 1950," *Journal of the Society for the Study of Architecture in Canada* 24, 2 (1999): 61-69.

9   Winnipeg Council of Social Agencies, Committee on Housing, *Report: Housing in Winnipeg* (Winnipeg: The Author, 1943), 20. By the end of the war, the press constantly drew attention to the city's housing shortage: "New Construction Lags Behind Need for Accommodation," *WT*, 18 January 1941; "Marriages in 1941 Far Outdistanced Boom in Building," *WT*, 22 January 1942; "City Housing Survey Reveals Shortage at Desperate Stage," *WT*, 18 January 1946; "City's Housing at All Time Low," *WT*, 20 January 1944.

10 Val Werier, "Sun and Gadgets: Musts for the Modern Home," *WT*, 8 November 1952.

11 "Fast Building," *WT*, 18 February 1950. For an overview of housing and suburbanization in Canada, see Richard Harris, *Creeping Conformity: How Canada Became Suburban, 1900–1960* (Toronto: University of Toronto Press, 2004); and Michael Doucet and John Weaver, *Housing the North American City* (Montreal and Kingston: McGill-Queen's University Press, 1991).

12 "Building Exceeds Pre-War Demand," *WT*, 18 February 1950.

13 "Suburban Building in 1950 Tops '49 despite Floods," *WT*, 19 January 1951; "Building at Near-Record Level in '60," *WT*, ? December 1960 [file 1777].

14 "Individuality and Housing," *WT*, 12 February 1949. Serge Chermayeff, *Oral History of Serge Chermayeff*, interviewed by Betty J. Blum, Chicago Architects Oral History Project (Chicago: The Art Institute of Chicago, 1986), 69–71 (available on-line: http://www.artic.edu/aic/libraries/caohp/chermayeff.pdf). Serge Chermayeff and Christopher Alexander, *Community and Privacy: Toward a New Architecture of Humanism* (Garden City, NY: Doubleday, 1963); Serge Chermayeff, *Design and the Public Good: Selected Writings 1930–1980*, ed. Richard A. Plunz (Cambridge: MIT Press, 1983); Alan Powers, *Serge Chermayeff: Designer, Architect, Teacher* (London: RIBA, 2001).

15 A number of useful studies have investigated Wildwood Park: Faculty of Architecture, University of Manitoba, *A Study of Wildwood Park* (unpublished research report, ca. 1972); Carl R. Nelson, Jr., and Donald G. Crockett, *Wildwood Park Study* (Winnipeg: Carl R. Nelson, Jr., 1984); Mavis Reimer, *Wildwood Park through the Years* (Winnipeg: Wildwood History Book Committee, 1989); Michael David Martin, "The Landscapes of Winnipeg's Wildwood Park," *Urban History Review / Revue d'histoire urbaine* 30 (October 2001): 22–39.

16 "325 Houses to be Built in Ft. Garry," *WT*, ? 1945 [file 3589–1].

17 Lillian Gibbons, "It's Wildwood Park," *WT*, 7 August 1948.

18 "Wildwood Shopping Centre Is Unique in Dominion," *WT*, 30 October 1947.

19 "$18 Million Plan for 'Shopperville' Announced in City," *WT*, 12 November 1952; "Everything Is Available for a Modern Family at Grant Park Plaza," *WT*, 26 August 1969.

20 "Polo Park Centre Now One Year Old," *WT*, 31 August 1960.

21 George Froehlich, "Plaza Expansion Nears Completion," *WT*, 13 August 1969. On the developing association of women with shopping, see Joy Parr, *Domestic Goods: The Material, the Moral, and the Economic in the Postwar Years* (Toronto: University of Toronto Press, 1999), 200.

22 "Protests at No Shop Centre," *WT*, 10 March 1960; "1000 in Charleswood Seek Shopping Centre," *WT*, 24 May 1960.

23 "$500,000 Polo Park Enclosed Mall," *WT*, 17 September 1963; "Urban Shopping," *WT*, 18 September 1963.

24 "Beautiful Shop Centre a Challenge to Artists," *WT*, 12 November 1958; "A Gong and a Concrete Tree," *WT*, 18 November 1958.

25 "Eaton's to Build $5 Million Store in Polo Park," *WT*, 20 May 1966.

26 "Polo Park Is Sold to Montreal Firm," *WT*, 11 August 1961; "Polo Park Sale Nears Completion," *WT*, 19 June 1961.

27 "8,000,000 Will Visit Polo Park in '68," *WT*, ? 1968 [file 6111].

28 "Co-op Centre Sod Turned," *WT*, 27 September 1957; "3.5 Million Dollar Grant Plaza Shop Centre," *WT*, 4 April 1962; "New Commercial Centre Opens," *WT*, 29 October 1963; "Big Shopping Centre Planned in Transcona," *WT*, 4 April 1964; "Northgate Plaza Offers the Ultimate in Comfort," *WT*, 24 November 1964; "New Shopping Centre Development," *WT*, 27 February 1965; "20 Stores in Crossroads Centre," *WT*, 23 November 1966.

29 "$30 Million Spent on New Homes Is Changing the Face of the City," *WT*, 18 June 1955; "Opening Seen by Sept. 1957," *WT*, 28 September 1956.

30 Its plan was adopted in 1945, based on a design drafted for a smaller subdivision on Lyndale Drive in the Norwood district. The Norwood plan was designed by C.L. Fisher of the Metropolitan Planning Commission, which had been a consultant on the Wildwood development. "Norwood Plan for Housing Approved," *WT*, 11 May 1945. It was used elsewhere on a smaller block scale in one or two areas of the city, such as Cabana Place and Gaboury Place, developed in the mid-1950s off Desmeurons Street in St. Boniface.

31 "Huge Housing Scheme Studied," *WT*, 1 September 1954.

32 "1,500-Home Plan O.K.'d for Suburb," *WT*, 28 October 1952; "West Kildonan Approves $16 Million 'Garden City'," *WT*, 21 December 1953; "Giant Project Will Include Homes, Shops," *WT*, 22 March 1954; "$15 Million Co-op House Project for St. Boniface," *WT*, 21 October 1955; "Only One Job Bigger in Canada," *WT*, 19 January 1956; "New Homes for 5,000 People," *WT*, 10 August 1956. On "The Front of the House," see Peter Ward, *A History of Domestic Space: Privacy and the Canadian Home* (Vancouver: University of British Columbia Press, 1999), 134–39.

33 "All the Same But What to Do?" *WT*, 10 August 1961.

David Burley

34   Royal Architectural Institute of Canada, Committee of Inquiry into the Design of the Residential Environment, *Report*
     (Ottawa: Royal Architectural Institute of Canada, 1960).

35   "Architectural Stethoscope: They'll Study Sick Spots," *WT*, 26 September 1959.

36   "Sewers Win Out over Happiness," *WT*, 30 October 1959.

37   "Architects Report: 'Drab' Life in Suburbia," *WT*, 9 February 1960.

38   "Architect Says People Select Location First," *WT*, 29 October 1959; "Judging Housing Standards," *WT*, 28 August 1961.

39   "Stereotypes Not True: Prof Blasts Bias against Suburbs," *WT*, 11 February 1960. For his extended critique of the stereotype
     of the suburb, see S.D. Clark, *The Suburban Society* (Toronto: University of Toronto Press, 1966). Clark was especially critical
     of the study of one Toronto suburb by J.R. Seeley, R.A. Sime, and E.W. Loosley, *Crestwood Heights: A Study of the Culture of
     Suburban Life* (New York: Wiley, 1956).

40   "Group Deplores Home Standards," *WT*, 1 June 1960. Cf. Rhodri Windsor-Liscombe, "The Female Spaces of Modernism:
     A Western Canadian Perspective," *Prospects* 26 (2001): 667–700.

41   "Group Deplores Home Standards," *WT*, 1 June 1960.

42   "Blight in City Centre Price of Suburban Sprawl," *WT*, 1 June 1960.

43   "Architects Told Fight Bad Design: Better Town Plans Urged," *WT*, 2 June 1960.

44   "Winnipeg Architects Win 5 Medals," *WT*, 3 November 1961; "Two Winnipeg Architects Win Home Design Awards,"
     WT, 30 November 1962; "City Builder Takes Award Once Again," *WT*, 6 April 1967; "Southwood Green Crates New Concept
     in Elegant Town House Living," *WT*, 9 September 1967; "MTS Building Tops Architectural Contest," *WT*, 27 January 1968.
     Cross, "Creating Domestic Space in 1950s Canada," *Architecture and Arts* 1 (1996): 90–99.

45   The city's manufacturing payroll rose $42.4 million in 1946 to $133.4 million in 1971 (the equivalent $61.3 million in
     1946 dollars). See Alan F.J. Artibise, *Winnipeg: An Illustrated History* (Toronto: Lorimer, 1977), 106, 170, 199; Gerald Friesen,
     The Canadian Prairie: A History (Toronto: University of Toronto Press, 1984), 419–20; Ruben Bellan, *Winnipeg First Century:
     An Economic History* (Winnipeg: Queenston House, 1978), 239–56.

46   Clarence Fairbairn, "Things Looking Up at City Centre," *WT*, ? 1965 [file 1778]. On modern apartments, see Ward, *A History
     of Domestic Space*, 88–97.

47   "Suburban Building in 1950 Tops '49 despite Floods," *WT*, 19 January 1951; "Building at Near-Record Level in '60," *WT*,
     ? December 1960 [file 1777].

48   "11-Storey Office Building for Edmonton-York Area," *WT*, 2 July 1960.

49   "Changing Face of Winnipeg: New Wheat Board Building," *WT*, ? 1963 [file 7128].

50   "Changing Face of Winnipeg: Our 'Donut' Loses its Hole," *WT*, ? December 1963, [file 7128].

51   "It Was a Record Building Year in '69," *WT*, 9 January 1970; Roger Newman, "A Silent Spring," *WT*, 28 April 1970.

52   "Projects May Cost over $136 Million," *WT*, 3 May 1969; "It Was a Record Building Year in '69," *WT*, 9 January 1970.

53   Harry Schachter, "Major City Construction on Schedule," *WT*, 10 August 1967; "Building Permits Increase," *WT*,
     20 April 1968.

54   Bob Hainstock, "Industry Heads Agree," *WT*, ? June 1969 [1778]; "Ottawa's Fiscal Policies Slow Down Construction," *WT*,
     27 September 1969.

55   Mel Jones, "$30-Million Plan Being Considered for Downtown Core," *WT*, 21 August 1969.

56   The contribution of planning and the planning profession to Winnipeg's modern urban landscape is another study, with its own
     complicated politics. The provincial government had wrestled with the problems of rational urban and suburban development.
     In 1943, at the initiative of its Committee on Post-war Reconstruction, the Province had created the Metropolitan Planning
     Committee to promote cooperative planning between Winnipeg and the suburban municipalities. The need for a more formal

organization resulted first in provincial incorporation of the Metropolitan Planning Commission in 1949 with responsibility for developing a metropolitan plan and advising the participating municipalities. Subsequently, in an attempt to give more political clout to planning, the provincial government of Duff Roblin in 1960 created a new level of municipal government, the Corporation of Greater Winnipeg, with control of certain essential services, including planning and zoning, water, sewers, transit, traffic control, major streets, and bridges, for the thirteen municipalities in the region. The hopes of many that planning would be a collaborative success and inspire municipal consolidation proved premature. The institutional structures introduced by the Province divided planning at a regional level from decision making at a municipal level, and rivalries, personal and institutional, often paralyzed implementation. Harold Kaplan, *Reform, Planning, and City Politics: Montreal, Winnipeg, Toronto* (Toronto: University of Toronto Press, 1982), 527–603; Artibise, *Winnipeg*, 184–86; R.D. Fromson, "Planning in a Metropolitan Area—The Experiment in Greater Winnipeg," MCP thesis, University of Manitoba, 1970; S. George Rich, "Metropolitan Winnipeg, 1943–1961," in *Cities in the West: Papers of the Western Canada Urban History Conference—University of Winnipeg, October 1974*, ed. A.R. McCormack and Ian MacPherson (Ottawa: National Museums of Canada, 1975), 237–68; Earl A. Levin, "City History and City Planning: The Local Historical Roots of the City Planning Function in Three Cities of the Canadian Prairies," PhD thesis, University of Manitoba, 1993.

57 "Outside Is Inside in Downtown Plan," *WT*, 5 June 1969; "Two-part Plan over 20 Years," *WT*, 5 June 1969.

58 Harry L. Mardon, "Building Boom Shows Revival of City Spirit," *WT*, 21 June 1969; "30-storey Building for Graham Avenue," *WT*, 25 July 1969.

59 "Architects President Pleads for Core Plan," *WT*, 9 May 1970.

60 "Architects Aim to Combine Needs," *WT*, 21 July 1966.

61 "More Urban Involvement Urged among Architects," *WT*, 5 May 1970; "Architect Says Cities in the Future to Be Tiered," *WT*, 21 January 1966.

62 "Architects Needed By Gov't: Steinkopf," *WT*, 18 January 1965.

63 "City Architects Criticized for Not Acting on Housing," *WT*, 29 October 1959.

64 "Report Criticizes Architects Stand," *WT*, 28 May 1966.

65 "Advice Given to Architects: 'Get With It,'" *WT*, 22 January 1966.

66 "City Through as Wallflower?" *WT*, 24 August 1967.

67 "Architects' Profit Secondary," *WT*, 3 June 1960.

68 "Role of Architect Changing; Expert Says," *WT*, 14 January 1965; "Committee Design Blocks Urban Beautification: Reid," *WT*, 15 June 1965.

69 "Architects President Pleads for Core Plan," *WT*, 9 May 1970.

70 "Give Leadership Architects Told," *WT*, 16 January 1965.

71 "Architectural Firm Announces Merger," *WT*, 5 March 1969.

72 "Architect Leaves Partnership to Start Own Practice in East," *WT*, 5 February 1971; "Smith Carter Shares New Venture," *WT*, 15 February 1972. On the significance of airports in the Modern movement, see Rhodri Windsor-Liscombe, "Grounding the New Perspectives of Modernism: Canadian Airports and the Reconfiguration of the Cultural and Political Territory," *JSSAC/ JSÉAC* 28 (2003): 3–15.

73 "What's Happened to the Building Boom?" *WT*, 30 May 1970.

74 Bob Hainstock, "Industry Heads Agree," *WT*, ? June 1969 [1778]; "Ottawa's Fiscal Policies Slow Down Construction," *WT*, 27 September 1969; "Cutback in Building Economic Indicator," *WT*, 25 August 1970; Don Atkinson, "Bleak Year for Construction Appears to Have Materialized," *WT*, 29 January 1971; "Private, Not Public, Buildings Highlight '71 Permit Picture," *WT*, 16 January 1972; "Building Trade Trends Termed Uncertain," *WT*, 13 October 1972.

David Burley

75   Roger Newman, "Three Projects Hint Highrise Building Slump Over," *WT*, 4 May 1971.

76   Gordon Shave, "Trail of Empty Office Space in Wake of City Building Spree," *WT*, 17 September 1963.

77   Ibid.

78   Bob Hainstock, "Industry Heads Agree," *WT*, ? June 1969 [file 1778].

79   Ibid.

80   "Winnipeg Downtown Construction Shows Signs of Regaining Strength," *Globe and Mail*, 3 August 1973.

81   David Walker, *The Great Winnipeg Dream: The Re-development of Portage and Main* (Oakville: Mosaic, 1979); Jonas
        Lehrman, "Downtown Winnipeg: A Need for New Goals," *Canadian Architect* (June 1975): 45–54.

82   Jonas Lehrman, "Disposable Buildings Next?" *WT*, ? December 1972 [file 1778]. Lehrman's proposal was reminiscent of the
        contemporary ideas of the English avant-garde group Archigram, which, in the 1960s, had advocated expendability,
        "throw-away architecture," as part of their conceptualization of the city as a living organism. As one member, David
        Greene, pronounced, "A new generation of architecture must arise with forms and spaces which seems to reject the precepts
        of 'Modern' yet in fact retains those precepts." "Archigram: Architects (1961–1974)," *Design in Britain*, <www.designmuseum.
        org/design/index.php?id=87> (accessed 11 February 2005). Also, see the Archigram Web site: <www.Archigram.net>
        (accessed 11 February 2005).

83   "The Philadelphia Story," *WT*, 2 April 1962.

84   "We're Paying to Preserve a Blight, Expert Claims," *WT*, 25 June 1960.

85   "City Renewal Scheme Started a Roblin Dream," *WT*, 3 June 1967; "City Centre No Longer Hub of Metro Area," *WT*, 24 June
        1967; "Study Reveals Crowded Houses," *WT*, 14 March 1967; "Low Income Families Would No Longer Be Placed in
        'Ghettos' on the Outskirts of the City," *WT*, 2 August 1967; "Metro Extension Pressed," *WT*, 2 August 1967; "Housing for All,"
        WT, 8 August 1967; Metropolitan Corporation of Greater Winnipeg, *Metropolitan Urban Renewal Study: Final Report*
        (Winnipeg: The Author, 1967).

86   On the relationship between urban renewal and public housing, see John C. Bacher, *Keeping to the Marketplace: The
        Evolution of Canadian Housing Policy* (Montreal and Kingston: McGill-Queen's University Press, 1993), 213–27; Kevin Brushett,
        "Blots on the Face of the City: The Politics of Slum Housing and Urban Renewal in Toronto, 1940–1970," PhD thesis, Queen's
        University, 2001; Kaplan, *Reform, Planning, and City Politics*.

87   "City Council Seeks Housing Authority," *WT*, 2 May 1950; "Housing Authority," *WT*, 3 May 1950; "Decision on Housing," *WT*,
        22 September 1952; "The Housing Project By-Law," *WT*, 22 October 1953; "Chamber Opposes City Low Rent Housing,"
        WT, 23 October 1953; Nick Hills, "Slum Clearance Three-Way Job," *WT*, 2 April 1962; "Eye-Opener for Winnipeg," *WT*, 30
        May 1962; Nick Hills, "We Need Overall Program to Clear Slums—Director," *WT*, 30 May 1962; "City Hall Blamed for Renewal
        Drag," *WT*, 7 June 1962; "Some Sober Second Thoughts," *WT*, 14 June 1962. See also Kaplan, *Reform, Planning, and City
        Politics*, 506–07, 509–12; N. Lloyd Axworthy, "The Task Force on Housing and Urban Development: A Study of Democratic
        Decision-making in Canada," PhD thesis, Princeton University, 1972.

88   Maureen Horsman, "Housing Cooperation Sought," *WT*, 24 November 1972.

89   "81 Groups Approve Resolution," *WT*, 23 April 1958. Elizabeth Lord, perhaps the city's only woman architect in private
        practice during the period under discussion, attracted an early feminist interest. In response to a statement from Bauhaus
        architect Marcel Breuer that there have been "no great women architects so far" and "the biggest problem of all is
        biological," the *Winnipeg Tribune* interviewed Lord in 1971. After twenty-five years in her practice, Lord admitted that
        her professional success exceeded her financial success. Still, she believed, "Women are ideally suited to architecture since
        they can empathize with their clients." But she added, "Competent women are a threat to men." Her remarks prompted
        denials of discrimination from local male architects. Michael Rattray, of Duncan, Rattray, Peters, and Searle, agreed with

Breuer and thought that family responsibilities presented problems for women: "You're either in this profession full-time or not at all. You can't switch back and forth between family and business—unless you're extremely talented." Roy Sellors, Dean of Architecture at the University of Manitoba, doubted that women were prepared to do the hard work required: "a number of girls," he explained, "have been discouraged by the volume of work. . . . There is no intentional discrimination against female architects in Canada, it's just a matter of tradition." Susan Janz, "Own Practice Long, Hard Pull Local Woman Architect Feels," *WT*, 16 April 1971; "No Great Women Architects So Far Says Marcel Breuer," *WT*, 16 April 1971.

90   Wolfgang Gerson, *An Urban Renewal Study for the City of Winnipeg: The C.P.R.-Notre Dame Area* (Winnipeg: CMHC, 1957), ii; "Report's History," *WT*, 17 September 1957; University of Manitoba, Faculty of Architecture, Planning Research Centre, *Low Cost Housing Study for Winnipeg: Interim Report* (Winnipeg: The Author, 1955); Welfare Council of Greater Winnipeg, *Housing Committee, Report* (Winnipeg: The Author, 1955); Winnipeg Emergency Housing Department, *Report: Housing Survey of Central Area of Winnipeg. Bounded by Main St., Sherbrook St., Notre Dame Ave., Canadian Pacific Railway Yards* (Winnipeg: The Author, 1955).

91   "Advisory Committee to Aid Slum Redevelopment Planning," *WT*, 3 August 1956; "Jim Hayes Cost $4 Million for One Section," *WT*, 2 February 1957; "City Seeks More Aid for Housing Survey," *WT*, 10 April 1957; "Close to 1,000 Families in Blighted Home Areas," *WT*, 17 September 1957; "'Worst Crowded' Notre Dame Area Requires Immediate Development," *WT*, 17 September 1957. In 1957 Gerson, an original resident of Wildwood, took up a faculty position at the University of British Columbia. He later reflected on the challenges of urban planning in *Patterns of Urban Living* (Toronto: University of Toronto Press, 1970). Gerson's contributions to modern architecture in Vancouver have been noted in Rhodri Windsor-Liscombe, *The New Spirit: Modern Architecture in Vancouver, 1938–1963* (Montreal: Canadian Centre for Architecture/Vancouver: Douglas and McIntyre, 1997), 19, 48, 62, 109, 111, 145, 146, 203.

92   "Board of 6 Citizens for Slum Clearance," *WT,* 5 September 1958; "Renewal Board Proposed 4-Stage Slum Clearance," *WT*, 27 November 1958.

93   Other members included William Gilbey of the Winnipeg and District Labor Council; R.H. Robbins, president of the Welfare Council of Greater Winnipeg; Harold J. Riley, QC; W.G. Malcolm of Malcolm Construction; and Elmer Woods, president of Monarch Life. Assisting them were officials of the city and metropolitan government. "Board of 6 Citizens for Slum Clearance," *WT*, 5 September 1958; "Renewal Board Proposed 4-Stage Slum Clearance," *WT*, 27 November 1958.

94   "Development Design Given to Local Firm," *Winnipeg Free Press*, 26 June 1965; "Rental Project Cost $5 Million," *WT*, 27 April 1966; Michael McGarry, "Shining Housing Project Rises from a City Slum," *WT*, 14 December 1967.

95   "Taxes Subsidize Big Landlords," *WT*, 14 October 1959; Jim Hayes, "Rules Halt Cure of Slum Cancer," *WT*, 15 October 1959; Jim Hayes, "City Funds Helped Draw this Portrait of a Slum," *WT*, 17 October 1959; "'Subsidized' Slums," *WT*, 17 October 1959; Tom Ford, "City Slums Take Huge Toll in Dollars and Bad Health," *WT*, 5 January 1957; "Taxes Subsidize Big Landlords," *WT*, 14 October 1959; "Slum Profiteers," *WT*, 15 October 1959.

96   "Chamber Supports Assault on Slums," *WT*, 15 September 1960; "A Profit in Subsidy Housing," *WT*, 15 September 1960; "Housing Study" and "Subsidy Is Good Business," *WT*, 16 September 1960; "Facts Just Facts Reversed a Policy," *WT*, ? September 1960 [file 3581].

97   Alan Mayne, *The Imagined Slum: Newspaper Representation in Three Cities* (London: Leicester University Press, 1993), 1–4.

98   "Frances Russell, "Slums—A City's Cancer," *WT*, 8 October 1966.

99   "Low Rental Housing Scheme Urged at Welfare Probe of Dalke Family" and "Public Welfare Practices Probe Urged by Joint Civic Committees," *WT*, 1 April 1948.

100   Jim Hayes, "Ald. Tennant Doesn't Know Owner Names," *WT*, 21 October 1959; "Jarvis Landlords Defended by Frith," *WT*, ? 1962 [file 3582]; "To Tour Jarvis Slum," *WT*, 6 November 1966.

David Burley

101   Gerson, *An Urban Renewal Study*, 30.

102   "70 Elmwood Residents at Meeting Protest Housing Project," *WT*, 8 March 1957; "Elmwood Bid Turned Down," *WT*, 28 May 1957.

103   "Housing Plan Corners Alderman in Living Room," *WT*, 1 October 1957; "Residents Aroused by Low-Rent Scheme," *WT*, 3 October 1957.

104   "Housewives Start Battle of Burrows," *WT*, ? March 1960 [file 3581].

105   "Neighbours Want Squalor Ended," *WT*, 27 September 1966; "Splitting up Poor the Cure?" *WT*, 4 October 1966; "Danzker on the Spot over 'Pigs' Remark," *WT*, 7 October 1966; Russell, "Slums—A City's Cancer."

106   Frank Jones, "Point Douglas Is the Scene of Slums and Fear of Them," *WT*, 11 July 1959.

107   "City Expropriation Policy 'Unfair, Ridiculous' Zuken," *WT*, 16 December 1966; "Ald. Seeks Report on Expropriation," *WT*, 4 January 1967; "Park Residents to Get Answers," *WT*, 17 May 1967; "150 Angry Residents Balk at Expropriation," *WT*, 21 December 1967; Michael McGarry, "You're Losing Your Home—in 3 Languages," *WT*, 8 February 1968; "Zuken Plan Would Free 'Trapped' Flora Residents," *WT*, 1 October 1969.

108   "Rent Project in Elmwood Urged to Replace Slums," *WT*, 20 October 1955; "Pilot Housing Backed," *WT*, 21 December 1955; Bob Metcalfe, "Elmwood to Get 30-Pilot Homes," *WT*, 14 February 1956; "Low-Rental Project Pronounced Success," *WT*, 17 April 1959; Wolfgang Gerson, Allan H. Waisman, and Jack Ross, "Triangle Gardens Housing Project Elwood [sic], Winnipeg, Manitoba," *Journal of the Royal Architectural Institute of Canada* (July 1958): 275–77; "Facts Just Facts Reversed a Policy," *WT*, ? September 1960 [file 3581].

109   Jim Hayes, "Mother of Seven Finds a New Life," *WT*, 24 October 1959; "Low-Rental Project Pronounced Success," *WT*, 17 April 1959.

110   Garry Lahoda, "Redevelopment—A Beginning Not a Miracle," *WT*, 7 June 1963.

111   Heather Robertson, "Urban Renewal Not the Answer for the 'Really Poor'," *WT*, 22 October 1966.

112   "Most Homes Are Neatly Kept in the Burrows-Keewatin Development," *WT*, 15 October 1966. A similar argument about the "territorial regulation" of moral character has been advanced by Sean Purdy in "From Place of Hope to Outcast Space: Territorial Regulation and Tenant Resistance in Regent Park Housing Project, 1949–2001," PhD thesis, Queen's University, 2003.

113   "City Renewal Scheme Started Roblin Dream," *WT*, 3 June 1967.

114   "Downtown Development Survey to Cost $200,000," *WT*, 23 August 1965; "Another Study," *WT*, 23 August 1965; Peter Raeside, "Govt. Approves Preliminary Plans for Main St. Changes," *WT*, 29 September 1965; Barry Came, "May Offer Lure to Developers," *WT*, 23 April 1966; City of Winnipeg, Urban Renewal and Rehabilitation Board, *South Point Douglas* (Winnipeg: The Author, [1959]).

115   "Two Firms to Plan Developments," *WT*, 15 February 1965; "$200,000 Tab on Urban Study," *WT*, 27 May 1966; "Renewal Financing Approved," *WT*, 15 July 1966.

116   "City Renewal Scheme Started a Roblin Dream," *WT*, 3 June 1967; Val Werier, "Mall on Market Street," *WT*, 10 June 1967; Val Werier, "An Arts Centre Needs People," *WT*, 8 February 1968; "City Core Facelift Proposed," *WT*, 13 February 1969.

117   "Government Precinct Near City Hall," *WT*, 24 January 1968; "Educational Park Gets Official Okay," *WT*, 24 January 1968; "A New 'Old Chinatown' Would Ban Vehicles," *WT*, 24 January 1968; Michael McGarry, "20-year Scheme Would Cost Millions," *WT*, 24 January 1968; "Report Follows Studies in 1966," *WT*, 24 January 1968; "A Multi-million Dollar Transplant of the City's Heart?" *WT*, 24 January 1968; "Housing for All," *WT*, 8 August 1967.

118   Jane Jacobs, *The Death and Life of Great American Cities* (New York: Vintage Books, 1961), 17.

119   Graham Fraser, *Fighting Back: Urban Renewal in Trefann Court* (Toronto: Hakkert, 1972); John Sewell, *The Shape of the City: Toronto Struggles with Modern Planning* (Toronto: University of Toronto Press, 1993).

120 Canada, Task Force on Housing and Urban Development, *Report of the Federal Task Force on Housing and Urban Development* (Ottawa: Queen's Printer, 1969), 65.

121 "Councils Shocked by Urban Aid Slash," *WT*, 15 August 1969; Gordon Pape, "Changed Housing Policy," *WT*, 18 August 1969; "Federal Spending Cutbacks Kill Urban Renewal Projects," *WT*, 20 August 1969.

122 "Happiness Is the Sunset at Burrows-Keewatin," *WT*, 8 February 1969.

123 "Slum Clearance Speedup Sought," *WT*, 1 July 1958; "Mayor Can't Give Answer to Slums," *WT*, 12 August 1960; "Slum Dwellers Unite," *WT*, ? 1960 [file 3581]; "Decision Follows 5 Women's Briefs," *WT*, 7 March 1961; "Question Sparks Council Argument," *WT*, 29 May 1962.

124 "Housing Decision Regretted," *WT*, 1962 [file 3581]; "Citizens to Have No Say in Scheme," *WT*, 3 September 1962.

125 *Report of the Federal Task Force on Housing and Urban Development*, 54, 56.

126 "CMHC Calls Suite Plan 'Ghetto', Refuses Funds," *WT*, 26 November 1969; Val Werier, "A Home Can Be Just as Cheap," *WT*, 19 December 1969.

127 Michael McGarry, "A Visiting Architect Looks at Winnipeg," *WT*, ? 1968 [file 7128].

128 Matoff's articles provoked a stinging rebuttal from architect H.H.G. Moody, who denounced his "rather twisted and half-cooked philosophy" and offered doubts about his ideas and teaching. "Criticism of Buildings Called Superficial," *WT*, ? 1965 [file 7128]. What Moody missed was Matoff's humanistic concern for the place of people within built space, which he thought best handled in the Canadian National Railway Station built in 1911. "A Stimulating, Imaginative space for People to Gather," *WT*, ? 1965 [file 7128].

129 "Fortunately It Will Be up to Date," *WT*, 2 June 1960.

130 Theodore Matoff, "City Hall: Prudence in Tyndall Stone Porridge," *WT*, ? 1965 [file 7128].

131 Theodore Matoff, "The Sorry State of Our Suburbia," *WT*, ? May 1965 [file 7128].

132 "A Case when More Means Less," *WT*, ? May 1965 [file 7128].

133 Werier wrote a series of articles on Portage and Main for the *Winnipeg Tribune*: "Spark Needed at Portage and Main," 1970 [file 7128]; "Ban the Cars, Not the People," 6 February 1971; "About Winnipeg's No. 1 Corner," 4 March 1971; "Support for the Portage Plaza," 11 March 1971; "Great Chance at No. 1 Corner," 16 March 1971; "For the City's 100th Birthday," 2 April 1971; "Support Grows for No. 1 Corner," 11 May 1971; "Mr. Richardson and No. 1 Corner," 11 December 1971; "Getting around Portage and Main," 20 December 1972.

134 Val Werier, "Experience Can Make a Difference," *WT*, 5 March 1975.

135 Val Werier, "A City Is Not a Packaged Product," *WT*, 19 May 1970.

136 David Walker, *The Great Winnipeg Dream: The Re-development of Portage and Main* (Oakville: Mosaic, 1979), 122–25.

137 Jan Kamienski, "Winnipeg's Old Architecture Is Valuable Heritage," *WT*, 1 March 1975.

138 Leonard Marcoe, "Splendid Past Is Antidote," *WT*, 26 February 1978.

139 Val Werier," Old Buildings Can Be Beautiful," *WT*, 22 May 1971; Val Werier, "We Have Princess, Vintage 1882," *WT*, 25 August 1972.

140 Pierre Berton, *Heritage Preservation*, Manitoba Historical Society, Transactions, Series 3 (1975–76 season), <http://www.mhs.mb.ca/docs/transactions/3/heritagepreservation.shtml>.

141 Garry Lahoda, "What This City Needs Is a Good Facelifting," *WT*, ? 1966 [file 7128].

142 Don Atkinson, "Architects Rearrange Sights," *WT*, 14 July 1962; Don Atkinson, "Storefront Architects: Continued Service Planned," *WT*, 27 October 1972; Bruce Little, "Now It's Storefront Architects," *WT*, 19 April 1973.

143 Val Werier, "Responsibility to the Community," *WT*, 16 February 1973.

David Burley

LIVING MODERNISM

Photographs by **Martin Tessler**
Introduced and Selected by **Herbert Enns**

Completed in the summer of 2005, this photographic essay by architectural photographer and journalist Martin Tessler of Vancouver documents exemplary Modernist projects in Winnipeg. The photographs capture the ongoing life and vitality of the buildings, and their continuing effective use and/or rehabilitation after more than forty years of service. Rae and Jerry's Steak House (fig. 3.1) has maintained its character and dining style with colours and materials that are back in vogue. The Blankstein residence on Waterloo Street (fig. 3.3) is ageless—an experimental Mies-inspired courtyard prototype for residential design. The Wolfgang Gerson residence (fig. 3.6) is one of a series of Modernist houses in Wildwood Park, and, like the Blankstein residence, demonstrates the wide array of architectural innovation at the domestic scale that evolved throughout the 1950s and 1960s. Both the Faculty of Architecture John A. Russell Building (fig. 3.4) and the Manitoba Health Service Building (fig. 3.5) have undergone significant renovations, completed in 2006. The Bridge Drive-In (fig. 3.7) and the St. Vital Pool (fig. 3.13) are living and viable Winnipeg summertime institutions. The well-used St. Vital Library and Community Centre (fig. 3.12), designed as a series of nested hexagons in plan, includes a wonderful double-height entry and checkout space. Much institutional architecture of the Modernist era remains. Winnipeg's utilitarian plus-fifteen walkways, a product of the 1980s, connect some buildings and interfere with others. Few conditions are as uncomfortable as the link that passes by the Winnipeg Clinic (fig. 3.10), a dignified example of early Modernist architectural experimentation at the institutional scale. Discreet and virtually invisible on Lombard Avenue, the Northern Sales Building (fig. 3.11) is a Modernist gem that frames an elegant northeast-oriented courtyard, and, while well maintained and timeless, has an unknown and perhaps dire future, as does the Winnipeg International Airport (fig. 3.2), which will be replaced in 2008. The Monarch Life Building (fig. 3.8, 3.9) is one of the best examples of Modernist detailing and urban design, and a model of Modernist preservation.

fig. 3.1
Rae and Jerry's Steak House (1957)
Smith, Carter, and Katelnikoff
Dennis Carter and Mike Krawitz principal design
with Doug Gillmor
Photograph: Martin Tessler (2005)

fig. 3.2
Winnipeg International Airport (1964)
Green, Blankstein, Russell, and Associates
Bernard Brown and David Thordarson principal design
Photograph: Martin Tessler (2005)

fig. 3.3
Blankstein Residence (1956)
Morley Blankstein principal design
Photograph: Martin Tessler (2005)

FUJIFILM RVP100F 40981 CF AREA

fig. 3.4
John A. Russell Building (1959)
School of Architecture, University of Manitoba
Smith, Carter, and Katelnikoff
James Donahue principal design with Doug Gillmor
Grant Marshall interior design

Reconstruction (2005-06)
LM Architectural Group
Terry Danelley and David Kressock principal design
Photograph: Martin Tessler (2005)

fig. 3.5
Manitoba Health Service Building (1959)
(second floor expansion 1967)
Libling, Michener, and Associates
Gerald Libling principal-in-charge
Étienne Gaboury principal design

Reconstruction (2006)
Stantec Architecture / GBR Architects
Verne Reimer principal-in-charge
Gail Little principal design
Photograph: Martin Tessler (2005)

fig. 3.6
Gerson Residence (1947)
Wolfgang Gerson principal design
Photograph: Martin Tessler (2005)

fig. 3.7
Bridge Drive-In (BDI) (1958)
Leslie Stechesen principal design
Photograph: Martin Tessler (2005)

fig. 3.9
Monarch Life Building (1959–61)
(Workers' Compensation Board)
Smith, Carter, Searle, and Associates
Dennis Carter partner-in-charge
James Donahue principal design
Photograph: Martin Tessler (2005)

fig. 3.10
Winnipeg Clinic (1942–62)
Frank and William Lount principal design
Photograph: Martin Tessler (2005)

fig. 3.11
Northern Sales Building (1953)
Waisman, Ross, and Associates
Charles Faurer and Allan Waisman principal design
Photograph: Martin Tessler (2005)

fig. 3.12
St. Vital Library and Community Centre (1963)
George A. Stewart principal design
Photograph: Martin Tessler (2005)

fig. 3.13
St. Vital Pool (1967)
(Centennial Pool)
Photograph: Martin Tessler (2005)

THE CAMPUS AS CITY

CENTENNIAL HALL AT
THE UNIVERSITY OF WINNIPEG

Serena Keshavjee

When Henry Duckworth inaugurated Centennial Hall at the University of Winnipeg in 1972, he spoke about reaching out to the community. (fig. 4.1, 4.2) His motto "the city is our campus" epitomizes the administration's efforts to promote the University of Winnipeg as an accessible and decentralized venue for higher learning, rather than competing with the more traditional model of education presented by the University of Manitoba. (fig. 4.3) Although faculty and staff at the University of Winnipeg had mixed feelings through the 1950s into the 1970s about its location in the core of an ailing city, they were determined to champion the potential advantages of this site. Efforts were made during this period to create an institution that would play a part in revitalizing the downtown of Winnipeg. The ideal of an accessible, urban university did not end with the university curriculum. Centennial Hall physically embodies the optimism that surrounded the University of Winnipeg in 1967 when it received its charter, the same year Canada was celebrating its centenary.

fig. 4.1
Centennial Hall (1972)
University of Winnipeg
Moody, Moore, Duncan, Rattray,
Peters, Searle, and Christie
James Christie partner-in-charge
Lewis Morse principal design
Photograph: Henry Kalen (1972)
1021D3-57 CN

fig. 4.2
Centennial Hall
Opening Ceremonies
with President Henry Duckworth
(23 September 1972)
Glenn Tinley Collection

fig. 4.3
"the city Is our campus" advertisement,
Winnipeg Tribune, 7 May 1971
University of Winnipeg Library

The story of how Centennial Hall (fig. 4.4) came to be built at the University of Winnipeg parallels the oft-repeated story of London's Crystal Palace. The prescient Crystal Palace was built for the Great Exhibition in 1851 because its designer, Joseph Paxton, promised a large structure with flexible interior spaces that could be erected quickly on a modest budget, inspiring Modernist utopian building for at least a century. These three constraints of size, time, and money likewise dominated Centennial Hall's construction.[1] According to Lewis Morse, the principal designer, budget restrictions controlled the building process, and yet, despite these limitations, Centennial Hall made the cover of no fewer than four architectural journals, including the premier international journal of the day, *Progressive Architecture*.[2] (fig. 4.5, 4.6) It was an ingenious solution to a challenging financial situation.

When its doors opened in 1972, Centennial Hall was perceived as a stylish, urban building, decorated with memorable super-graphics and filled with Canadian-designed furniture. Mechanical, heating, and electric elements were all exposed and integrated into the structural system, and large, unencumbered spaces flowed freely. (fig. 4.7) A facade made up almost entirely of glass exposed the colourful and busy inner workings of the institution to the outside community. As a mega-structure with a utopian iconographic program dedicated to social pluralism, Centennial Hall not only anticipated, both stylistically and symbolically, the Centre Georges Pompidou (1971-1977) in Paris (fig. 4.36), it was formulated on a common ground with it. The Pompidou, designed by Renzo Piano and Richard Rogers with Ove Arup and Partners as the engineers, became an internationally celebrated, iconic building representing late-Modernist architectural style, anticipating post-modern liberationist culture. Centennial Hall, on the other hand, conceived through strict budgetary constraints, continued to be governed by them. Over the next twenty years, the building was fundamentally modified through a series of "expedient and cost-effective" renovations that filled in the free spaces and covered up the glass facades, both of which were vital to the architect's conception.[3] These renovations, although done to service students' and faculty's need for more

fig. 4.5
Progressive Architecture
(March 1973)
Oliver Botar Collection
Photograph: Ernest Mayer (2006)

WINNIPEG MODERN
Architecture: 1945-1975

fig. 4.4
"Aerial View of Campus" (July 1971)
University of Winnipeg
Moody, Moore, Duncan, Rattray,
Peters, Searle, and Christie
James Christie partner-in-charge
Lewis Morse principal design
University of Winnipeg Library
SC-4-1, 84-107-6B

space and facilities, took no heed of the symbolic aesthetic program of the building, which was organized to reflect the administration's stated ideals of an accessible university in an urban centre. Based purely on financial and practical needs, the renovations demonstrated a lack of understanding of the building and a lack of interest in Modern architecture in general, and contributed greatly to Centennial Hall's general devaluation in the eyes of the faculty, staff, and students of the University of Winnipeg.

By 1957 United College had made the momentous decision not to join the University of Manitoba in its well-appointed suburban campus, as other affiliated colleges, St. Paul's and St. John's, had decided to do.[4] President Wilfred Lockhart's 1970 retirement speech revealed that there had been much pressure for United College to join the University of Manitoba. But once the decision to remain downtown was made, or, as Lockhart put it, "The die was cast and plans were made to remain an inner city centre of learning," the university promoters did everything to justify that decision.[5]

But, clearly, a university located in downtown Winnipeg during the 1960s was problematic. Duart Farquharson's survey of the state of Canadian cities for the *Winnipeg Tribune* declared that Winnipeg's "dying" downtown had been absolutely neglected during the 1960s.[6] As the City of Winnipeg's own report stated:

> Winnipeg's Downtown is going through the same changes as the Downtowns of other cities of this continent; it has lost most of its resident population; the people who are left are older and poorer than the 'average' in the city; it is losing its manufacturing, wholesaling, and warehousing industries; it is losing retail trade; only its services industries are holding their own but the volume and rate of new investment in the area are not sufficient to compensate for the losses. In short, Winnipeg's Downtown, like that of many North American cities is declining.[7]

WINNIPEG MODERN
Architecture: 1945–1975

Speeches by presidents Duckworth and Lockhart during the early 1970s made mention of the difficulties of having an urban campus. Duckworth stated:

> We began in the countryside, to serve a small segment of a particular denominational group, and at a time when life and work were simple. A great city is now our campus, and the community is our constituency, and life and work are *complex*. . . . Our downtown site gives rise to certain problems, but it provides peculiar advantages and potentialities as well. We are near the hub of a metropolitan transportation system, we are well placed to serve the educational needs of the downtown working force, the problems of the urban world are at our door step for constructive study and action, our specialized facilities are conveniently located for community use, and other specialized public facilities are readily accessible to our students.[8] (italics mine)

Lockhart also referred to the complexities of urban life, even as he tried to speak positively about the location: "The university is at the very centre of a vast human laboratory. The community around it, with all its *complexities*, offers the opportunity, especially for the social sciences, to bring research and learning into the worlds of human affairs"[9] (italics mine).

Advancing research and learning to the wider community became a key part of the administration's policy to establish the University of Winnipeg as Manitoba's unique metropolitan university, despite the fact that the University of Manitoba did maintain a downtown medical campus. Establishing a separate identity for the University of Winnipeg from that of the University of Manitoba by stressing its urban location was laid out as a strategy in the important 1967 report on campus development by the engineering firm Reid, Crowther, and Partners. In a section entitled "The Potential Downtown Role," Reid, Crowther, and Partners advised the university administration of the role it could play in the downtown community:

> The unique fact about United College is that it will be the only centrally located Winnipeg university and thus in a position not only to serve the

total metropolitan community but to initiate a vital relationship to the province as a whole. For the central "downtown", in which the College is located, constitutes the nerve centre of the governmental, business, cultural, educational and recreational systems of the city, the metropolitan area, and the province. This area contains a variety of intellectual, cultural and research resources not found in smaller communities and not surrounding any other university location in Manitoba.[10]

fig. 4.6
The Canadian Architect
(March 1973)
Neil Minuk Collection
Photograph: Ernest Mayer (2005)

The report goes on to suggest: "the urban university should understand the city, analyze its problems and conduct research into, and comment on them. It should commit university resources and enlist those of the community so that the quality of urban life can be improved."[11] The University of Winnipeg administration was made well aware of how important the university could be to the revitalization of city:

fig. 4.7
Centennial Hall Buffeteria, with moulded plastic chairs by Dudas, Kuypers, and Rowan (1972)
Moody, Moore, Duncan, Rattray,
Peters, Searle, and Christie
James Christie partner-in-charge
Lewis Morse principal design
Photograph: Henry Kalen (1972)

> Those responsible for the Planning and development of Greater Winnipeg are extremely aware of the role which United College could play in the future development of the core and the effects any decision by the College with respect to its role and function will have on the core. . . . Recent studies of the Metro Winnipeg area reveal an absolute necessity for public action in the core area in order to create an environment conducive to the encouragement of private and public investment and interest. The future of the core of Greater Winnipeg, a part of which is United College, is presently under active study. An approach to the development of a sound, living and rewarding core is, or ought to be, the objective of the total community of Metro Winnipeg and indeed the province of Manitoba.[12]

As the presidential speeches cited above demonstrate, by the 1970s, despite the problems of staying downtown, the university's location was being touted as its strength. As Lockhart put it, "In an age when it is obvious that learning must be more closely related to life, and since, for the majority that life is set increasingly in an urban context, the urban-based university offers possibility denied to more isolated institutions."[13] The goal of contributing to Winnipeg's revitalization created an ideal of the University of Winnipeg as an

WINNIPEG MODERN
Architecture: 1945–1975

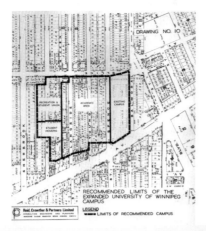

fig. 4.9
"Recommended Limits of the Expanded
University of Winnipeg Campus"
drawing no. 10
From "An interim report of the examination of
potential role, size and
campus development of
United College at Winnipeg Manitoba."
Reid, Crowther, and Partners (1967)
University of Winnipeg Library AC–22–2, file 2

fig. 4.8
Aerial View of the University of Winnipeg (c. 1971)
Photograph: David Portigal and Co.
Commercial Publicity Photographers
University of Winnipeg Library
SC–4–1, 84–107–11

fig. 4.10
"Suggested Development Concept for the
University of Winnipeg"
From "An interim report of the examination of
potential role, size and
campus development of
United College at Winnipeg Manitoba."
Reid, Crowther, and Partners (1967)
Photograph: Henry Kalen

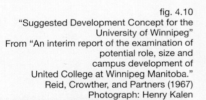

urban-based centre of learning. Creating an image to illustrate that ideal was the next stage in the university's development.

Ten years after the university had made the decision to stay centrally located, the extraordinary demand for university places, due to increased enrolment and changing attitudes towards higher education, led to United College's becoming a fully fledged, degree-granting institution—the University of Winnipeg. As the students kept coming, space shortages developed. Graham Hall (1962), Riddell Hall (1962-63), and Lockhart Hall (1969) were all built during the 1960s, and yet "with every addition to the physical plant students came to crowd the available space."[14] By the end of the decade it was obvious that the new University of Winnipeg needed much more space.

The pressing problem for the university administration was where to find this space. The University of Winnipeg campus is compressed into a narrow site, just over three hectares, in the middle of the city. (fig. 4.8) The Reid, Crowther report recommended expanding the low-density campus westwards.[15] (fig. 4.9, 4.10) More property would have to be acquired by buying out the surrounding sites. The report did not support the idea of a vertical expansion, but suggested that this was likely the only solution if the University of Winnipeg did not succeed in extending its site.[16]

Working within the original site was clearly the cheaper and faster solution and yet no one wanted to see a high-rise structure on a campus. It took Lewis Morse, a graduate from the School of Architecture, University of Manitoba, to think of a solution. Morse had just returned from a stimulating year in London, England (1968), where he worked first with the British-Hungarian modernist Ernö Goldfinger, and then with Arup and Associates, Ove Arup and Partners' architectural arm.[17] He remembers being intrigued by the parameters of the University of Winnipeg expansion, and he produced some sketches for the Number Ten Architectural Group, for whom he worked at the time, which involved "going over and around the existing buildings and utilizing the spaces

Serena Keshavjee

fig. 4.11
The Firm of Moody, Moore, Duncan,
Rattray, Peters, Searle, and Chrisie
in front of Lockhart Hall
Photograph: Henry Kalen (1969)
1268W–4

fig. 4.12
Sketch of Centennial Hall Exterior (c. 1970)
Lewis Morse
Slide of original sketch (1971)
Glenn Tinley Collection

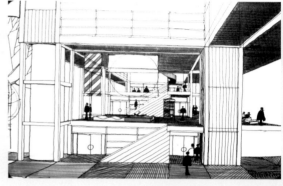

between and above. . . ."[18] The idea of a low-rise building that developed beside existing structures had already been successfully utilized by Moody, Moore, Duncan, Rattray, Peters, Searle, and Christie in the Lockhart Hall extension (fig. 4.11), and so when Moody, Moore, and Partners were awarded the new contract for Centennial Hall in 1970, Morse took his ideas to them.[19] (fig. 4.12, 4.13)

Morse's ideas did not follow those of Reid, Crowther for a low-density expansion, with numerous, new, small-sized buildings. Instead, he turned the idea of the skyscraper on its side by focussing on a large, multi-purpose "groundscraper," a relatively low-rise, horizontally oriented building, which rose over the existing buildings and created usable space between them. (fig. 4.14) No one could have hoped for a more ingenious, preservationist, or economical plan than this one. Because the new building was being piggybacked above the existing campus, the university could function more or less normally during the period of construction. An infill structure meant that no more land had to be bought, which avoided the difficulties of finding land in a built-up neighbourhood. Of course, it also saved money. Morse's and engineer William Milley's innovative construction method of prefabricated steel parts reinforced with concrete was very reasonably priced at twenty-five dollars a square foot.[20] Finally, as an aesthetic consideration, a megastructure superimposed on the smaller buildings offered the hope of both visually and practically uniting the very physically diverse campus. (fig. 4.15) Although it was not his intention, Morse's design also preserved the older buildings and, in doing so, preserved the history of United College. "Expansion 70," as this project was dubbed, was a 250,000-square-foot, $8.5 million building project, the expedient goals of which were to meet the needs of the continually expanding student body with more space for classrooms, laboratories, a cafeteria, an updated library, multimedia resource centre, student activity areas, as well as indoor and outdoor lounges.[21]

fig. 4.13
Sketch of Centennial Hall Exterior (c. 1970)
Lewis Morse
Slide of original sketch (1971)
Glenn Tinley Collection

WINNIPEG MODERN
Architecture: 1945-1975

fig. 4.14
Lewis Morse, Glenn Tinley, and David Tranter
with the Model of Centennial Hall (c. 1971)
Glenn Tinley Collection

fig. 4.15
Centennial Hall (1972)
Moody, Moore, Duncan, Rattray,
Peters, Searle, and Christie
James Christie partner-in-charge
Lewis Morse principal design
Photograph: Henry Kalen (1972)
1021D3–62

During its 100-year history, the learning institution that would become the University of Winnipeg was made up of several colleges with stylistically unconnected buildings of different materials, sizes, and scales. Morse thought these cobbled-together structures were unappealing and disconnected, and he wanted to break away from the traditional campus scheme by offering a huge, multi-purpose warehouse rather than creating more separate buildings. He was also interested in incorporating the urban precinct into the design. A non-traditional university model for the new University of Winnipeg fit the recommendations of the Reid, Crowther report and the anonymous report written around 1950, entitled *Some Important Historical Facts about United College*, both of which emphasized the importance of the University of Winnipeg's maintaining a separate identity from the University of Manitoba.[22] In Morse's mind, the older University of Winnipeg buildings underneath and beside his new ground-scraper would eventually be replaced with "architecturally interesting" new buildings, as the university could afford it.[23]

In the meantime, however, Morse's chief concern was connecting the diverse buildings on the small campus with a dynamic structure. Morse envisaged a dominant monolithic building, which would function as the "connective tissue" between the north (Lockhart Hall) and south (Wesley Hall) poles of the campus by filling in the space between the existing buildings and creating new floors above them.[24] (fig. 4.4) As the partner-in-charge, James Christie, put it, "this at once leapfrogging and unifying concept resulted in spectacular appearance, good internal communications and permitted the existing university to continue to operate while the construction took place."[25] Christie's comment that the building was spectacular in appearance was no exaggeration. Centennial Hall clearly stood out in Manitoba's built environment in the early 1970s. The futuristic-looking structure gained international recognition for realizing some of the more experimental architecture and ideas being proposed by firms like the London-based Archigram and the Japanese Metabolists.[26] The colourful interior was greatly admired for its original and functional super-graphics and its Canadian furniture.[27] Visiting German

british columbia business Journal

APRIL 1972

- STEEL STEEL STEEL
- Triumf Project Pioneers New Science

Glenn Tinley

fig. 4.16
Centennial Hall Staircases (1972)
British Columbia Business Journal (April 1972)
Moody, Moore, Duncan, Rattray,
Peters, Searle, and Christie
James Christie partner-in-charge
Lewis Morse principal design
Photograph: Glenn Tinley
Glenn Tinley Collection

architecture critic Hienrich Engel commented: "The megastructure built onto the University of Winnipeg is something truly unique. . . . This is the first time I've ever seen anything like this and it works. This is a good example of the integration of an old structure with historical significance combined with futuristic design into a megastructure which other architects should learn from."[28]

As Morse describes it, the "futuristic" high-tech aesthetic of the building is key. Every structural and mechanical element was uncovered, acting both functionally and decoratively. Thus, the huge, exterior, steel towers house floating stairways that were meant to be encased in glass, as the interior, yellow, spiral staircases currently are. Had administration allowed for the cost of the glass, the towers would have framed the stairs as pieces of glowing yellow sculpture.[29] (fig. 4.16, 4.17) Mechanical, electrical, and ventilation systems, as well as tubular steel trusses and supports, are openly exposed inside the building in an effort to "honestly" express the process of building and engineering. One reviewer stated: "The structure never yields! Its pattern is all-pervasive, always apparent. The building makes no attempt to conceal its bowels."[30] Nothing would be hidden in the physical building, setting the example for the administrators to manage the university in an equally transparent manner.

The engineering aesthetic that Morse utilized here, and earlier in Riverside Elementary School in Thompson, was meant to symbolically reflect the educational reforms that were being institutionalized during the 1960s.[31] The liberationist movements representing minority rights, whose voices began to be heard during the 1960s cultural revolution, valued inclusivity, which ushered in the post-modern movement and profoundly influenced notions of teaching and learning in the Western world. By the time Centennial Hall was being built, it was widely acknowledged that universal popular education should be extended to a wider, less privileged, audience for a longer period; that the structure of authority had to be democratized; that the ideological basis of

111

fig. 4.18
Centennial Hall Lounge (1972)
Moody, Moore, Duncan, Rattray,
Peters, Searle, and Christie
James Christie partner-in-charge
Lewis Morse principal design
Photograph: Henry Kalen (1972)
1021D3–91

fig. 4.17
Centennial Hall Building in Progress (1970–71)
Moody, Moore, Duncan, Rattray,
Peters, Searle, and Christie
James Christie partner-in-charge
Lewis Morse principal design
University of Winnipeg Library
SC–4–1, 84–104–11

curricula was being challenged by minority cultures; and that knowledge must be made more relevant to life and not simply memorized.[32] The use of a transparent, exposed mechanical aesthetic and flexible spaces became the architectural signifiers of the democratization and decentralization of education. Morse purposefully utilized the symbolism of the engineering aesthetic to reinforce the idea of a rational, flexible, and accessible learning university.

The rationale that structure could be decorative as well as functional was also applied to the space. Moody, Moore, Duncan, Rattray, Peters, Searle, and Christie denied the notion of a patriarchal "master plan," and instead promoted flexibility of space as a fundamental principle of design and teaching:

> In considering the future growth of the University of Winnipeg beyond the Expansion 70 programme, the architects have avoided the temptation to develop some form of "master plan," attempting instead to design a flexible system which can eventually adapt itself to changing functions in the years ahead. . . . [C]hange in enrollment patterns, change in teaching patterns, introduction of new courses and the abandonment of old ones, led to the recognition of the importance of flexibility. . . . The present system has been designed to anticipate and accept the fact that continuous evolution and change takes place in the learning process and in the growth of universities.[33]

That space should be user-determined rather than predetermined was a popular idea during the 1970s. Clients' needs had become so complex, it was suggested, that space had to be made versatile or it might become useless soon after the building's completion.[34] Christie refers to Centennial Hall as being built from a "Meccano set," meaning that it is easier to change and rearrange this type of structure than a traditional building with predetermined spaces.[35] The 250,000-square-foot building had vast spaces on each floor to be used in a multitude of ways. Large, open areas were assigned to the cafeteria and lounge spaces, which could accommodate students in less formal settings. (fig. 4.18) Morse planned for complete flexibility, even to the extent of some

fig. 4.19
Mobile Unit (c. 1970)
Lewis Morse
Slide of original drawing (1971)
Glenn Tinley Collection

moveable workstations, designed from prefabricated trailers, rather than stationary, preset, professors' offices.[36] (fig. 4.19) The Meccano set-like flexibility of the building proved immensely useful and economical as the University of Winnipeg student body kept expanding. It did nothing, however, to keep the architects' careful conception of open spaces intact. The ease with which the free spaces could be filled in meant that, in reality, slowly but surely, the universal space was designated and thus eradicated.

Typical of many utopian Modernist buildings is the concept of transparency, a fundamental element of the original conception of Centennial Hall. The fifth-floor library stacks use transparency to provide exterior circulatory elements and visual interest in the subdued atmosphere of an academic reading room. (fig. 4.20) Large stack rooms flow one into the other, linked by glass-walled walkways with exterior courtyard spaces and stunning views of Winnipeg. But it was in the south facade that the most clearly conceptual use of transparency was evident. (fig. 4.21) In 1972 the physical contrast between Centennial Hall and Wesley Hall (1896) was considerable. Centennial Hall was built up of an exposed, slender, steel frame, and its main-floor walls and entranceway were of glass, expressly countering the thick, stone, castellated facade of Wesley Hall. As Jonas Lehrman described it, "Entering the new building from the direction of Wesley Hall and ascending to the fourth floor by escalator is an exciting spatial experience, full of promise, which is fulfilled in the subsequent views of interpenetrating internal levels and exterior courtyards."[37] Following the changes in pedagogical practice during the late 1960s and early 1970s, the glass entranceway and second-floor outdoor lounge, made lively with students using the stairway in-between, was meant to be not only visually interesting, but transparent and inviting, breaking through the crenulated stone fortification of Wesley Hall and the nineteenth-century model of education it represented. (fig. 4.22) Morse's goal was an egalitarian and democratic building. Centennial Hall was a manifesto of a new post-modern era, in contrast to the crumbling stone walls of Wesley Hall.[38]

fig. 4.20
Centennial Hall Library Walkway (1972)
Moody, Moore, Duncan, Rattray,
Peters, Searle, and Christie
James Christie partner-in-charge
Lewis Morse principal design
Photograph: Henry Kalen (1972)

fig. 4.21
Centennial Hall (1972)
Moody, Moore, Duncan, Rattray,
Peters, Searle, and Christie
James Christie partner-in-charge
Lewis Morse principal design
Photograph: Henry Kalen (1972)
1021D3–61

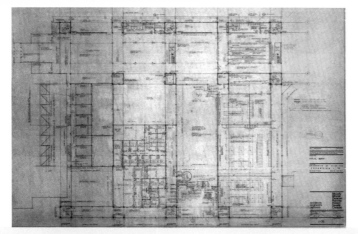

fig. 4.24
Plan of the Fourth Floor (1970)
Centennial Hall
Moody, Moore, Duncan, Rattray,
Peters, Searle, and Christie
James Christie partner-in-charge
Lewis Morse principal design
Digital Scan: Brad Russell (2005)
James Christie Collection

Architectural historian Jean Lauxerois notes that transparency and flexibility of space were key characteristics of historical, Modern, utopian building from the Crystal Palace to the Centre Georges Pompidou: "Le verre est cette immatérielle matierè qui, . . . signifie le principe de l'absolue visibilité, garantit la transparence du système et activie la fluidité des circulations."[39] By the late 1960s, issues of social pluralism and relativity are reflected in architectural concepts of flexible, open space, transparency, and the exposed aesthetic of the High-Tech Style, which had become signifiers of democracy, anticipating post-modernism, all of which are embodied in Centennial Hall.

fig. 4.22
Wesley Hall, University of Winnipeg (c.1969)
Glenn Tinley Collection

The idea of opening up the building to more pluralistic and non-hierarchical educational methods penetrated the university system. Henry Duckworth, who was inaugurated as president along with the new building in 1972, seemed to embrace these cultural changes, adopting the catchy motto "the city is our campus," organizing credit courses under the auspices of a "University at Noon" to be held in department stores, office buildings, and a downtown church, and continuing the Institute for Urban Studies. As a gesture symbolic of his good faith in reaching into the community, he had the fence that surrounded the University of Winnipeg removed. (fig. 4.22) He characterized this move as an attempt to "share our patch of green with our neighbours."[40] Influenced by the success of the Open University in the United Kingdom, in his inaugural speech, Duckworth spoke of changing the curriculum in order to make the university experience a more relevant one.

fig. 4.23
Plug-In City
University Node—Elevation (1965)
Monochrome print
Peter Cook, Archigram
The Archigram Archives

> With Arts and Science, the curriculum traditionally has been disinterested and liberal, deriving in part from the ancient view that University students come from a select group and deliberately withdraw from society for a few years to read, to discuss, to reflect—before returning to assume positions of privilege. As universities become increasingly egalitarian and graduates are expected increasingly to work for a living, it is not surprising that our Arts and Science curriculum has been adding a here-and-now component as an optional supplement to its traditional, timeless core . . . what might be called 'An Education for Today and Tomorrow, . . . [41]

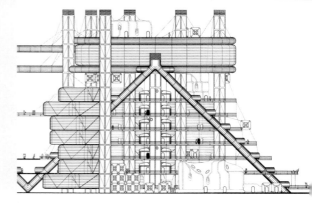

116

fig. 4.26
Main Floor Entrance
Centennial Hall (1972)
Moody, Moore, Duncan, Rattray,
Peters, Searle, and Christie
James Christie partner-in-charge
Lewis Morse principal design
Photograph: Henry Kalen
Glenn Tinley Collection

fig. 4.25
Interior Design for Main Floor Entrance (c. 1971)
Centennial Hall
Ursula Ferguson
Ink and collage on paper
Glenn Tinley Collection

fig. 4.27
Interior Design for Buffeteria (c. 1971)
Centennial Hall
Ursula Ferguson
Ink and collage on paper
Glenn Tinley Collection

fig. 4. 28
Centennial Hall Buffeteria (1972)
Moody, Moore, Duncan, Rattray,
Peters, Searle, and Christie
James Christie partner-in-charge
Lewis Morse principal design
Photograph: Henry Kalen

Morse was also interested in an egalitarian, decentralized university experience and he used the model of the city as his inspiration for the physical structure of Centennial Hall at a number of different levels. Centennial Hall paralleled other late-1960s experimental, urban architectural conceptions such as Archigram's Plug-In City, where living pods could be rearranged within a metal skeleton, especially the University Node of Plug-In City from 1965 (fig. 4.23), and the University of Alberta's covered street student centre, Hub Mall, designed by Diamond and Myers between 1969 and 1973.[42] With its warehouse feel of exposed pipes, Centennial Hall was to relate to the urban environment in which the students were immersed. Morse conceived of the building itself, like Hub Mall, as a street linking all the separate older buildings.

As with any city, circulation was a challenge for the university because of the volume of students travelling through the building at set times. Because Centennial Hall has few of the traditional markers of hallways and corridors, and because it connected a number of buildings, directing the human traffic became vital.[43] "Pedestrian Streets," as described by Christie, led the students through the building to the central meeting places.[44] (fig. 4.24) Both main pedestrian circulation routes were marked by colourful super-graphic arrows, designed by Ursula Ferguson, which pointed out the key directions. (fig. 4.25, 4.26) When one entered the building, the double bank of escalators immediately directed users up to the main student areas on the fourth floor—the buffeteria (fig. 4.27, 4.28), which was to serve as the city's main square, and the library—considerably reducing the congestion on the main floor. A second thoroughfare took students through the building's north-south axis to the Lockhart lobby. The conceit of a city with "streets," street signs, and walkways was continued into outdoor and indoor courtyards. Morse conceived of the outdoor courtyards in the fourth and fifth levels as a series of exterior circulatory elements to bring in natural light and add some visual variety to the interior of the library. (fig. 4.29, 4.30) Centennial Hall was designed as a mini-city in the core of a bigger city. It was a newly designed, fully functioning city with fresh paint, and a growing, youthful population, in other words,

117

Serena Keshavjee

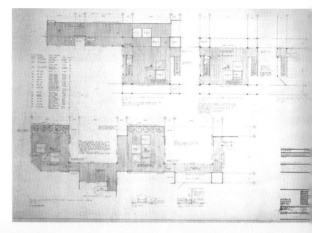

fig. 4.29
Plan of Courtyards (1972)
Centennial Hall
Moody, Moore, Duncan, Rattray,
Peters, Searle, and Christie
James Christie partner-in-charge
Lewis Morse principal design
Digital Scan: Brad Russell (2005)
James Christie Collection

everything Winnipeg was not. Just as the utopian choice of the "honest" High-tech Style and open plan set the tone for the administration of the university, so too was the building meant to function symbolically as a model of a thriving city within a decaying one.

Exposing the infrastructure of the building exaggerated the Modernist desire for frankness to material, structure, and use. A building where nothing structural or mechanical is hidden, where space is determined by few walls, where the inside and the outside flow into each other, and where glass dominates, was very much in tune with the cultural changes of the 1960s. Centennial Hall embodied in its physical structure and layout utopian ideas of equality and liberation. As the author of the *Progressive Architecture* article states, the architects "[s]et out to design a system, not a building—an encapsulation of university activities."[45]

And yet, the conception for the building as an inviting metropolitan centre open to the community did not happen to the degree desired. It was President Duckworth's decision in 1977 to fill in the facade of Centennial Hall by closing off the second-floor courtyard and entrance to make room for a much needed large lecture theatre (later to be named the Eckhardt Grammate Hall) and classroom. Duckworth thought the second-floor entrance was underutilized, he described it as "dead-space," and thus he went ahead with a practical and cost-efficient scheme that fundamentally modified the entranceway.[46] (fig. 4.31, 4.32, 4.33) The large, existing trusses at the entranceway easily supported an enclosed space, and his decision to place Eckhardt Grammate Hall there was logical. (fig. 4.34) Yet, covering over the second-floor courtyard and much of the glass of the facades that face Portage Avenue and especially Spence Street dramatically changed the street presence of the building, turning it away from the city. The advertised Meccano-like quality of the structure lived up to its conception of being a flexible system, easily adapting itself to client's need as the architects had advertised, but in the end this very flexibility contributed to the building's devaluation, as renovations, easy and cheap

fig. 4.30
Courtyard (c. 1970)
Centennial Hall
Slide of original drawing (1971)
Lewis Morse
Glenn Tinley Collection

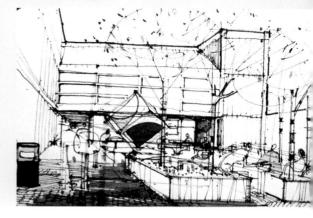

FOURTH MEZZANINE COURTYARD

fig. 4.31
Design for Second Floor Courtyard (c. 1971)
Centennial Hall
Ursula Ferguson
Ink and collage on paper
Glenn Tinley Collection

to facilitate, slowly filled in glass walls, student lounges, courtyards, and the other free spaces, dramatically altering the visual impact of the interpenetrating indoor/outdoor spaces. By the end of the 1970s, Centennial Hall became as much a fortress as Wesley Hall was. (fig. 4.35)

During the next ten years, Centennial Hall was under attack by the faculty and staff who had become disgruntled with the building, especially its style. The brightly coloured graphics seemed out of date and were painted over, eradicating the directional signs in the building and confusing traffic flow.[47] The carefully thought-out furniture and carpets wore badly under the stress of cigarette burns, dust collected on the exposed trusses and pipes, and the lounge and courtyard spaces, so crucial to the architect's conception of a city within the campus, were whittled away by more prosaic demands. Professors complained of noise due to exposed pipes, and the joins between Centennial Hall and the older buildings were never properly completed, remaining awkward. The administrative decision to value cost-effective renovations over the architect's conception, the modus operandi from day one, steadily dismantled the building's aesthetic program. Today, the building is rundown, chopped up in terms of its spatial layout, and badly cluttered with inappropriate furniture and corporate-style renovations. It is reviled at worst and ignored at best. Ironically, the campus that was to be a model for the declining city was allowed to decline itself. Commenting in the 1960s, Duart Farquharson of the *Winnipeg Tribune* implied that the neglect of Winnipeg had gone on for so long that it was going to be difficult to correct it, a legacy Winnipeggers still live with today. The situation is parallel for Centennial Hall. Luckily, its structure and engineering design do remain in good condition, even if they are obscured by the pastel washes of the 1980s makeovers.

fig. 4.32
Second Floor Courtyard
Centennial Hall (1971)
Moody, Moore, Duncan, Rattray,
Peters, Searle, and Christie
James Christie partner-in-charge
Lewis Morse principal design
Photograph: Henry Kalen
1021D3–121

In his book *The Making of the Beaubourg* about the Centre Georges Pompidou, Nathan Silver notes that "the developing architectural culture of the early 1970s was converging. Between 1972 and 1974, architects who knew nothing of the Beaubourg competition" were designing related buildings.[48] (fig. 4.36)

119

fig. 4.33
Second Floor Courtyard (c. 1971)
Centennial Hall
Moody, Moore, Duncan, Rattray,
Peters, Searle, and Christie
James Christie partner-in-charge
Lewis Morse principal design
Photograph: Henry Kalen
Glenn Tinley Collection

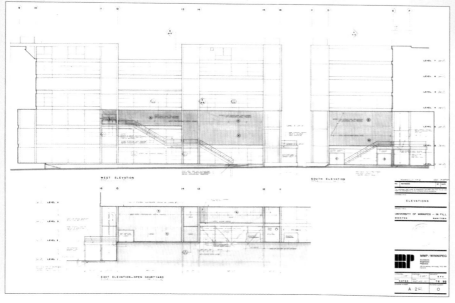

fig. 4.34
Renovation Elevation (1977)
Centennial Hall
MMP Architects, Engineers
Archives of Manitoba

fig. 4.36
Centre Georges Pompidou (1971–77)
Renzo Piano and Richard Rogers
Photograph: Oliver Botar (2003)

Centennial Hall is clearly one of those buildings, and not surprisingly so since Morse trained for one year in 1968 with Arup and Associates, the architectural division of Ove Arup and Partners, who, between 1971 and 1977, organized the engineering for the Centre Georges Pompidou with architects Renzo Piano and Richard Rogers. While it might be assumed that Centennial Hall was inspired by the more famous Pompidou, in fact, the competition for the Beaubourg was not announced until January 1971—by which time the University of Winnipeg plans were well finished.[49] What Morse did glean from Arup and Associates was a collaborative working method between engineers and architects, which saw the integration of structure with mechanics, an interest in an "honest" architecture, and the engineering aesthetic suitable for a flexible multi-use space. But it was Morse's coming of age in the 1960s that motivated him, as it did Piano and Rogers, to create a non-elitist institution accessibly located in the middle of the city. The Pompidou Centre was acclaimed for opening up culture to a wide audience—a "supermarket of culture," as it was called.[50] The architects described it as "'a live centre of information, entertainment and culture' the building to be both a flexible container and a dynamic machine, highly serviced and made from prefabricate pieces, aimed at attracting as wide a public as possible by cutting across the traditional cultural institutional limits."[51] Claude Mollard, the general secretary of the Pompidou Centre, wanted it to be "a house for everyone which will be open to all forms of cultural expression, whatever their origin."[52] As we have seen, these goals were also ascribed to Centennial Hall.

The cultural revolution of the 1960s demanded changes in attitudes towards education, and Centennial Hall and the Pompidou directly reflect those changes. For architectural historians Alan Colquhoun and Jean Lauxerois, the Pompidou's functionalism, flexibility, and transparency align it with the Modern utopian tradition of iron and glass buildings.[53] The Modernist notion of open, flexible space had come to represent a post-modern, non-hierarchical structure and social pluralism. In Centennial Hall and the Pompidou, glass, space, and exposed structural elements were used to symbolize accessibility

Serena Keshavjee

and a decentralization of culture and education and, thus, of power. Along these lines, both Centennial Hall and the Pompidou were planned to play a revitalizing role in downtown neighbourhoods and the success of the Pompidou in this endeavour is evident in the immense popularity of the area around Les Halles. Both buildings are horizontal megastructures in tune with the height of the older buildings around them, despite the exposed steel frame of their machine aesthetic, which in both cases was used to render a traditional type of institution more up-to-date and reflective of twentieth-century urban values. The facade of the French museum was made lively through the bright colours, exposed escalators, and glass walls. The original facade at Centennial Hall used a bright yellow on the exposed, open stair rail, the walls were all glass, and the second-level entrance courtyard was filled with locally designed, organically shaped, vibrantly coloured furnishings.

The similarities between the Pompidou Centre and Centennial Hall end there. The building of the Pompidou has been well preserved over the past twenty-five years and just celebrated its anniversary with a careful renovation by one of the original architects, Renzo Piano. The new renovation, however, has been criticized for destroying the spirit of the original concept by imposing charges for the scenic escalator rides up the exterior wall, and remodelling the casual cafeteria into a exclusive restaurant no longer priced for the general public. Interestingly enough, the case of the University of Winnipeg is almost opposite. The University of Winnipeg continues to uphold its promise of accessibility to students and pays attention to its inner-city, heterogeneous student body and urban environs, yet the potential relevance of the very structure within which the university's avowed program is housed is diminished and dismissed.[54]

fig. 4.35
Centennial Hall after 1977 Renovation
MMP Architects, Engineers
University of Winnipeg Archives

ENDNOTES

Acknowledgements: I would like to thank Peter McCormack, who carried out an independent study on the assigned topic of a comparison of Centennial Hall and the Centre Georges Pompidou under my direction in 2003. His excellent paper uncovered the basic archival sources and issues for me to begin my work. I thank my research assistant Aldona Dziedziejko for interviewing Lewis Morse on my behalf in 2004 and gathering articles for me. I want to thank those who read and commented on my paper: Oliver Botar, Henry Duckworth, Steven Coppinger, and Daniel Stone. I would also like to thank Peter James for his guidance in navigating the University of Winnipeg Archives, and Jude Romualdo for scanning some of the images for this article. Brad Russell, University of Winnipeg's map librarian, must also be thanked for his assistance with the scanning of the large plans of Centennial Hall. Lewis Morse, James Christie, and Glenn Tinley offered up their archives and their ideas willingly and I very much appreciated their time and information. In addition to the University of Winnipeg Archives and private archives, I also researched at the Archives of Manitoba, looking at the papers of Moody, Moore, and Partners. I thank Christopher Kotecki, Reference Services Assistant, for his help.

1   See James Christie, "University of Winnipeg," *Western Construction and Industry* (August-September 1972): 5; no author, "Expansion of University of Winnipeg Building Continues in 1971," *Winnipeg Free Press*, 7 May 1971, p. 36; J.M., "Without Grounds: University of Winnipeg," *Progressive Architecture* (March 1973): 80–85. Author's interviews with Lewis Morse, 8 March 2005 and 19 January 2004. Morse has consistently stressed to me that the solution for Centennial Hall came out of the restraints of not enough money, not enough land, and not enough time.

2   See the cover of *Progressive Architecture* (March 1973). Centennial Hall was also featured on the cover of *Canadian Architect* (March 1973), *Western Construction and Industry* (August-September 1972), *Design in Steel* (January 1975), and the *British Columbia Business Journal* (April 1972) with a cover photograph by Glenn Tinley.

3   Steven Coppinger, Special Projects Officer, University of Winnipeg, notes to the author, October 2005.

4   Regarding the decision not to join the University of Manitoba, see *Some Important Historical facts about United College* (Winnipeg, c. 1950), "The Proposed Fort Garry Site," University of Winnipeg Archives, AC–38–1, file 1, p. 14. This document outlines the province's offer of seven acres at the Fort Garry campus for United College if they were to move out there. For a chronology of these events, see Gerald Bedford, "One Hundred Years of History," *The University of Winnipeg: The Commemorative Journal 1888–1988* 4, 2 (Summer 1988): 8, University of Winnipeg Archives; and A.G. Bedford, *The University of Winnipeg: A History of the Founding Colleges* (Toronto: University of Toronto Press, 1976), chapters 12, 13, and 14. Wesley and Manitoba colleges joined to become the United College in 1938. Also of interest, Wilfred C. Lockhart, "The Sixteen Years," in *Winnipeg: University of Winnipeg* (1971), University of Winnipeg Archives, AC–37–1, file 3, p. 8. On the history of the University of Manitoba campus, see J.M. Bumsted, *The University of Manitoba: An illustrated History* (Winnipeg: University of Manitoba Press, 2001), especially chapters 5 and 4.

5   Lockhart, "The Sixteen Years," 8. He continues, "The decision to stay, however, was not made on the basis of abstract principle. It was a very pragmatic choice. To move required a purchaser for the property and sufficient extra dollars to re-establish the institution in Fort Garry. Neither were available and no-one was able to suggest where such additional funds were procurable."

6   See Duart Farquharson, "Winnipeg Has Failed its Citizens," *Winnipeg Tribune*, 28 April 1970, pp. 1–2.

7   Metropolitan Corporation of Greater Winnipeg Planning Division, Downtown Winnipeg 1967, *Report* (Winnipeg: The Author, 1969), 1.

8   "Address by Dr Henry Edmison Duckworth on the Occasion of His Installation as President and Vice-Chancellor," in *A Souvenir of the 100th Birthday*, ed. Joy S. McDiarmid (Winnipeg: University of Winnipeg, 1971), University of Winnipeg Library, AC–18–1, file 4, p. 12.

9   Lockhart, "The Sixteen Years," 9.

10   Reid, Crowther, and Partners, *An Interim Report of the Examination of Potential Role, Size and Campus Development for the University of Winnipeg*, parts 1 and 2 (Winnipeg, Manitoba, 1967), 25, University of Winnipeg Archives, AC–22–2, files 1 and 2. Thanks to Peter McCormack for finding this report. The c. 1950 report *Some Historical Facts about United College* also points out some of the advantages of a downtown location over University of Manitoba's suburban location ten kilometres south of the city, see pp. 1–2.

11   Reid, Crowther, and Partners, *An Interim Report*, 24.

12   Ibid., 54.

13   "Summer Sport for Lockhart Autumn Years," *Winnipeg Free Press*, 7 May 1971, p. 25; Lockhart, "The Sixteen Years," 8–9.

14   Lockhart, "The Sixteen Years," 8. As Lockhart stated in 1955, fewer than 6 percent of 18–24-year-olds were in university; by 1971 the rate was over 13 percent. In 1957 there were 1100 full- and part-time students at the University of Winnipeg; by 1970 that number had risen to 7000 (Lockhart, "The Sixteen Years," 1–2). Also see Bedford, *The University of Winnipeg*, 380ff, and Reid, Crowther, and Partners, *An Interim Report*, Part 1, 8. For general statistics on the population growth in universities in the late 1950s and 1960s, see Edward F. Sheffield, *University Development: The Past Five Years and the Next Ten* (Ottawa: Canadian University Foundation, 1961), 3.

15   Reid, Crowther, and Partners, *An Interim Report*, 51, 99.

16   Ibid., 51. A.G. Bedford mentions that a site north of Ellice Avenue was considered for the University of Winnipeg, see *The University of Winnipeg*, 380. Ruth Cawker and William Bernstein, *Contemporary Canadian Architecture: The Mainstream and Beyond* (Markham: Fitzhenry and Whiteside, 1988), mention that there was a suitable large site available across Portage Avenue, but "its owner wanted double what the university could afford to pay," 167.

17   Lewis Morse was awarded the national Pilkington Traveling Scholarship in 1968, which funded him for a trip to London, England, where he worked for Arup and Associates. With Arup and Associates he was on the design team for the Biochemistry Building System at Cambridge University. When he returned to Winnipeg, he worked for Number Ten Architectural Group, with whom he designed an open-concept elementary school, Riverside, Thompson, Manitoba (1969). For information about the architectural award the school won, see, Anonymous, "Riverside Elementary School Addition, Thompson, Manitoba, Architects: No. 10 Architectural Group," *Canadian Architect Yearbook 1969: Annual Awards* 14, 2 (February 1969): 39–43. Peter McCormack mentions the influence of Arup and Associates' Mining and Metallurgy Building in Birmingham (1968) in his independent study for me in 2003. Morse told McCormack that he felt that the one-and-a-half-storey Riddell Hall inefficiently occupied a major section of the campus and "to go above it just made sense" (Peter McCormack and Lewis Morse, 13 April 2003). I thank Lewis Morse, Peter McCormack, and Aldona Dziedziejko for helping me gather this information.

125

Serena Keshavjee

18   Lewis Morse in conversations with Aldona Dziedziejko on 28 April 2004, and with the author on 8 March 2005. Morse thinks he may have read the Reid, Crowther report, although James Christie, the partner-in-charge of the project, does not remember the report. Quotation from James Christie, "University of Winnipeg," *Western Construction and Industry* (August-September 1972): 5.

19   Cawker and Bernstein, *Contemporary Canadian Architecture*; regarding the competition, see p. 167. Also on this page, note their discussion regarding why Centennial Hall was such an ingenious solution for University of Winnipeg.

20   J.M., "Without Grounds," 85.

21   Joy S. McDiarmid, "University of Winnipeg Opens Centennial Hall," News Release, 14 September 1972, University of Winnipeg Archives, AC–37–1, file 4.

22   *Some Important Historical facts about United College*, part VI, 15–18. This early report (p. 17) stresses the needs of the Church: "The choice before us is which is the wiser policy from the standpoint of the Church; to have under our control a smaller body of students in an environment which we are absolutely free to condition for religious ends, or to be in proximity to a greater mass of students in an environment which is not under our control and which is imbued with a strong tendency to secularism?" Only twenty years later in the Reid, Crowther report, the considerations are no longer religious, but socio-economic.

23   Lewis Morse interviews, 13 April 2004 with Peter McCormack, 28 April 2004 with Aldona Dziedziejko, and 8 March 2005 with Serena Keshavjee. The older buildings were not replaced as Morse had hoped.

24   James Christie, "University of Winnipeg Expansion '70 programme," 23 April 1971, University of Winnipeg Archives, UW–3–1, file 4, p. 2. Morse explained to me that he conceptualized Centennial Hall as the "glue" that would connect the existing structures. He did not conceive of it as a separate structure, but a connecting structure; author's interview with Lewis Morse, 19 January 2004. In support of this idea, it is interesting to note that Lockhart Hall and Centennial Hall both pay homage to Wesley Hall's castellated towers. There are precedents for megastructures in Canadian universities, as John Andrew's work at Scarborough College in Toronto (1964), Arthur Erickson's University of Lethbridge (1968), and the University of Alberta's Hub Mall (1969–1973) in Edmonton, by Jack Diamond and Barton Myers, demonstrate.

25   James Christie, "Centennial Hall University of Winnipeg," *Design in Steel* (January 1975).

26   *Contemporary Structures* (Washington, D.C: American Iron and Steel Institute, c. 1972), example 17. Morse is adamant that this building was not influenced by Archigram as *Contemporary Structures* suggested. He explains that he did learn about Archigram at the Faculty of Architecture, but was more interested in built projects. He suggests more important sources for Centennial Hall were the Japanese Metabolists and the late work of Corbusier. Morse mentioned, in particular, the plans for Corbusier's unbuilt hospital in Venice, and the Heidi Weber Pavilion, both of 1965. He also talked about the concepts behind the Berlin Free University. One can make interesting comparisons between Centennial Hall and all these buildings. The literature about the hospital in Venice stresses the building's relationship to its urban environment and the importance of circulation within the building, both key to Centennial Hall. The Heidi Weber Pavilion utilizes flexible space and colour panels. As well, the concept of the Berlin Free University was based on a decentralized model of a university, in which Morse was very interested. Most important for his work, according to Morse, however, was the approach of Arup and Associates to integrate the mechanical elements into the building's structure.

27 Ursula Ferguson was in charge of the interior design for Centennial Hall. While some of the furniture was standard Herman Miller, such as the fibreglass swivel chairs, much of it was Canadian-designed (i.e. Nienkämper shelving and the moulded Polypropylene chairs by Dudas, Kuypers, and Rowan), and Manitoban-designed (i.e. Moyer Vico Limited's revised Harvard chair). For the furniture contracts, see University of Winnipeg Archives, file M6912. The study carrels and organic-shaped indoor and outdoor furniture were designed by Moody, Moore, and Partners, somewhat influenced, I would suggest, by Verner Panton's "Phantasy Landscape Visiona II" for the Cologne Furniture Fair in 1970. For indoor seating, Moody, Moore ordered the moulded Polypropylene chairs by Dudas, Kuypers, and Rowan, designed for the Habitat housing development at Expo '67. For information on these chairs, see Virginia Wright, *Modern Furniture in Canada 1920–1970* (University of Toronto Press, 1997), 186–87; and Rachel Gotlieb and Cora Golden, *Design in Canada: Fifty Years from Tea Kettles to Task Chairs* (Toronto: Knopf, 2001). For a critique of Centennial Hall's interior design, see Marcia E. Secter, "Centennial Hall Interiors," *Canadian Architect* (March 1973): 37–39.

28 "Winnipeg Lacks Face," *Winnipeg Free Press*, 6 March 1973.

29 Conversation, Lewis Morse, 8 March 2005. Secter, "Centennial Hall Interiors," 39.

30 Secter, "Centennial Hall Interiors," 37.

31 See Anonymous, "Riverside Elementary School Addition," 39–43.

32 Organization for Economics Co-operation and Development, "Introduction," in *The Teacher and Educational Change: A New Role* (Paris: Organization for Economics Co-operation and Development, 1974). Earlier important developments included the 1972 International Commission on the Development of Education, which called for the "decentralization of decision making, of responsibilities and resources and broad participation of those concerned at all levels and in all areas, in determining and carrying out educational activities." *See 50 Years of Education*, p. 4, at <Unesco.org.> (accessed 19 December 2005). It was also in the 1960s that Unesco founded the International Institute for Educational Planning.

33 James Christie, "University of Winnipeg," *Western Construction and Industry* (August-September 1972): 4–9, quotation, pp. 8, 6, and 9.

34 Alan Colquhoun, "Critique," *Architectural Design* 47, 2 (1977): 96–103, 100.

35 James Christie, e-mail to author, March 2005.

36 This information and the image come from Glenn Tinley, who worked with the original design team for Centennial Hall and who designed the model. I thank him for sharing his archive and information with me.

37 Jonas Lehrman, "Centennial Hall University of Winnipeg," *Canadian Architect* (March 1973): 33.

38 See *Some Important Historical Facts*, p. 11, where it is noted that the walls were already crumbling. Lewis Morse states that he was well aware of the changes in pedagogy during this period, which attempted to use open space and less formal structures for teaching within the university as a way of inspiring students to learn. Author's interview, 8 March 2005. In an interview of 19 January 2006, he used the words "egalitarian" and "democratic" to explain what type of building he wanted to create.

39 Jean Lauxerois, *L'Utopie Beaubourg, Vingt Ans Après* (Paris: Centre Georges Pompidou, 1996), 28, quotation 30.

40 For Duckworth, see "Address by Dr. Henry Edmison Duckworth," 13. Also see Henry E. Duckworth, *One Version of the Facts: My Life in the Ivory Tower* (Winnipeg: University of Manitoba Press), 247. Regarding University of Winnipeg's

Serena Keshavjee

outreach, see Joy McDiarmid, "The University of Winnipeg Announces University at Noon," Public Service Announcement, 8 October 1971, University of Winnipeg Archives, WW–3–1, file 1. President Wilfred Lockhart was less easy with what he described as the cultural "dissent" and the "turbulent campus" of the 1960s. See Lockhart, "The Sixteen Years," 1–2, 5–6, 14–15. He complained about the changes that university campuses had undergone in his farewell speech of 1971:

> the growth of the student population brought with it not only a period of frantic planning and construction of new university facilities but the turbulent campus. . . . It is regrettable that such growth occurs at a time when the community at large is undergoing a somewhat dramatic revolution in its value and belief system . . . a revolution with youth as its most vociferous spokesman. Universities and colleges, therefore, have been natural centres for its expression and the focal point for the most open dissent and disruption. . . . The campus became a highly volatile community which, at times, appeared committed to its own self-destruction. At the same time, it demonstrated phenomenal growth and an amazing capacity for change. (1–2)

> . . . this somewhat irrational yet profoundly disturbing revolution affecting youth . . . has had its effect in the field of continuing education and will continue to do so. Feeling alienated, many students attack education as irrelevant if it does not appear to have an immediate application to life. . . . If this alienated youth culture continues to flourish and becomes a determinative force in the future, universities will continue to have a difficult time. (14–15)

41 See "Address by Dr. Henry Edmison Duckworth," 14. Duckworth was influenced by the great success of the United Kingdom's Open University (1971), which offered university services to part-time students through distance education (Duckworth to Keshavjee, October 2005, and *One Version of the Facts*, 260–61). The Open University's objective was to promote the spread of egalitarianism in education. See Daniel Schugurensky, "1971: U.K. Open University opens its doors," in *History of Education: Selected Moments of the 20th Century*. URL http://fcis.oise.utoronto.ca/_danile Schugurensky/ assignment1/1971 (accessed October 2005).

42 To see examples of Archigram's Plug-In City, see Design Museum Archigram at www.designmuseum.org/designerex/ archigram.htm (accessed September 2005).

43 See Lehrman, "Centennial Hall University of Winnipeg," 33, column 2. See Cawker and Bernstein's comments on the circulation in Centennial Hall, based on "automobile circulation where roads vary according to the flow and speed of traffic. . . ." in *Contemporary Canadian Architecture*, 168, and how this greatly improved connections between various parts of the campus, Also, Secter, "Centennial Hall Interiors," 39; J.M., "Without Grounds," 81. Peter McCormack also noted the importance of the pedestrian arteries.

44 James Christie, "University of Winnipeg," 5.

45 J.M. "Without Grounds," 81.

46 Duckworth in conversation with the author, October 2005.

47 Peter Sampson, Prairie Architects, in conversation with the author, November 2005. Sampson also feels that positioning student spaces on the fourth floor did little to make the building inviting to the public.

48 Nathan Silver, *The Making of the Beaubourg: A Building Biography of the Centre Pompidou Paris* (Cambridge: MIT Press, 1994), 184.

49   This was my assumption when I assigned Peter McCormack this topic in 2003 as part of an independent study he was doing with me. He quickly found out otherwise. I thank him for his diligent work on this topic and his initial contact with Lewis Morse and James Christie. I have since seen the plans in James Christie's archive and they were signed in 1970 (Centennial Hall, Fourth Floor 17/9/1970), with some revisions made between 1971–72. McCormack and Morse set the following chronology: the initial design was submitted towards the end of 1969, and the model was finished by late February 1970.

50   Alan Colquhoun, "Critique," *Architectural Design* 47, 2 (February 1977): 87–90, quotation 98, "What evidently appealed to the jury was the uncompromising way in which the building interpreted the centre as a supermarket of culture. . . ."

51   "Centre Georges Pompidou Piano and Rogers: A Statement," *Architectural Design* 47, 2 (February 1977): 87–90, quotation 87.

52   "The Centre Pompidou's Role," *Architectural Review* 16 (May 1977): 286–87.

53   Colquhoun, "Critique," 100.

54   From the quotations typically heading University of Winnipeg e-mail from the Communications Office in 2005 to 2006, the ideology of pluralism and democracy is still important to university administration: "The University of Winnipeg boasts a unique location in the heart of the city. We're proud to be considered part of the community, working together with our neighbours to revitalize the downtown." As well, note, "located in the urban heart of downtown, The University of Winnipeg is a compact, diverse, multi-cultural academic community committed to excellence and access." President Lloyd Axworthy was quoted in the 8 November 2003 press release regarding *The Annual Maclean's Ranking of Canadian Universities 2003*: "The University of Winnipeg is in the process of redefining its role while celebrating what makes this University distinctive: its history of excellence; social consciousness; and, its student body, drawn from a diverse population of ethnicities, income levels, ages, and cultures," said Axworthy. "Its belief that a liberal education, when taught in an exacting, creative, and humane way, can have transforming effects on individual lives, and on society as a whole."

Serena Keshavjee

THE MEANING OF WHITE

Kelly Crossman

The moment when Winnipeg's architectural culture shifted irrevocably towards the modern can be identified quite precisely. In 1951 the Elizabeth Dafoe Library opened its doors to faculty and students at the University of Manitoba. (fig. 5.1, 5.2) It had a surface of stone, a structure of steel, and walls of floor-to-ceiling glass. The space inside was open and expansive, offering visitors an experience few had encountered before. One part of the building seemed to flow into the next; even on the coldest day of winter it would be easy "to move about, to see new vistas from one space to another."[1] This, as we now know, was only the beginning.

fig. 5.1
Elizabeth Dafoe Library
University of Manitoba (1951)
Green, Blankstein, Russell, and Associates
David Thordarson principal design
Photograph: Henry Kalen (c. 1951)
156D5.3–01

fig. 5.2
Elizabeth Dafoe Library
University of Manitoba (1951)
Green, Blankstein, Russell, and Associates
David Thordarson principal design
Photograph: Henry Kalen (c. 1951)
156D5.3–10

fig. 5.3
Rae and Jerry's Steak House (1957)
Smith, Carter, and Katelnikoff
Dennis Carter and Mike Krawitz principal design
with Doug Gillmor
Photograph: Henry Kalen (1960)
123B5.3–3

From 1951 on, there appeared in Winnipeg a steady stream of Modernist schools, churches, stores, houses, apartments, and commercial and public buildings, which quickly changed the face of the Manitoba capital—most emerging from the drawing boards of five firms: Green, Blankstein, Russell, and Associates; Smith, Carter, Searle, and Associates; Waisman, Ross, and Associates; Libling, Michener, and Associates; and Moody, Moore Architects. These new buildings won awards and provided a graceful, elegant, and generally sympathetic counterpart to the surrounding Edwardian/jazz age neighbourhoods and streets. Buildings like Rae and Jerry's Steak House (fig. 5.3, 5.4), the University of Manitoba School of Architecture (fig. 5.5), or the Monarch Life Building (fig. 5.6) were up-to-date and stylish, offering Winnipeggers the kinds of spaces seen in films like Alfred Hitchcock's thriller *North by Northwest*, in magazines, or on vacations in New York or southern California.

By the end of the 1950s, as these architects and the Modern movement itself matured, the scene shifted again, becoming more complex and pluralist. During the 1960s, the Manitoba school of Modernism, which by now had taken firm root in its prairie soil, enjoyed a period of unparalleled prosperity and accomplishment. New talents and offices emerged, such as Étienne Gaboury, Gustavo da Roza, and the Number Ten Architectural Group. Winnipeg was widely recognized as an important centre of Canadian Modernism.

Today, the novelty of Modernist spatial experience has long since disappeared. While Winnipeg's architects—and the Dafoe Library is a case in point—might have been successful at creating conditions in buildings more convenient and comfortable in a city with long winters and often uncomfortably warm summers, walls of glass and open, unencumbered space are now found everywhere in the modern world. They are taken for granted or seen as symbols of a mid-twentieth-century mindset now firmly in the past. In a world of computers and Ipods, virtual reality, and the fantastical forms of Frank Gehry, architectural taste and invention have moved on. And yet, Winnipeg's encounter with architectural Modernism, and particularly that movement's engagement with

fig. 5.4
Rae and Jerry's Steak House (1957)
Smith, Carter, and Katelnikoff
Dennis Carter and Mike Krawitz principal design
with Doug Gillmor
Photograph: Henry Kalen (1960)
123B5.3–2

fig. 5.5
School of Architecture (1959)
(John A. Russell Building)
University of Manitoba
Smith, Carter, and Katelnikoff
Ernest Smith partner-in-charge
James Donahue principal design with Doug Gillmor
Grant Marshall interior design
Photograph: Henry Kalen (1962)
249D5.2–31

the *here*, with connections between past and present, is a story that still has the power to deepen our understanding of the world in which we live. With the acuity of a great writer, the Winnipeg novelist Carol Shields has shown us why this is so. In her novel *The Republic of Love*, Shields describes Winnipeg as light-filled, "a city of wide formal boulevards lined with handsome stone buildings," a city that, despite "its city-share of graffiti-spattered back alleys" and its "grid of streets, bridges, shopping centres, traffic lights and pedestrian crossings," is one Tom, her main protagonist, quite clearly loves.[2] Throughout the novel, the question Carol Shields implicitly raises is, why? What is it that makes us love a person, a place, a thing? And, by way of an answer, we are pointed in a certain direction (which is not so obvious) towards the nature of our human response to the physical world, and towards a consideration of how things in their combination—the particular, the general, the ordinary, the special, the presence of the past, and the varying intensity of the present—come together to form a specificity and so to register, often below the surface of human consciousness, as expectation, recognition, memory.

Memory. Despite its short history, Winnipeg, in 1951, the moment architectural Modernism began to alter the city's cultural and physical landscape, was already a place with a distinguishable and identifiable architectural culture. Not only did it have local brickyards and builders, but also, northeast of the city, at Garson, Manitoba, quarries that produced a distinctive fossilized limestone. This "Tyndall" stone had been used in the region since pioneer days and gave the architecture of its public buildings a characteristic hue and harmony—is it coincidental that Carol Shields chose this stone as a symbol for her next and most famous novel, *The Stone Diaries*? Winnipeg had also been lucky. Its wealth and position as the unrivalled metropolis of the Northwest meant it was a city able, especially from the mid-1890s on, to attract an impressive array of architectural talent from New York, Chicago, Montreal, and Toronto. By the late 1920s, within the space of a generation, and in a very North American way, its citizens had built an urban culture of broad avenues, great department stores, fine churches, salubrious suburbs, and impressive civic and public

Kelly Crossman

fig. 5.7
View of Portage Avenue
from Main Street, Winnipeg
Photograph: Henry Kalen (1965)
645.W-4

fig. 5.8
"Aerial View of the Red and Assiniboine River"
Central Winnipeg North (c. 1947)
City of Winnipeg Archives and Records Control
Box P2, File 77

buildings (fig. 5.7). All this occurred in an era when architecture and planning in North America was—with Chicago and New York as its epicentres—among the finest and most innovative in the world. And it was lucky, too, that, unlike many North American towns planned grid-form by pragmatic surveyors, Winnipeg grew large from an organic template able to accommodate the needs of a twentieth-century metropolis. The famous corner of Portage and Main was once the meeting point of ancient prairie trails. The flow of traffic west and north still mirrors the path of the city's rivers; ever-shifting streetscapes follow the lot lines of the Red River settlers. (fig. 5.8) Winnipeg remains one of a relatively small number of cities on the continent whose morphology is even now determined by figures from the pre-industrial past.

Winnipeg's historical and geographical specificity were clearly understood by young architects in the 1950s. They were well aware of the city's storied past, its links to the advanced architectural culture of late nineteenth-century Chicago, and especially the tradition of rationalism and structural expression that Chicago-style architecture represented.[3] And yet, this reminiscence of a local tradition and sense of place leads to an obvious question. If architectural Modernism in Winnipeg, as elsewhere, was not a local but an international movement—which it unequivocally was—why was it so appealing to a young Manitoba architect or architectural student in 1951? Is it possible to speak of a Manitoba school of Modernism? Can we say that Modern architecture in Winnipeg was distinct in any meaningful way from elsewhere on the continent?

In trying to answer those questions, we can do no better than begin by turning to an explanation given by the Toronto-based architect John C. Parkin when the impact of the Modern movement was at its height. Speaking in Minneapolis/St. Paul to the annual conference of the Society of Architectural Historians in 1961 on the subject of Canadian architecture, Parkin noted that "while it was on the Prairies that one might expect to see the influence of Frank Lloyd Wright the strongest, it was here in fact that one found it the least." The reason for this, he said, was that:

fig. 5.9
Donahue Residence
Fulham Avenue (1950)
James Donahue principal design
Journal, Royal Architectural Institute of Canada
(December 1950)
Photograph: Bob Talbot (2006)

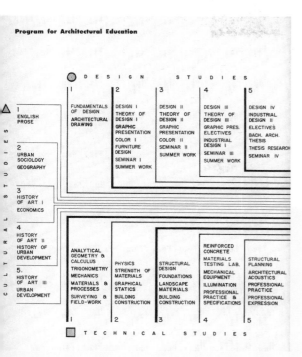

fig. 5.10
Program for Architectural Education, Curriculum
"Architectural Education at the University of Manitoba"
Journal, Royal Architectural Institute of Canada
(March 1954)

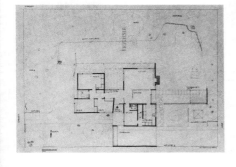

HOUSE OF MR. A. J. DONAHUE, WINNIPEG, MANITOBA; A. J. DONAHUE, ARCHITECT

406

In my opinion the great opposite force exists in one of our most important Schools of Architecture, 400 miles immediately north of here. The presence, at Winnipeg, of the University of Manitoba School of Architecture, of a dedicated teacher, John Russell (of American birth) and his driving encouragement of post-graduate training in design, has resulted in a dominant Internationalist influence in architecture on the Prairies, and most certainly in Winnipeg itself. Few schools in North America could claim so high a percentage of post-graduates of Harvard, MIT, and interestingly, of the Illinois Institute of Technology, as can Manitoba. Most have returned to the Prairies, but others of us have scattered to the eastern and western extremities of Canada—each an "internationalist" (if I may say) in viewpoint.[4]

Although based in Toronto, Parkin knew what he was talking about. He had been raised in Winnipeg and attended the School of Architecture at the University of Manitoba (the only architecture school in western Canada at that time) before leaving for graduate work at Harvard in 1945. As Parkin pointed out, both the nature of Modern architecture in Winnipeg as well as the way it developed cannot be understood without taking into account the architecture program at the university and especially the work of John A. Russell. In the mid-1940s Russell, who had been teaching at the school since the 1920s, had begun to modernize the university curriculum, bringing it in line with worldwide trends. Parkin had been a member of the first graduating class to benefit. Others in the class of 1945 included Harry Seidler, who would ultimately settle in Australia, as well as Ernest Smith, who, like Parkin, subsequently left for graduate work at the Massachusetts Institute of Technology. But this was only a beginning; as Parkin suggests, his in-depth understanding of Modernist architectural thought was largely a result of post-graduate work, something Russell very much encouraged among his students. But Russell was also intent on bringing Boston to Winnipeg in the form of new faculty. When enrolment in the School of Architecture jumped as veterans from Europe registered at the university (a rise of 125 percent from 1945 to 1946),[5] Russell hired the Architectural Association-trained Wolfgang

137

Kelly Crossman

fig. 5.11
Donahue Residence (1955)
Hosmer Boulevard
James Donahue principal design
Photograph: Henry Kalen (1961)
222B1–2

Gerson as well as A.J. (Jim) Donahue, a Saskatchewan-born architect with a B.Arch. from Minnesota and M.Arch. from Harvard. Planners Victor Kostka and Herschel Elarth followed in 1948 and, by the early 1950s, design studios at the university were invigorated by the contributions of a stream of alumni—Roy Sellors, Ernest Smith, Dennis Carter, and Douglas Gillmor among them.[6]

The decision to hire Jim Donahue was especially instrumental in the establishment in Manitoba of a school in the Modernist mode and the subsequent exploration and development of Modernist ideas in built form across the city. Russell, a graduate of MIT, had strong links to American schools and "could pave the way" for his students' post-graduate study there, but Donahue, as well as being one of the first graduates (1942) trained by the German émigré Walter Gropius at the Harvard Graduate School of Design, was also a talented architect and designer in his own right. His work provided a direct model for his students: an example of what could be done. Once in Winnipeg, Donahue built a Modernist frame house for himself on Fulham, little known in the literature (fig. 5.9). Other houses by Donahue followed, including one in Edmonton, as well as apartment buildings and, in 1958, a design for the Russell Building at the University of Manitoba (with Smith, Carter, and Searle). Donahue's rigorous, formalist approach to design was immediately reflected in the fully resolved Modernism of student work at the school and also by the establishment in 1952 of a comprehensive and thoroughly reorganized curriculum. (fig. 5.10)

fig. 5.12
Donahue Residence (1955)
Hosmer Boulevard
James Donahue principal design
Photograph: Henry Kalen (1961)
222B1–16

The desire for rigour in architectural design—a rigour analogous to the analytical methods of science—had led Donahue's teacher, Walter Gropius, first in Germany at the Bauhaus, and then at Harvard, to structure architectural conceptualization as the union of three autonomous fields: science (engineering), art, and what one might call humanities, or, more broadly, human culture. In this way the dominant force of the modern world—science—could be brought into the realm of art as a kind of objective subjectivity. However, as Gropius, Mies, and others of their generation understood, it was also essential that architecture find a place for advances in philosophy, history, and

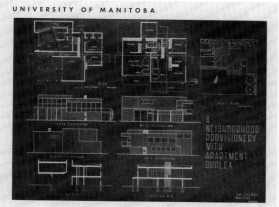

A NEIGHBOURHOOD PROVISIONERY WITH DUPLEX APARTMENT
D. N. Chapman
ARCHITECTURAL DESIGN II
FOUR WEEKS

This provisionery is to be constructed in the isolated section of the new Wildwood Development in Fort Garry. The store itself will be semi-self-service. In addition to the necessary service and storage areas on the first floor, an apartment duplex is to be provided on the second level — one apartment being for the provisioner and the other for rental purposes. This preliminary design stage was followed by a five week development of working drawings and details in conjunction with Building Construction I.

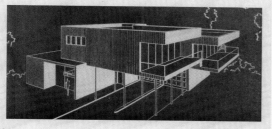

148   Journal, Royal Architectural Institute of Canada, M

fig. 5.13
"A Neighbourhood Provisionery with
Duplex Apartment"
D.N. Chapman
Journal, Royal Architectural Institute of Canada
(May 1947)

the social sciences; architecture, despite its links to art, could not exist as a purely autonomous realm, divorced from the conditions of ordinary life. Recent scholarship has shown, for example, that even within the work of a single architect like Mies van der Rohe, many competing ideas, influences, and theoretical positions came into play.[7] It is an indication of the influence of these ideas on Donahue and others teaching at the University of Manitoba that the architectural program there, as reorganized in the early 1950s, followed the pedagogical principles of the Bauhaus/Harvard quite closely. The influence of Gropius's methodological structure as well as the complexity of Modernist thought can be seen in the division of the university curriculum into three fields: Technical Studies (mathematics, building construction, mechanics, structural design, etc.); Design Studies (architectural drawing, studio, graphics, colour, theory of design, etc.); and Cultural Studies (history of art, English prose, economics, sociology, urban development).

In 1954 Jim Donahue left his first house to build a new residence in the southwest Winnipeg suburb of Tuxedo Park. The Fulham house had taken advantage of the register of passing seasons by means of low, sheltered spaces. Now he was to live in a house—still frame—that was compact and geometrically reductive (essentially a rectangular box) with most of the living space on a raised floor. (fig. 5.11, 5.12) Donahue explained that he had done this to create a view across the prairie landscape toward Assiniboine Park, a view that was, no doubt, more expansive in the mid-1950s than it is today. But it would not have passed unnoticed by his students that the new house, with its dark timber walls, fireplace, screened porch, ground-level entry, protected parking pad, and careful distribution of private and public space blended so softly onto the site as to be almost invisible, giving the sense that here, unlike the case with most suburban houses, a pre-existing growth of oak trees had been scarcely disturbed; nor that this had been accomplished using elements that, as can be seen from a student design of 1947, were quite straightforward and that they had been exploring in their architecture studios. (fig. 5.13) They could see quite clearly that Donahue's Modernist training and design methodology had allowed the production of a house of modest cost,

which was nonetheless elegant, fashionable, and, in a kind of way, provocative. For a young architect in the early 1950s, looking to build a practice and a career, this was tremendously exciting.

In foregrounding issues of context—albeit within the frame of an ostensibly universalized architectural language—Donahue's house, with subtlety and adeptness, had addressed an aporia that lay at the heart of "international" Modernism—to use John C. Parkin's phrase—and which, since it reflected an ongoing tension within modern culture, could not be resolved as such but only accommodated. This tension was the need to balance, in a science-based, economically minded culture, expectations of pragmatism and efficiency with the equally important need for integration into daily life of aspects that lay outside the quantitative and quantifiable: the poetic, the personal, the subjective. Although, as the Manitoba curriculum demonstrates, architectural thought recognized the importance of "cultural studies," an allocation expressly intended to address these issues, during the 1950s and 1960s the rise of the social sciences seemed to suggest that human needs could also be understood rationally and scientifically, so that from a rigorous analysis and computation of all the functional requirements of a building (including "human" ones), the most rational and efficient architecture would emerge: the building as "machine," one might say. But for some people, there was a problem with this notion. If architecture was about to become a scientific practice with universal values and techniques, then what of local history, climate, customs, way of life? How and in what way could these values be brought into the process of design? Was it inevitable that a building in Wyoming be the same as one in Winnipeg?

Jim Donahue's house, despite the debt it owed to the Modernist architectural culture of Harvard, seemed to show that the language of Modernism, while it might be based, like mathematics or engineering, on universal principles, could, if used thoughtfully, produce an architecture highly attuned to specific conditions and needs. And even more, Donahue and other talented Modern architects seemed to be saying that the particular nature and gift of Modernism

140

fig. 5.16
Green, Blankstein, Russell, and Associates Office Building (1951)
Osborne Street North
Green, Blankstein, Russell, and Associates
and
Manitoba Medical Service Building (1952)
Northwood and Chivers
Photograph: Henry Kalen (1961)
269U3–7

fig. 5.17
Green, Blankstein, Russell, and Associates Office Building (1951)
Green, Blankstein, Russell, and Associates
Morley Blankstein principal design
Photograph: Henry Kalen (c. 1961)
157F1.2–4

fig. 5.18
Northern Sales Building (1953)
Waisman, Ross, and Associates
Allan Waisman and Charles Faurer principal design
Photograph: Henry Kalen (1962)
381F3–1

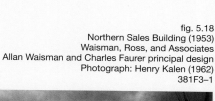

to contemporary life, because of its freedom and technological ingenuity, was to take what traditional architecture left behind—cheap materials, industrial processes, leftover spaces, worn-out types—and transform them. Later in the decade, in 1958, in the design of a building for the School of Architecture, Donahue (with Doug Gillmor and Smith, Carter, and Searle) combined new technology to make an internal light court (a little-used afterthought in conventional Winnipeg buildings of the time) the heart of a rejuvenated faculty, providing natural light in the depths of winter, shelter from the prairie winds, and a haven for birds at dawn and dusk. (fig. 5.14) In central Winnipeg, Donahue's rethinking of the conventional office type produced in the Monarch Life Building a series of complex and varied spaces, which remain a delight and inspiration to this day. (fig. 5.15)

Perhaps because of Donahue's example, perhaps because of the conditions in which the young graduates of the University of Manitoba worked—a sophisticated and competitive environment, building conditions at the extreme end of the normative envelope—it seems to us today that they were engaged in a kind of conversation, with themselves and with each other, over how to incorporate the best new ideas worldwide while creating buildings of a certain and, in their own terms, convincing specificity to the Winnipeg region. The presence of these two distinct, though not necessarily opposed, tendencies played an important role in encouraging architectural innovation in Winnipeg during the 1950s and 1960s, even within the work of a single firm. A series of low-scale buildings facing Memorial Park in central Winnipeg tells the tale. In 1951 Morley Blankstein and Isadore Coop, both Manitoba graduates recently back from post-graduate work at Illinois Institute of Technology in Chicago, built a new office for their firm, Green, Blankstein, and Russell (GBR), at 222 Osborne Street. (fig. 5.16, 5.17) The building was simple: a façade of glass enclosed by two thin, brick walls. It was a striking departure from other, neighbouring buildings, many of which also were built in the late 1940s/early 1950s but which were heavier in appearance and covered in Tyndall stone. The GBR office, in its interest in transparency, looked forward to GBR's winning Miesian design in the 1953

141

fig. 5.19
Winnipeg General Post Office (1953–55)
Green, Blankstein, Russell, and Associates
Morley Blankstein principal design
Photograph: Henry Kalen (c. 1953)
146L1–3–21

fig. 5.20
Man with an Axe (Clifford's Clothing) (1958)
Blankstein and Coop
Isadore Coop principal design
Photograph: Henry Kalen (c. 1961)
151G1–2

fig. 5.21
Norquay Building (1959)
Green, Blankstein, Russell, and Associates
David Thordarson principal design
Photograph: Henry Kalen (c. 1959)
216L1.2–13

competition for the National Gallery of Canada. Its vocabulary of brick and glass is also related to the slightly later, more fully resolved Modernism of Waisman, Ross's Northern Sales Building on Lombard Street of 1955. (fig. 5.18) Following the National Gallery competition, GBR flourished, soon emerging—apart from the occasional hiccup, like overheated workers in an un-air-conditioned (by order of Treasury Board) General Post Office (1953) (fig. 5.19)—as one of the most successful Modernist firms in the city.[8] However, within a few years Blankstein and Coop were gone from GBR; practising on their own, producing work like Man with an Axe (Clifford's Clothing) (1958) (fig. 5.20) and then in 1964 joining with Waisman, Ross to form Number Ten Architectural Group.

The team of Blankstein/Coop was one influence on the early work of GBR, but there was another. In the mid-1950s GBR produced a design for a government office building—the Norquay Building (1959)—also in the Osborne Street/Memorial Park area. (fig. 5.21) Dominated by a façade of glass, it featured a veneer of smooth limestone, which blended easily with surrounding civic and commercial office buildings on Osborne Street and recalled the limestone surface of the Dafoe Library built earlier in the decade. The Dafoe Library had itself complemented earlier stone buildings on the University of Manitoba campus. At another GBR building of that era, St. George's Anglican Church in Crescentwood (fig. 5.22), limestone was used to cover a structure of steel and brick and to provide a visual link with an existing parish house and office.

All these projects—the Dafoe Library, the Norquay Building, St. George's—are credited to GBR, but today we know that their design was largely the work of David Thordarson, a University of Manitoba graduate who joined the firm in the summer of 1949 at the age of twenty-three, immediately following graduation. David was an architect sensitive to the innate qualities of materials and, although a Modernist like his contemporaries, Blankstein, Coop, Waisman, and Ross, he was especially drawn to Manitoba limestone. In his hands this became a material capable of great beauty and refinement, and a means, arguably, by which Modern architecture in Winnipeg could be linked with its geographic and socio-cultural context.[9]

Kelly Crossman

fig. 5.23
St. George's Anglican Church (1956–57)
Green, Blankstein, Russell, and Associates
David Thordarson principal design
Joan Harland interior design
Photograph: Henry Kalen (1961)
204N1.2–8

The Church of St. George's, Crescentwood, was by no mean the most important of GBR's projects from the 1950s, but the circumstances surrounding the design help us understand the architectural challenges of that time. The project of 1956 was to replace an earlier church of frame and stucco from the 1920s. Many parishioners wanted a neo-Gothic church, both to match the parish house and to evoke the long association of Canadian Anglicanism with Gothic forms. But the slightly earlier parish house (1952–53) had been expensive, and its abrupt details, unconvincing buttresses, and scant mouldings demonstrated how difficult, economically and logistically, it would be to construct a new church in the Gothic mode in Winnipeg in middle of the twentieth century.[10] So the parish opted for a modern design that would nonetheless accommodate the forms and practice of the past. The new church was organized as a series of related but contrasting rectangles—on plan, as volumes, and in elevation, as a series of rising forms—which, clothed with a cool palette of bluish limestone and filled with panels of glass, expressed the underlying structure and blended softly and gently into the mainly residential neighbourhood. The new church contained the traditional elements of the ancient basilican plan—narthex, nave, aisles, east window, west window, bell tower—all given serenity by the simple repetitive elements of the plan, the stained glass, and the coloured mosaics, which were the work of Winnipeg artist George Swinton. (fig. 5.23) While St. Georges's recalled the work of Eliel Saarinen (a debt Thordarson willingly acknowledged[11]), we can see, half a century later, that it marked the growing maturity of a distinct architectural voice whose interest in the abstract qualities of light, form, and tectonic expression, by means of the persistent motif of the frame covered in buff limestone, would soon ennoble many of Winnipeg's most important public buildings, including the Winnipeg Civic Centre complex and the Winnipeg International Airport. Thordarson's use of local stone also prefigured the immense limestone surfaces of architect Gustavo da Roza's Winnipeg Art Gallery.[12]

fig. 5.22
St. George's Anglican Church (1956–57)
Green, Blankstein, Russell, and Associates
David Thordarson principal design
Joan Harland interior design
Photograph: Henry Kalen (1961)
204N1.2–4

fig. 5. 24
Perth's Dry Cleaners
Waisman, Ross, and Associates
Photograph: Henry Kalen (1962)
399H4–3

"In winter when the snow arrives, only white can settle a house so completely into its environment. What elsewhere is rationalised as a device for setting a building apart from nature, in Canada, becomes the means of integration."[13] That remark by John C. Parkin describes how—and his understanding of how—the semantics of the built environment can shift from place to place with a subtlety that often passes unnoticed, so that meaning and affect are slowly and cumulatively altered. It is an insight worth keeping in mind today as one considers the legacy of the Manitoba Modernists. Each of the important Winnipeg firms, and in, some cases, each of the principals in those offices, developed an identifiable architectural manner, related to but distinct from that of their peers. Some were interested in structural expression; others were attracted by the pleasures and possibilities of transparency, the tactility of surfaces, or the manipulation of spatial volumes. But taken as a group, and in a way that ultimately derived its meaning from the interaction of their work with the particulars of the place in which they lived, they gradually moved Winnipeg's experience of itself forward so that today, the architecture of the 1950s and 1960s is rivalled only by that of the Edwardian period for its quality and cumulative impact on the city's neighbourhoods and streets. As this anthology and related exhibition shows, the range of Modern buildings the Manitoba Modernists produced was broad and impressive. It included virtually every building type, from small-scale projects in the 1950s—drive-in shops for Perth's dry cleaners (fig. 5.24) or Tilden Rent-a-Car—to large-scale urban renewal projects in the 1960s like the City Hall/Public Safety complex (fig. 5.25), or the Centennial Concert Hall and Manitoba Museum of Man and Nature. (fig. 5.26)

In his early 1960s account of Canadian architecture, John C. Parkin made the case, even if indirectly, that the underlying principles and internationalist character of the Manitoba school were also the dominant values in Canadian architecture at that time. "It is my view," he said, "that there is almost a national motif in our architecture in the widespread expression of the post and lintel connection. . . . I would suggest that the majority of our contemporary Canadian architects, whether romantics or classicists, all join in the

146

seemingly common conviction that a building must honestly advise how its structure holds."[14] Parkin's insight was a reflection of the influence of rationalism and especially structural rationalism on Canadian practice. It was a theme in Modernist architectural culture, which came naturally to prairie boys like himself, if only because it was an approach so widely seen in the city and countryside in which he grew up: not just in Chicago-style warehouses and office buildings but in the directness and simplicity of the region's ordinary wood-frame farm buildings and houses.

It was also an approach that—although Parkin could not have known this—was at the height of its influence in the early 1960s. By the end of the decade, American architecture was on the verge of the Post-Modern reaction, many of the great Modernist pioneers were retired or gone, and both Parkin and Jack Russell were prematurely dead. In Winnipeg, the architectural scene had become more diffuse and complex. Some practitioners such as Allan Waisman at Number Ten Architectural Group explored new materials (concrete) and languages (brutalism) in buildings such as the Manitoba Theatre Centre (fig. 5.27); others had left the city (Jim Donahue). Younger talents such as Étienne Gaboury and Gustavo da Roza had emerged and with them an approach more sculptural and overtly organic than anything championed by their immediate predecessors. The completion of important projects such as the Richardson Building by the American firm Skidmore, Owings, and Merrill LLP (in association with Smith, Carter Partners) signalled a change in the city's cultural climate: from now on and in a way reminiscent of an earlier era, local architects would face stiff competition from central Canadian or American firms.

These developments point to a reality: in Winnipeg, Mid-Century Modernism can be seen as a particular and reasonably discrete—insofar as any cultural manifestation can be separated from its chronological surroundings—moment in time. It lasted roughly from the design of the Dafoe Library at the University of Manitoba in 1951 to the death of John Russell in 1966. Within this time

147

Kelly Crossman

frame, it is possible to identify key players, a more or less unified body of work, a recognizable architectural language, and an institutional centre; one could make the case that this cohesiveness describes a localized movement. More importantly, it reminds us that in an age that still sometimes sees architectural Modernism as a kind of monolith of discredited practices, distinctions need to be made; not just between individual practitioners, but also between the projects and work of planners and architects, architects and builders, developers and independent clients.

The work of the talented young Winnipeg-trained architects who came of age in the early 1950s should be seen as related to, but necessarily apart from, the great mass of ordinary building from that time. The degree to which these men and women were able, or interested—as a group—in creating an immediately recognizable regional architecture is difficult to assess. At the very least, this was an idea of greater interest to some than others. What is everywhere evident in their work is the desire to make human life, in a city where building is difficult and great wealth rare, more comfortable, more enjoyable, more potently connected to the expression and resolution of its own realities.

The Manitoba Modernists sought out the possibilities inherent in Winnipeg's morphology and topography. For them, architectural Modernism was a means of discovery; its utility, a mode of experience and model. Their achievement was to show, by means of the evolving practices of an ancient art, that even a prairie landscape offers the potential for views and delicate changes of grade; that light and life can be brought deep into the heart of buildings.

Even in the midst of the long northern winter's white, buildings can help create communities. Looking back, the work of Manitoba's Modernists is evidence, if evidence is needed, that all places, whether remote or at the centre of the world's artistic and economic life, have tradition and materials and culture enough to generate an architecture of their own if they so desire.

fig. 5.26
Centennial Concert Hall (1967) and
Manitoba Museum of Man and Nature (1970)
Associated Architects for the Manitoba Cultural Centre:
Green, Blankstein, and Russell
Moody, Moore, and Partners
Smith, Carter, Searle, and Associates
Photograph: Henry Kalen (c. 1969)
851E–59

ENDNOTES

1   A.F. Ackerman, B.H. Green, M.R. Johnston, D.A. McQuaig, K.R. Webber, with H.A. Elarth, "Red River Skyline," *Journal, Royal Architectural Institute of Canada (JRAIC)* 31, 3 (March 1954): 85.

2   Carol Shields, *The Republic of Love* (Toronto: Random House, 1992), 99–100.

3   Ackerman et al., "Red River Skyline," 81–85.

4   John C. Parkin, "Architecture in Canada since 1945," *Journal, Royal Architectural Institute of Canada,* 39 (January 1962): 35.

5   "Annual Report of the School of Architecture and Fine Arts 1946–47," University of Manitoba Calendar, 1947, p. 5; "Annual Report of the School of Architecture and Fine Arts," University of Manitoba Calendar, 1946–47; 1947–48; 1948–49; 1949–50; 1950–51; 1951–52; 1952–53.

6   Adele Freedman, "West Coast Modernism and Points East," in *The New Spirit, Modern Architecture in Vancouver 1938–1963*, ed. Rhodri Windsor-Liscombe (Montreal: Centre for Canadian Architecture/Vancouver: Douglas and McIntyre, 1997), 14–15; 18.

7   See, for example, Terence Riley and Barry Bergdoll, *Mies in Berlin* (New York: Museum of Modern Art, 2001, 2002); Phyllis Lambert, ed., *Mies in America* (New York, H.N. Abrams, 2001).

8   Eric W. Thrift, "Manitoba," *Journal, Royal Architectural Institute of Canada* 35, 9 (September 1958): 354.

9   Kelly Crossman, "North by Northwest: Manitoba Modernism, c. 1950," *Journal of the Society for the Study of Architecture in Canada* 24, 2 (1999): 66–67.

10   Joan Harland, "St. George's Church, Crescentwood, Architectural Design," www.stgeorges.mb.ca/download/historypdf.

11   Author's interview with David Thordarson, December 1998.

12   The Winnipeg Art Gallery was designed by Gustavo da Roza, with Number Ten Architectural Group as Associate Architects.

13   Parkin, "Architecture in Canada," 39.

14   Ibid.

fig. 5.27
Manitoba Theatre Centre (1970)
Number Ten Architectural Group
Allan Waisman principal design with Michael Kirby
Photograph: Henry Kalen (c. 1969)
1103E6–38

WIDE OPEN SPACE

MANITOBA'S MODERNIST LANDSCAPES

Herbert Enns

The settlement of the vast, unspoiled, and unexploited lands of western Canada yielded a unique Modernist architecture in Manitoba. Imported ideals and a foreign imagination reformed the idea of land from being a vague and largely mythical pre-colonial state to the pioneer vision of space, liberty, adventure, peace, and prosperity. The doctrine of Modernism—a series of intentions and a strategy of beliefs—was lucidly articulated in the 1930s, 1940s, and 1950s, and became evident in the manifestos of Le Corbusier, and in the writings of Nicholas Pevsner, Siegfried Giedion, Peter Collins, and Reyner Banham.[1] These new ideals, approaching perfection and excellence, were invented and articulated in Europe during the late nineteenth and early twentieth centuries. Exported to the new world, they mixed easily with rapid settlement and the intellectual advance of a new prairie culture. The distance and space afforded by the prairies provided the necessary context for Modernism's fruition in western Canada. The desire to formulate a philosophy of architecture and a body of work inspired by place—at some considerable distance from America's centres of Modernist exploration, such as New York, Boston, and Chicago, and at an even greater distance from the European establishments of culture and criticism where it was born—led to a rich and inventive hybrid condition in Manitoba. (fig. 6.1) The significant legacy of Modernist architecture in this region bears witness to the impact of the westward unfolding of imported Modernist ideals as they encountered the fertile and expansive tabula rasa of the spatially and philosophically unencumbered prairies.

fig. 6.1
Winnipeg International Airport (1964)
Green, Blankstein, Russell, and Associates
David Thordarson and Bernard Brown principal design
Photograph: Henry Kalen (1964)

While the subjects of geography and landscape are rarely broached in writings on Modern architecture, post-World War II architectural invention in Manitoba resonated with, and was influenced by, the land history of western Canada. Influences such as the Hudson's Bay Charter of 1670, the inspiring consequences of the unique spatial perceptions available on the prairie, the strategic requirements of new settlements and inventive systems of survey, the remarkably neutral topography, and the rapid deployment of new economic, social, and political models and systems gave shape and dimension to the "idea of land."

This idea can be summarized as having three distinct aspects: the mirage of hope and unbounded prosperity; opportunity and prosperity linked to pragmatism and a work ethic; and success based on mechanical advantage through technological invention. In the late nineteenth and early twentieth centuries, western North America was promoted as a new dreamland of "lemonade springs and cigarette trees and jails made of tin."[2] The western landscape—Wallace Stegner's "Geography of Hope"[3]—was configured by invention and willpower for its utilitarian benefits. (fig. 6.2) Complex land management organized the open prairie as a commodity to be parcelled out for agricultural, commercial, and institutional use. Young architects—graduates of the University of Manitoba School of Architecture under the direction of John A. Russell—were inspired by the geometry of the section grid, an infinite range of light quality, emptiness (and openness) as both perceived and absolute, and the momentum of pioneer self-sufficiency. (fig. 6.3) The abstract and perceptual qualities of the land were manifest in a series of sophisticated Modernist architectural projects.

The landscape was an external stimulus for design, and was supplemented by the influences of existing unselfconscious industrial architecture and an integration of the arts. Manitoba's School of Architecture, supported by a faculty of strong Modernist persuasion, graduated students who were single-minded in their dedication to Modernist ideals. The newly settled land of

fig. 6.2
Silo Construction (c. 1920)
Archives of Manitoba
69—17226

fig. 6.3
Cultivator (Van Brunt) (1910)
Archives of Manitoba
18—N17031

the Modernist era was a perfect setting for an architectural philosophy that favoured utilitarianism, industrialization, strategic programming, and structural clarity.

The economic explosion of building at the turn of the century that inspired the collection of Chicago-style warehouses gave form to Winnipeg's ambition to be a major centre in western Canada. However, economic and cultural expansion stalled as a Depression-inspired dormancy between the world wars. Post-World War II development gave rise to both a second economic boom and a resurgence in the role of all the arts. A cross-pollination of artistic exploration and economic advance reinforced the West as a place where Modernist experimentation and application were possible. A desire for permanence—marking the end of the pioneer era—coincided with the maturing and consolidation of architecture and the allied arts (theatre, dance, music, and fine art) as the primary means of cultural expression, communication, identity, and, most importantly—once and for all—arrival.

The key Manitoba Modernist projects, while maintaining strict adherence to functional intentions and Modernist theory, emphasized poetic traits and expressed possibilities inspired by local conditions. The University of Manitoba's School of Architecture (1959), the Manitoba Health Service Building (1959), and the Winnipeg International Air Terminal (1958 to 1964) are three effective representations of a hybrid of Modernist philosophical sensibilities and constructions, beholden to Modernist dictums of light, space, and openness, but also inspired by a new land culture and identity. In these buildings in particular, the correspondence between the settlement of the West and evolving Modernist strategies became tangible. Each addressed new land ideals in innovative ways. These projects exploited and amplified the potential of the land's most important cultural corollaries—space and myth—including careful material selection, the use of systems of geometry and proportion derived from the basic design teachings of the Bauhaus, structural invention and integration, site orientation and landscape, responses to direct and ambient light and view, and the manipulation of spatial order. The results transcended dogmatic interpretations of Modernist ideology and demonstrated the possibilities of a hybrid Modern and Western inventiveness applied on a clean-slate landscape.

William Herbert New has attempted a postcolonial definition of land in his *Land Sliding: Imagining Space, Presence, and Power in Canadian Writing* (1997).

> Yet land can also function not just as the revelation of the status quo, but also as the space or place or site of challenge to the accustomed borders of power. It shifts, in this context, from a designation of locality to a (perhaps more abstract) designation of activity. Land functions in cultural discourse, therefore (and in other cultural practices: mining, farming, real estate sales), both as an icon of stability and as a medium of change. Fixity vies recurrently with fluidity, position with positionality, the place of social residence with the condition of being there.[4]

New's transference from "land" to the "idea of land" as a medium for change, or from surface, topography, material, and deed to a condition of living and a cultural space of operations, is central to Manitoba's Modernist architectural evolution.

Aboriginal peoples understood the land as inclusive of earth, water, and sky. Land (and water and sky) had spiritual significance. Their beliefs were manifest in cosmological constructs and narratives, in their considered use of physical resources, and in the marking of places of social gatherings for rituals and ceremonies. Their relationship with landscape involved complex and interdependent constructs that gave them identity and gave the land meaning. The ideal of individual ownership of land—central to European culture and mission—was unknown to them.[5]

fig. 6.4
Aboriginal People at Port Nelson (1912)
Archives of Manitoba
17–18013.

The sixteenth-century invasion of European traders, land speculators, settlers, politicians, and government agents subordinated First Nations nomadic life. (fig. 6.4) The exclusion and suppression of the First Nations, as instituted in the treaties from 1870 and onwards, created the conditions for Western colonization, settlement, and industrialization. Susanna Moodie witnessed the darker side of the Western land dream in Canada and recorded her abhorrence for speculators and land dealers in *Roughing it in the Bush* (1852):

> Oh, ye dealers in wild lands—ye speculators in the folly and credulity of your fellow men—what a mass of misery, and of misrepresentation productive of that misery, have ye not to answer for! You had your acres to sell, and what to you were the worn-down frames and broken hearts of the infatuated purchasers? The public believed the plausible statements you made with such earnestness, and men of all grades rushed to hear your hired orators declaim upon the blessings to be obtained by the clearers of the wilderness.[6]

If God was in the details, the Devil was in the land deal. Five years after Leo Tolstoy wrote his famous story,[7] just how much land a man needed became evident in the remote and far-flung reaches of the Canadian West. Representatives of the Crown—expanding the global reach of the British Empire—concluded Treaty #1 in 1871 with the Aboriginal peoples for what is now Manitoba.[8]

The land was given commercial value, and made available for settlement and investment at ten dollars per 160-acre quarter section.[9] New corporate identities, national jurisdictions, and governmental entities were invented to manage the land revolution. The open lands of the First Nations peoples were displaced by the massive 200-million-acre survey system, the world's largest legal survey. The West, the surveyors calculated, had the capacity to host 1.25 million homesteads on quarter-section plots.[10]

158

With the construction of the Canadian Pacific Railway from 1881 to 1885, the lands attained commercial promise.[11] As settlers and supplies were freighted into the West on the new railroad, wheat poured out. By 1924, sixty million acres on the prairies had been accessed for agriculture, with annual total wheat production reaching 500 million bushels; Canada contributed 40 percent of the world's wheat exports.[12] The land was more than commercially valuable, as it turned out. The dealers and speculators were right. With an immigrant population defined by the very commodities they produced, the land revolution was complete. Evolving from a sophisticated speculative stratagem, the land's capacity to support organized and purposeful economic expansion gained legibility.

But what of the more profound interpretations of land encouraged by William New? Once the strategies for effective, functional, and profitable land use were firmly entrenched, and the economic and political functions of a new city were consolidated by edifices of timber, brick, and stone, the "condition of living" and the "cultural space of operations" of the post-war period required redefinition. And this is where Modernist architecture found a purposeful and poetic niche. By shaping the renewed post-war cultural institutions and demonstrating a more refined and reflective framework for intellectual discourse, Modernist architecture reformed the idea of land from being the site of hinterland colonization and the stone, timber, and masonry warehouses and banks to being a new plateau of intellectual sophistication and artistic and design experimentation and excellence.

The change in land identity and the philosophical shift to the "idea of land" may be illustrated by comparisons between the design developments in Europe and colonial advances. Peter Behrens (1868 to 1940) was a young man of seventeen when news reports from Canada arrived announcing the Last Spike and the completion of the Canadian Pacific Railway in 1886. It is doubtful that Behrens would have known of the opening of the first hydroelectric generating station on the Winnipeg River at Pinawa in June 1906 (fig. 6.5), preceding his Modern masterpiece—the High Tension (Turbine) Factory in Berlin-Moabit—by three years. As the distribution of free agricultural land through the Dominion Lands Act concluded in 1930, the Bauhaus organized by Walter Gropius and Adolf Meyer (1926) was already four years old. Indeed, the Beaux Arts-based School of Architecture at the University of Manitoba, started in 1913, must have been oddly out of synch with the homesteaders consolidating their farms on the frontier of western Manitoba. In an era when Mies van der Rohe completed his pavilion for the Deutscher Werkbund at the International Exhibition in Barcelona (1929), and Siegfried Giedion published *Befreites Wohnen* (*Liberated Living*) (1929),[13] settlers were still homesteading on the western prairie. (fig. 6.6)

These comparisons represent the extremes, but they illustrate the space and distance between the two settings at the turn of the century: one, the Modernist leading edge of a new philosophical and technological force in Europe; and the other, the waves of settlers spilling out of train cars onto Winnipeg's warehouse-lined streets, gathering sharpened tools and supplies with which to forge their dreams of prosperity.

Changes in land perception occurred as a new western Canadian culture emerged. Modernist critics and scholars, such as the Europeans Siegfried Giedion and Reyner Banham, and the Canadian Peter Collins,[14] discussed new ideals, values, and techniques concomitant with new ways of living. They were interested in how Modernist architecture could be embodied through glass and steel, informed by industrial processes, and inspired by the principles of mass production. They promoted designs that privileged access to light and air (lightness and atmosphere). The central axis of their argument was the celebration of open and unencumbered spaces. This new space was flexible, adaptable, ambiguous, and liberating. New technology provided the means, and political and social changes provided the impetus.

fig. 6.5
Power Station and Dam on the
Winnipeg River (c. 1920)
Pinawa
Archives of Manitoba
N21639

fig. 6.6
Ambroise McKay Sod Barn (1932)
St. Laurent
Archives of Manitoba
N21468

An important distinction between European Modernist architecture and Manitoba Modernist architecture was the Canadian access to a new kind of vista and prospect. Westward expansion presented a new panoramic context for Modernist momentum and its preoccupation with a scale of operations that emphasized the immediate foreground and middle distance. The appropriation of vast tracts of landscape required new techniques of representation, and new metaphors and spatial analogies. In contrast, European modernists Theo van Doesburg and Piet Mondrian expressed geometric relations through compositional structures, and made visible formerly subconscious spatial sensibilities in the De Stijl movement.[15] Spatial relations in their work were explored at an intimate scale—the scale of an interior, or the scale of a work of art. The most effective architectural manifestation of De Stijl's spatial imagination was the Schröder House designed by Gerrit Rietveld (1924-25), preceded by his famous Red/Blue Chair of 1918. Lacking the expansive western North American spatial comprehension, the idea of space as stemming from a greater land-view eluded van Doesburg and his contemporaries, and was precluded by the introspective attraction of their compositional experiments.

Nicholas Pevsner briefly explored the western North American architectural preoccupation with "the conquest of space" in his *Pioneers of the Modern Movement*. He touched on ideas of regional and master planning, describing the aloofness of modern architects in the face of broader planning objectives:

> Here too is the conquest of space, the spanning of great distances, the rational co-ordination of heterogeneous functions that fascinates architects. The profound affinity of this passion for planning with the characteristics of the twentieth-century style in architecture and with the eternal concern of Western architecture with the conquest of space is evident.[16]

In western Canada, inventions in geometry and survey were converted into new scientific models of space at a grand scale that represented a philosophical break from the circumscribed European frame of reference. While Modern architectural theorists and designers in Europe were interested in explorations of space at an intimate scale, the primary western Canadian spatial constructs were centrifugal, linear, and continental. The scale of the landscape required organizing structures that allowed for uncomplicated navigation, precision, exactitude, and individual autonomy.

Western North American spatial resolution can be traced back to the great North American land charters: the Hudson's Bay Company Charter (1670),[17] the Louisiana Purchase (1803), the Convention of London (1818), and the Dominion Land Act (1872). They represent the transformation of land perception from geographically based generalizations to highly abstract (and highly precise) legal entities that spanned the continent. The Convention of London, for example, represented the first purely geometric transcontinental articulation of territory on the prairies, and called for the formal survey of a boundary—the 49th Parallel—from the western end of Lake of the Woods to the Pacific Ocean, with no proviso for geographic exigencies and anomalies. This projection of spatial geometry in advance of discovery represented a complex shift in perspective, still horizontal and linear, but informed by new survey techniques and unfettered by the conventions of waterway travel and geographic limitations.

Cartographer Philip Turnor delineated coastal fringes and waterways for the Hudson's Bay Company. (fig. 6.7) The Hind Map of 1870, a cartographic sketch, locates the Prime Meridian, upon which the townships, ranges, and sections of the prairie grid were generated. (fig. 6.8) In the Surveyor General of Canada's map of Manitoba (1872), the organizing structure of the grid supercedes waterways, and is ambivalent to the undulating Red and Assiniboine rivers and natural features. (fig. 6.9) Expanding the survey westward, the Russell 1878 map of the North-West Territory records surveyors' triangulations following the Assiniboine River. From these river-based benchmarks, the meridians and parallells were projected westward across The Great Plain of the Souris. (fig. 6.10)

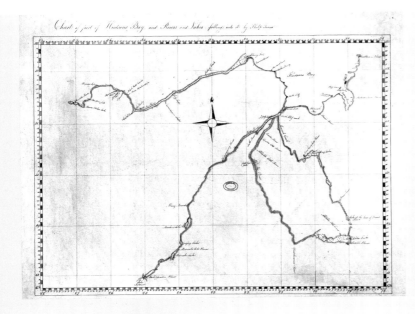

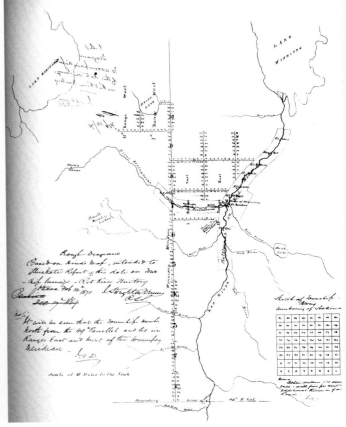

fig. 6.7
"Chart of part of Hudsons Bay and
Rivers and Lakes falling into it."
Philip Turnor cartographer
Hudson's Bay Company Archives HBCA G.1/1
Archives of Manitoba

fig. 6.8
Rough diagram, based on Hind's Map
intended to illustrate
*Report on Townships Surveys and
Red River Territory* (1870)
National Archives of Canada NMC 7065–H12/740/Red River
Settlement/1870–27994

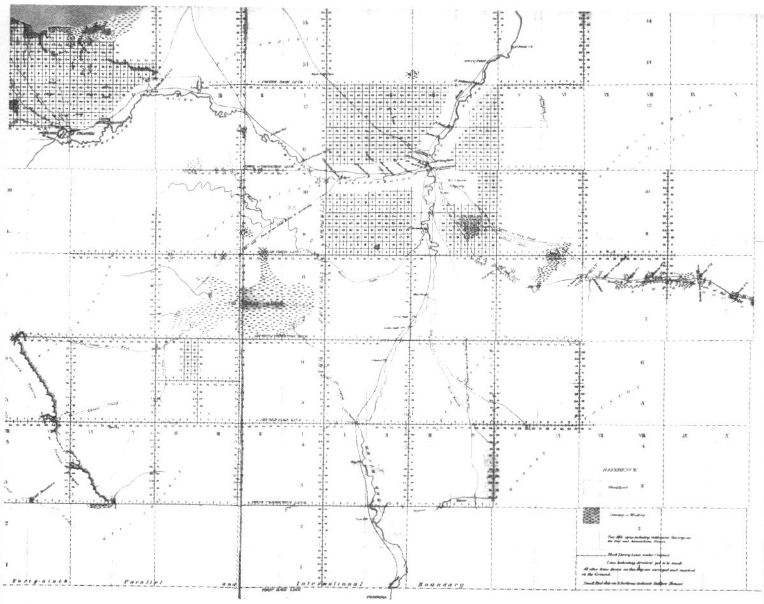

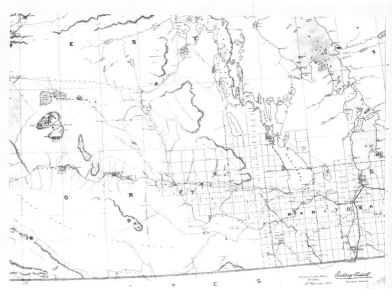

fig. 6.9
"Map of the Province of Manitoba,
showing the surveys effected in
1871 and 1872" (1872)
National Archives of Canada
NMC 26690–55582–H2/501/1872– 27086

fig. 6.10
"Map of Part of the North West Territory
Shewing the Operations of the
Special Survey of Standard
Meridians and Parallels for
Dominion Lands" (1878)
National Archives of Canada
NMC 11638–H1/701/1878–41876

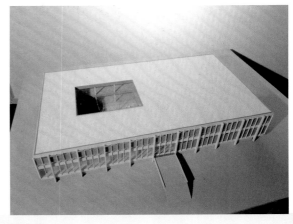

fig. 6.11
Project Model (1957)
School of Architecture (1959)
(John A. Russell Building)
University of Manitoba
Smith, Carter, and Katelnikoff
Ernest Smith partner-in-charge
James Donahue principal design with Doug Gillmor
Grant Marshall interior design
Photograph: Henry Kalen (1957)

The Dominion Land Act (1872) reduced the landscape by scientific means: it assigned a grid of ranges and townships extending from the Principal Meridian—167 kilometres west of the Manitoba/Ontario border—across the western lands to form, as John A. Macdonald boasted in the House of Commons, "one great country before us to do as we like . . . and one vast survey system, uniform over the whole of it."[18]

Until the advent of aerial photography, westward expansion privileged the horizon line and linear perception. Most decisions affecting land control in the West were made well before the invention and proliferation of aerial photography. The earliest maps of La Vérendrye, for example, were two-dimensional distortions of horizontal passage. The Canadian Pacific Railway (CPR) and Canadian National Railway (CNR) rail line and their sinuous beltways intertwined with the landscape and privileged linear perception and control.

Advances in scientific land survey methods—and a mechanism for the complex spatial appreciation of large landscapes—came with the formal introduction of aerial photography. Captain E.G.D. Deville, Surveyor General of Canada, developed a method of mapping landscape from mountaintop observations (a challenge on the prairies) that was expanded to a formal program of national air photography in the early 1920s.[19]

In the 1950s and 1960s architecture of Winnipeg, the buildings that best demonstrate the influence of a new land ideal are the John A. Russell Building at the University of Manitoba, designed by James Donahue with Doug Gillmor and Grant Marshall (interior design) for Smith, Carter, and Katelnikoff, 1959 (fig. 6.11, 6.12); the Manitoba Health Service Building on Empress, designed by Étienne Gaboury for Libling, Michener, and Associates, 1959 (fig. 6.13, 6.14); and the Winnipeg International Airport, designed by David Thordarson and Bernard Brown for Green, Blankstein, and Russell, 1966. (fig. 6.15, 6.16) Unconventional for their distinction from literal contextual references, these buildings are derived from (and inspired by) the larger landscape and

166

fig. 6.12
Courtyard
School of Architecture (1959)
(John A. Russell Building)
University of Manitoba
Smith, Carter, and Katelnikoff
Ernest Smith partner-in-charge
James Donahue principal design with Doug Gillmor
Grant Marshall interior design
Photograph: Henry Kalen

detached from the inner workings they house. Like the survey grids of the western Canadian landscape, they offer neutral systems of organization that suggest a refined composition of lines and geometry of infinite prospect. They modulate light by combinations of ephemeral and diaphanous facades—translucent, transparent, and screened. Their neutral spaces allude to the emptiness of the landscape. They are inventive, complex, and self-made experiments in design.

"Multi-use," a catchphrase in the 1960s, is not what was intended in these structures. Rather, the buildings were ambivalent to use, privileging only space, structure, order, and light—the light, space, and openness[20] that Siegfried Giedion championed in 1929—which were the very constituents of Western spatial constructs and mythology. The Manitoba architects designed for a new culture, reflecting the opportunity provided by the rapid explosion of development around them. Like the landscape itself, and the first surveys before aerial photography, they mark a minimalist response to space and geometry.

One can argue that the wood-panelled walls of the Russell Building Centre Space hearken back to the primitive pre-colonial forests of Canada. This is particularly true when the lights are dimmed for illustrated lectures, with soft light filtering in from the lobby around the extended folding screens. The Centre Space, while located in a high-Modernist building, is, in essence, a cave, as so ably demonstrated by Dennis Crompton of Archigram in the spring of 2002, when he lit the oak veneer-panelled space with a single candle to begin his lecture. The courtyard is the opposite: an uncontested and open apparatus of proportion and light. Like its geometrically precise predecessor—the section grid of the prairies—it establishes a neutral baseline that frames daily life and links diverse functions by representational means. Its central axis is the sky, relating the building to climate, latitude, and light. It is redolent with the haunting likeness of a pre-Modern stockade, this one made

167

Herbert Enns

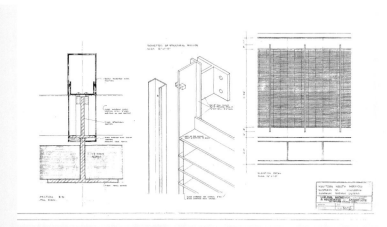

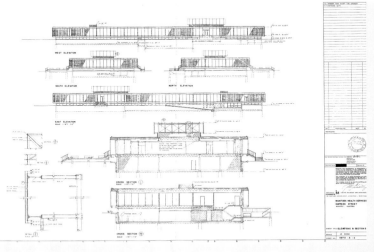

fig. 6.13
Aluminum Screen Details (5872—Jul 64)
Manitoba Health Service Building (1959)
Libling, Michener, and Associates Architects
Gerald Libling principal-in-charge
Étienne Gaboury principal design
Collection of the Province of Manitoba

fig. 6.14
Elevations and Cross Section (1958)
Manitoba Health Service Building (1959)
Libling, Michener, and Associates Architects
Gerald Libling principal-in-charge
Étienne Gaboury principal design
Collection of the Province of Manitoba

fig. 6.15
Winnipeg International Airport (1964)
Green, Blankstein, Russell, and Associates
Bernard Brown and David Thordarson principal design
Photograph: Henry Kalen (1964)
1217K3.2–24

fig. 6.16
Winnipeg International Airport (1964)
Green, Blankstein, Russell, and Associates
Bernard Brown and David Thordarson principal design
Photograph: Henry Kalen (1964)
217K3.2–16

of 1959 aluminum and glass. If the Centre Space hearkened back to the past, the courtyard signalled a bold step into the future. (fig. 6.11, 6.12)

The Manitoba Health Service Building (1959) responds to ideas of spatial metaphor with a subtle shift. Rather than framing a courtyard, this building is wrapped externally by an envelope of filtered space. Ambivalent in texture and density, the space is neither inside nor out, a hybrid interstitial zone. Like the Russell Building, this project floats above a horizontally recessed plinth. The perimeter screen, however, is an invention of lightness. The screen recalls sculptural values, blurring the spaces of engagement. The means of this elaborate spatial device are clear enough: straightforward connections of aluminum bar stock and matter-of-fact details that are simple connections relate to the whole, as well as to the landscape beyond. The metaphors are compounded: an aspen forest of aluminum, a barbed-wire fence, or an aluminum bird's nest with a glass liner floating above the meticulously proportioned landscape.

For the Winnipeg International Airport, design architects David Thordarson and Bernard Brown disengaged horizontal space from the surface of the earth and floated it as a mezzanine above a ground plane of terrazzo and below a monolithic, luminous, artificial-sky ceiling: an heroic and abstracted space suspended in the terminal between the city to the east and the runways and setting sun to the west. (fig. 6.15, 6.16) It was an act of multiplication and expansion, not appropriation. To understand the genius of this response is to recognize the spatial liberties inherent in the West.

Thus, the architects of the Modernist era in Manitoba were heavily committed to experiments with space, geometry, structure, and light. Filtering the European Modernist impetus, they explored the cerebral and intellectual intentions of Modernist architectural theory with a high degree of subtlety, refinement, and sophistication. The architects were in step with the burgeoning artistic class of a settled and committed community. The Modernist precepts

Herbert Enns

were adopted and transformed in profound ways, and were tempered by an altogether unique spatial sensibility that transcended the preconceptions of the Modern masters, generating a distinct lightness and ease of fit, durability, and programmatic clarity for a progressive artistic community. This movement reached its crescendo and generated its most compelling examples at the end of the 1950s and the beginning of the 1960s. The last decade of Modernism in Manitoba—from approximately 1965 to 1975—was a period of increasing stasis, of heavy materials, an architecture symbolizing permanence and increasingly self-conscious prosperity.

The poetry of Robert Kroetsch, from his book *Seed Catalogue*, highlights the compound mythic-poetic/pragmatic impulse for defining a new land ideal.

> . . . Son, this is a crowbar.
> This is a willow fencepost.
> This is a sledge.
> This is a roll of barbed wire.
> This is a bag of staples.
> This is a claw hammer.

We give form to the land by running
a series of posts and three strands
of barbed wire around a 1/4-section.

> First off I want you to take that
> Crowbar and drive 1,156 holes
> in that gumbo.
> And the next time you want to
> write a poem
> we'll start the haying.

How do you grow a poet?

> This is a prairie road.
> This is the shortest distance
> Between nowhere and nowhere
> This road is a poem[21]

170

In the course of a century, the Western spatial imagination had evolved from natural geographic identifiers (waterways and mountain ranges), through the scientific and abstract coordinates of descriptive geometry, trigonometry, and new survey conventions, to a more holistic documentation that mapped the world fully in both two and three dimensions. Identity was anchored as fence posts across the prairies were driven a section at a time into the ancient and fertile grassland topsoil. These new perspectives coalesced ownership and control (as expressed by legal description) with resource potential, and rendered the landscape as having material benefit beyond a mytho-poetic terra icognita.

The will to develop a range of spatial cognition capable of maintaining an image of Western distance, range, and possibility was a pioneer feat. A vast and indefinite perspective was condensed into a more European-like middle distance by two influences: advances in communication (Alexander Graham Bell's telephone, 1876), and advances in transportation (Canadian Pacific Railway, 1885). The collapsing of background and middle ground into foreground by technology and media—and its ultimate decentralizing effect on culture—was the focus of the meditations of Herbert Marshall McLuhan, who devoted his life to larger questions of spatial identity and perception. A review of his chapter headings in his book *Understanding Media* reveals the subjects of his studies that ushered the western Canadian landscape into the twentieth century, from Roads, the Motor Car, the Telegraph, and Telephones all the way to Automation: Learning a Living. His was the story of Western evolution by mechanical and technical means. Starting on the remote prairies, he was, in a spatial sense, working his way back (eastward) into the world's consciousness.

In Europe, the machine also dominated architectural inspiration. In *Mechanization Takes Command*, Siegfried Giedion extended the mechanical muse of Modernism to the western landscape, discussing agricultural practices and the Pullman passenger car as he documented his first trip onto the Great Plains:

When, through the Pullman window, a traveler sees the sun sink beneath the cornfields of Illinois, and the next morning rise again on cornfields as if the train had not moved from the spot, he experiences the meaning of dimension as figures can but thinly convey.[22]

Giedion had some idea of the social consequences of technological progress—and referred to John Steinbeck's *The Grapes of Wrath* in describing the impact of technology on tenant farmers—but he was preoccupied with industrial ingenuity and emphasized causes of mechanized agriculture over their effects. His writings implicate land use and resource management, though he steers clear of references that are anything other than anecdotal about the role that land might play. For him (and for Le Corbusier), the mighty grain structures and unselfconscious industrial architecture of purely functional origins were more inspirational than the underlying intentions of agricultural practices, resource development, and empire building. (fig. 6.17, 6.18)

Reyner Banham, in his introduction to *Theory and Design in the First Machine Age* (1960), anticipates his later *Los Angeles: The Architecture of Four Ecologies*,[23] the environmental movement, and the overlap between environment and design. By referring to the "new paths of choice in the ordering of our collective identities," Banham suggests that a greater moral good be considered in the adaptation of the machine age into all aspects of our lives. "Our accession," he continues, "to almost unlimited supplies of energy is balanced against the possibility of making our planet uninhabitable."[24] Banham captures the essence of post-World War II technical audacity and warns against future environmental consequences. He points to the space age as liberating us from the exhausted earth, but this is an overstatement. The kernel of truth in his introduction is his willingness to consider—if only briefly—the environmental consequences of modernity.

172

fig. 6.17
Three Grain Elevators, Niverville (c. 1911)
Archives of Manitoba
Niverville Collection, 3

fig. 6.18
Barn Raising, Ninette (1901)
Archives of Manitoba
F.H.H. Lowe Collection, 9

The late twentieth century was notable for the rediscovery of the seventeenth-century idea of land as being geographically distinguished by waterways and watersheds, and as having ecological wholeness as understood by the First Nations. Their way of understanding land anticipated the environmentalist movement. It was the harnessing of Manitoba's northern rivers (the Winnipeg, the Nelson, and the North Saskatchewan, for example) for hydroelectric power that re-established a spatial conception of the landscape derived from geographic systems. The corporate derivative of this modern geographic and land-centric registration of Western land values is Manitoba Hydro, and its central architectural symbol is the authoritative and sophisticated main head office on Harrow Street and Taylor Avenue (circa 1957). Here is a modern institution that depends solely on the lands as defined by the 1670 Hudson's Bay Charter: the continental drainage system that collects the water pouring through its turbines from as far away as the Rocky Mountains constitutes a modern-day manifestation of the edict "all the waters that flow into Hudson's Bay."[25]

Manitoba Hydro played an instrumental role in providing power for the expanding post-war economy of Manitoba. Heavy rainfall in western Saskatchewan means profit for the corporation downstream. A list of dams and generating capacity developed between 1945 and 1975 gives some indication of the reciprocity between power and architectural expansion:

Slave Falls Generating Station	Winnipeg River	1948	499 million kW·h
Pine Falls Generating Station	Winnipeg River	1952	620 million kW·h
Seven Sisters Generating Station	Winnipeg River	1952	990 million kW·h
McArthur Generating Station	Winnipeg River	1955	380 million kW·h
Kelsey Generating Station	Nelson River	1961	223 million kW·h
Grand Rapids Generating Station	Saskatchewan River	1968	479 MW
Kettle Generating Station	Nelson River	1974	1220 million kWh [26]

The Winnipeg Floodway is likewise governed by the snow pack and spring melt rates in the Dakotas and northwestern Minnesota. A forty-eight-kilometre seasonal control canal, it redirects Red River valley spring floods around Winnipeg.

The paradigms of control are now shifting from ownership and profit to environment and conservation—as Reyner Banham predicted in his introduction to *Theory and Design in the First Machine Age*. Notwithstanding the defiance and ambivalence of the hard-lined, non-negotiable, surveyed boundaries of states, provinces, and countries "conceived," as Rudy Wiebe wrote, "in the imagination of officials who had never and had never intended to see it,"[27] we are becoming increasingly conscious of land as an ecological and biological entity, with limits and powers that supersede the abstract land dispensations of western settlement. In this sense, the geographically based spatial instincts of King Charles and Prince Rupert were prophetic.

Modernist architecture marked the end of the pioneer expansionist era, as itinerant pioneers filled out the landscape and consolidated their interests and institutions in the sprawling cities of the Canadian West. The formerly horizontal and linear spatial biases of pioneer culture matured. Having settled the prairies by a rapid agricultural expansion that tested the limits of soils, temperature, and rainfall, western land-centric agricultural desires were exhausted, and perpetual westward movement came to a halt. Nomadic settlers admitted commitment and stasis, and marked the end of their roaming by the geometry of permanence: the Z-axis was added to the X and the Y.

In 1965 in Blanchard, North Dakota, 200 kilometres south of Winnipeg, the KTHI television transmission tower (now renamed the KVLY-TV tower) claimed the title of the tallest structure in the world at 628.8 metres, a record that still stands.[28] (fig. 6.19, 6.20, 6.21) In Winnipeg, the Richardson Building by Skidmore, Owings, and Merrill LLP and Smith, Carter Partners was the first skyscraper in the city at thirty-four storeys and 124 metres high. (fig. 6.22, 6.23, 6.24) Started in 1966 and completed in 1969, it was a magnificent testament to the energy of the prairie's agricultural and economic capacity. Winnipeg entered into a phase of cultural institution building, leading to the Canadian

175

fig. 6.20
Cables / Site
KTHI (KVLY-TV) Transmission Tower (1965)
Blanchard, North Dakota
Photograph: Herbert Enns (2005)

fig. 6.19
Cable Stayed Transmission Mast
KTHI (KVLY-TV) Transmission Tower (1965)
Blanchard, North Dakota
Photograph: Herbert Enns (2005)

fig. 6.21
Concrete Cable Anchors / Dampers / Transmission Mast Base
KTHI (KVLY-TV) Transmission Tower (1965)
Blanchard, North Dakota
Photograph: Herbert Enns (2005)

fig. 6. 22
"November 4, 1968 James A. Richardson & Sons Ltd.
Topping Off Ceremony"
(George Richardson, James Richardson,
Mayor Steven Juba, and Premier Walter Weir)
Richardson Building (1969)
Smith, Carter Architects
Skidmore, Owings, and Merrill LLP
James Searle partner-in-charge
Valdis Alers and John Turner principal design

fig. 6.23
Model
Richardson Building (1969)
Smith, Carter Architects
Skidmore, Owings, and Merrill LLP
James Searle partner-in-charge
Valdis Alers and John Turner principal design
Photograph: Henry Kalen (1964)
863F-24

fig. 6.24
Richardson Building (1969)
Smith, Carter Architects
Skidmore, Owings, and Merrill LLP
James Searle partner-in-charge
Valdis Alers and John Turner principal design
Photograph: Henry Kalen

Centennial projects, the international confirmation of the Pan Am Games, significant expansion to the universities, the move of the Hudson's Bay Company headquarters to Winnipeg from London in 1970, and the design and construction of the Winnipeg Art Gallery. If aluminum, glass, and steel suited a mobile, expanding, and itinerant culture, these late-Modernist projects—confirming the hype of the Dominion Land-grab boosters—were rendered in the materials of permanence. The Richardson Building was clad in precast concrete panels with granite aggregate supported by concrete caissons bearing on bedrock. The Winnipeg Art Gallery, an impenetrable and immovable monolith of Tyndall stone with glacial references, was most importantly an architectural signature of permanence.

In the September 1972 issue of *Westways* magazine, Wallace Stegner wrote an essay entitled "Thoughts in a Dry Land." Reprinted in 1992, Stegner's meditations articulate the effects of land on culture:

> That is only one sample of how, as we have gone about modifying the western landscape, it has been at work modifying us. . . . Our first and hardest adaptation was to learn all over again how to see. Our second was to learn how to like the new forms and colors and light and scale when we had learned to see them. Our third was to develop new techniques, a new palette, to communicate them. And our fourth, unfortunately out of our control, was to train an audience that would respond to what we wrote and painted.[29]

fig. 6.25
Winnipeg International Airport (1964)
Green, Blankstein, Russell, and Associates
Bernard Brown and David Thordarson principal design
Photograph (detail): Henry Kalen (1964)

The necessary ingredients—learning how to see; appreciating the new forms, light, colour, and scale; developing a new language adapted to these insights; and educating a receptive audience to communicate these insights to—constituted a complex abstract vision of the idea of land. And this is where Modernist architecture in Manitoba gained its mid-century power and density. Its architects projected the possibilities of a new language of form and content, drawing on mythical, mechanical, and spatial tropes to constitute an inventive architecture rooted in and informed by the idea of land.

Among the more delicate, sophisticated, and influential buildings of Manitoba's Modernist era, the Winnipeg International Airport's future is uncertain at this time (fig. 6.25), while the Manitoba Health Service Building (fig. 6.26), and the John A. Russell Building (fig. 6.27) are undergoing careful planning and renovation programs that will leave their land-lessons visible and intact for this and future generations.

These buildings are Manitoba's Modernist embodiment of Siegfried Giedion's 1929 call for light, air, and openness. They are also inspired by new perceptions of land, and by new spatial appreciations stemming from context and from integration and interaction with the arts. They embody the new colours and forms and light and scale that Stegner pointed to, a vision to which we, the once pioneer and now fully fledged cultural audience, are still growing accustomed.

fig. 6.26
Manitoba Health Service Building Reconstruction (2006)
Stantec Architecture / GBR Architects
Verne Reimer principal-in-charge
Gail Little principal design
Photograph: Martin Tessler (2005)

fig. 6.27
John A. Russell Building Reconstruction (2005–06)
University of Manitoba
LM Architectural Group
Terry Danelley and David Kressock principal design
Photograph: Herbert Enns (2005)

179

Herbert Enns

ENDNOTES

1   Nicholas Pevsner, *Pioneers of the Modern Movement*, 2nd ed. (London: Faber and Faber, 1936), *Pioneers of Modern Design* (New York: Museum of Modern Art, 1949); Siegfried Giedion, *Mechanization Takes Command: A Contribution to Anonymous History* (New York: W.W. Norton & Company, 1969); Peter Collins, *Changing Ideals in Modern Architecture* (London: Faber and Faber, 1965); Reyner Banham, *Theory and Design in the First Machine Age* (New York: Praeger, 1960).

2   Harry McClintock, "The Big Rock Candy Mountain," Track 5 in *Folk Song America* Vol. 1 (Washington, DC: Smithsonian Collection 461). Performed by Harry McClintock.

3   Wallace Stegner, "A Geography of Hope," in *A Society to Match our Scenery* (Boulder: University of Colorado Press, 1991).

4   William Herbert New, *Land Sliding: Imagining Space, Presence, and Power in Canadian Writing* (Toronto: University of Toronto Press, 1997), 5–6.

5   For an excellent recent survey of First Nations spatial and environmental perception, see I. Davidson-Hunt and F. Berkes, "Learning as you journey: Anishinaabe perception of social-ecological environments and adaptive learning," *Conservation Ecology* 8, 1 (2003): 6. Available on-line http://www.consecol.org/vol8/iss1/art5/ Center for Community-based Resource Management, Natural Resources Institute, University of Manitoba (accessed 15 April 2005).

6   Susanna Moodie, *Roughing it in the Bush* (London: Richard Bentley, 1852).

7   Leo Tolstoy, "How Much Land Does a Man Need" (1886), in *Leo Tolstoy: Stories and Legends*, illus. Alexander Alexeieff, trans. Louise and Aylmer Maude, intro. Dorothy Canfield Fisher (New York: Pantheon Books, 1946), 49. "But the Devil had been sitting behind the stove, and had heard all that was said. He was pleased that the peasant's wife had led her husband into boasting, and that he had said that if he had plenty of land he would not fear the Devil himself."

8   Marion V. C., *Indian treaties and surrenders: from 1680 to 1890* (Saskatoon: Fifth House, 1992). Canada Dept. of Indian Affairs?—cf. Higgins, Canadian government publications, 1936, p. 260. Originally published: Ottawa: Queen's Printer, 1891. "Articles of a Treaty made and concluded this twenty-first day of August in the year of our Lord one thousand eight hundred and seventy one between Her most gracious Majesty the Queen of Great Britain and Ireland by Her Commissioner Wemyss M. Simpson Esquire of the one part and the Chippewa Tribe of Indians, inhabitants of the country within the limits hereinafter defined and described by their Chiefs chosen and named as hereinafter mentioned of the other part."

9   Lewis H. Thomas, ed., *Dominion Lands Policy* (Toronto: McClelland and Stewart Limited, 1973), 146. By 1880, 3,750,000 acres had been distributed. It is interesting to note that for a period in the 1880s, the customs and excise revenues generated by the rapid immigration of homesteaders were more profitable than land sales.

10 Library and Archives Canada, http://www.collectionscanada.ca/02/02011101_e.html#records (accessed 15 April 2005).

11 Land distribution through the railway charters of 1879 assigned a beltway of 220 miles (110 miles to the south and 110 miles to the north of the track), which was valued according to proximity to the railway itself:

        Belt A (5 miles wide / $6.00/acre)

        Belt B (15 miles wide / $6.00/acre)

        Belt C (20 miles wide / $3.50/acre)

        Belt D (20 miles wide / $2.00/acre)

        Belt E (50 miles wide / $1.00/acre)

12 Gerald Friesen, *The Canadian Prairies: A History* (Toronto: University of Toronto Press, 1984), 329.

13 Siegfried Giedion, *Befreites Wohnen* (Zürich / Leipzig: Forell Füssli Verlag, 1929).

14 Peter Collins addressed space in the final chapter of his *Changing Ideals in Modern Architecture*, 285–93. In naming Frank Lloyd Wright as the inventor of modern space, Collins's history of modern architecture was framed objectively and anchored in case studies and precedent. Following Siegfried Giedion's *Space, Time and Architecture,* and Reyner Banham's *Theory and Design in the First Machine Age*, Collins's *Changing Ideals* proclaimed a Modernism emanating from a theoretical core (from the inside out). Thus, the record of large-scale cognition as manifest in the prairies is lacking in the lexicon of Modernist literature.

15 Paul Overy, *De Stijl* (London: Thames and Hudson, 1991), 100. Of particular interest is Piet Mondrian's drawings for the Ida Bienert, 1926, and its reconstruction by Pace Gallery, New York, 1970.

16 Pevsner, *Pioneers of the Modern Movement*, 216. The attraction of built objective projects as Modernist referents was irresistible, and in the text he quickly abandons his spatial conjectures, returning to the world of industrial architecture and ideas of opportunity and power. He concludes his essay with a reference to Gropius and Meyer's Model Factory for the 1914 Werkbund Exhibition in Cologne.

17 Charter and supplemental charter of the Hudson's Bay Company. Charters, 1670–1884 & 1892. [Hudson's Bay Company] By laws. [Hudson's Bay Company] reports, HBC Coll.FC 3207.4 H8 [1910] 1875–1910, Publisher S.l. : Hudson's Bay Company, 1875–1910. Notes inside front cover: "F.G. Ingrams, 1910" [secretary, Hudson's Bay Company, 1911–1923].

18 Sir John A. Macdonald, *Debates of the House of Commons* (Canada, 1883).

19 It is worth noting that a concomitant vision of colonial interests relayed by scientific means was being exercised in India. Colonel George Everest led the attempt to measure the earth's diameter through longitudinal triangulations in a survey known as the Great Trigonometrical Survey of India. This was completed in 1866, and laid the trigonometric foundations for calculating the height of Mount Everest. These major events in the history of survey sought (and found) a knowable, and, hence, exploitable, landscape.

20 Giedion, *Befreites Wohnen*.

21 Robert Kroetsch, *Seed Catalogue: Poems* (Winnipeg: Turnstone Press, 1986), 17.

22 Giedion, *Mechanization Takes Command*, 142.

23 Reyner Banham, *Los Angeles: The Architecture of Four Ecologies* (London: Allen Lane, 1971).

24 Banham, *Theory and Design*, 9.

25 Charter of the Hudson's Bay Company.

26 Manitoba Hydro: http://www.hydro.mb.ca/about_us/history/history_timeline.html (accessed 15 April 2005).

27 Rudy Wiebe, *Playing Dead: A Contemplation Concerning the Arctic* (Edmonton: NeWest Publishers, 1989), 9.

28 Site visit by the author, 20 May 2005, Blanchard, North Dakota.

29 Wallace Stegner, "Thoughts in a Dry Land," in *Where the Bluebird Sings to the Lemonade Springs: Living and Writing in the West* (New York: Penguin Books, 1992), 52. First published in *Westways* magazine (1972).

Herbert Enns

THE WINNIPEG AIRPORT

MODERNISM,
CULTURE,
AND THE
ROMANCE OF
AIR TRAVEL

Bernard Flaman

When the Winnipeg airport terminal opened in 1964, it was hailed as one of the most remarkable structures in the city. Designed by a local architectural firm, Green, Blankstein, and Russell, it was described as a "tonic for anyone who sweeps in across the prairie."[1] Spacious, sophisticated, and modern, it fed the romantic expectations of air travel in the early days of the jet age.[2] (fig. 7.1, 7.2) The Winnipeg terminal was part of a network of major terminals built across the country between 1958 and 1968 by the Canadian Department of Transport. Each was resolutely Modern, each incorporated the latest Canadian and international furniture, and each terminal evoked the interior of an art gallery by displaying the largest public art project ever realized in Canada.[3] These extraordinary efforts represented a desire on the part of the federal government to convey a thoroughly modern and up-to-date national image that would serve as an introduction to Canada and its culture for the foreign traveller. The architecture and artworks were also meant to represent a unifying force for the citizens of a large and diverse nation composed of several different linguistic and cultural groups as well as numerous topographic regions.

fig. 7.1
Man with fedora (1964)
Wnnipeg International Airport
Photograph: Henry Kalen (1964)
217K3.2–45

The airport terminal program came on the heels of a milestone in Canadian cultural history, the publishing of the Royal Commission on National Development in the Arts, Letters and Sciences, in 1951, also known as the *Massey Report*, named after its chairperson, Vincent Massey. The report was an attempt to "forge and project a Canadian culture that resulted in the creation of the Canada Council for the Arts and the National Library, and directed cultural production in Canada until the 1970s."[4] At the heart of the report was the promotion of a recognizable expression of "true Canadianism."[5] The airport terminals, with their coordinated approach to architecture and public art, are one of the tangible examples of directives articulated in the *Massey Report*. The Winnipeg terminal was built during arguably the high point of the building program and was designed and constructed at the same time as terminals at Toronto and Edmonton. Direction on the architectural image, the interior design, and the public art program had developed to a level where it received a great deal of official support from the Department of Transport. By this point, major terminals had been completed at Gander, Halifax, Montreal, and Ottawa, with the Vancouver terminal still in the planning stages.

With the design of the Toronto, Winnipeg, and Edmonton terminals, the public art program became official policy when Deputy Minister of Transport John R. Baldwin convinced the Minister of Transport in the Diefenbaker government, Leon Balcer, to allocate one-half of one percent of the construction budget to art.[6] Rather than selecting artists through a limited competition, similar to the one that resulted in Kenneth Lochhead's mural at Gander, Baldwin solicited the collaboration of Charles Comfort, director of the National Gallery, John A. Russell, director of the School of Architecture at the University of Manitoba, and John C. Parkin, director of the National Design Council and the architect for the Toronto terminal. Comfort and Parkin were asked to compile a list of prominent Canadians who would compose three committees responsible for selecting the artists for the public art program.[7] Responsibility for guiding the architectural and interior design direction rested with the Department of Transport Air Services branch under Chief Architect W.A. (Alex)

184

fig. 7.2
Winnipeg International Airport (1964)
Green, Blankstein, Russell, and Associates
Bernard Brown and David Thordarson
principal design
Photograph: Henry Kalen (1964)
217K3.2–57

Ramsay. The branch was directly responsible for designing smaller, regional terminals and for guiding the work of consulting architects commissioned for the design of the large terminals. Stanley White, employed by the Air Services branch, became an important figure during the design phase. A graduate of the University of Toronto School of Architecture in 1949, he served as secretary of the fine art committee and was responsible for coordination of the interiors. He was described as "an accomplished designer-director in the amateur theatre, who has provided much of the impetus for a vastly improved standard of design."[8]

The set of three terminals at Toronto, Winnipeg, and Edmonton became the first in Canada to be designed for jet passenger aircraft. The technical objectives for the so-called "jetports" were not yet completely formulated and the design process exhibited exploration and experimentation with the basic building footprint and passenger flows. The result was three different approaches that shared the common programmatic elements of ticket concourse, public lounge, VIP lounge, arrivals area, restaurant, and lunch counter.

Originally conceived as the first of several aeroquays, the Toronto terminal was based on a circular plan form to minimize walking distances from the drop-off curb or from the parking garage that was an integral part of the building. (fig. 7.3) Passengers arrived by a roadway that dipped below the aircraft ramp, similar to Heathrow airport in London during the early stages of its development, and emerged in front of the departure concourse in the centre of the building. From there it was a short walk to the check-in counters and departure lounges that ringed the concourse area. The Edmonton terminal was based on a simple linear design with a separate departures and arrivals level roadway. (fig. 7.4) Although much less daring than the design for Toronto, the linear nature and two-level roadway embodied aspects of terminal design that would become common in the future. The multi-storey administration tower slab, set perpendicular to the terminal and clad in a glass curtain wall, added symmetry and monumentality to the design. The structural design was

fig. 7.3
Toronto International Airport (1964)
John B. Parkin
Photograph: Panda Fonds
Canadian Architectural Archives

fig. 7.4
Edmonton International Airport (1964)
Rensa and Minsos
Provincial Archives of Alberta

186

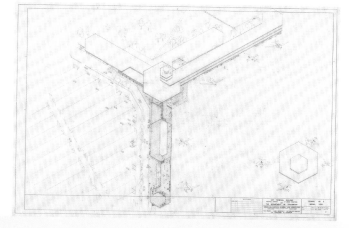

fig. 7.5
Scheme 2 (July 16, 1957)
Winnipeg International Airport
Perspectival drawing
Green, Blankstein, Russell, and Associates
Bernard Brown and David Thordarson
principal design
Archives of Manitoba

conventional with a "domino" steel frame. The volume of passenger traffic at the Winnipeg airport was deemed too small by the Department of Transport for an aeroquay scheme or a two-level roadway, resulting in a single-level concept that allowed for expansion and the eventual construction of a two-level roadway. The final scheme was the result of a three-year design process that stretched from early 1957 to late 1959 and can be analyzed and understood through an excellent record of archival drawings.

Scheme number 2 illustrates an approach that could be interpreted as naïve in relation to the future accommodation of jet aircraft. (fig. 7.5) The Y-shaped plan defines three separate wings: a departures wing with check-in counters; an arrivals wing with luggage pick-up; and a wing for aircraft loading and unloading. The most surprising aspect of this scheme, especially in the context of the final building, is the architectural expression, which displays an overt influence of the work of renowned American architect Frank Lloyd Wright. Scheme number 4 explores an aeroquay scheme with a series of separate, circular terminals similar in concept to the Toronto design. (fig. 7.6) The drawing set includes a perspective rendering by Bernard Brown, and depicts jet aircraft parked on the tarmac. Brown worked in the office of John B. Parkin Associates, the designers of the Toronto terminal, and his experience in that office may be why an aeroquay scheme was explored. Scheme 7 is perhaps the most interesting of the series. (fig. 7.7) Highly ambitious, it includes a terminal, office building, parking garage, and hotel in a symmetrical, axial arrangement with each element connected by enclosed, elevated walkways. It also displays a novel arrangement of separate arrival and departure roadways on a single level. Architecturally, it presents an extremely compelling collection of forms, combining a cylindrical hotel tower, a semicircular parking garage, and a terminal that spreads across the prairie landscape, capturing space within open courtyards between the departure lounges and the main terminal structure. The rest of the design process, culminating in scheme 13R, illustrates a rearrangement and consolidation of the basic design of scheme 7. (fig. 7.8) The courtyards are still evident, but are radically reduced in size; the

fig. 7.7
Scheme 7 (July 10, 1958)
Winnipeg International Airport
Photograph of original drawing
Green, Blankstein, Russell, and Associates
Bernard Brown and David Thordarson principal design
Archives of Manitoba

187

Bernard Flaman

fig. 7.6
Aeroquay Scheme 4 (1958)
Winnipeg International Airport
Perspectival drawing by Bernard Brown
Green, Blankstein, Russell, and Associates
Bernard Brown and David Thordarson
principal design
Photograph: Ernest Mayer (2006)
Stantec Architecture/ GBR Collection

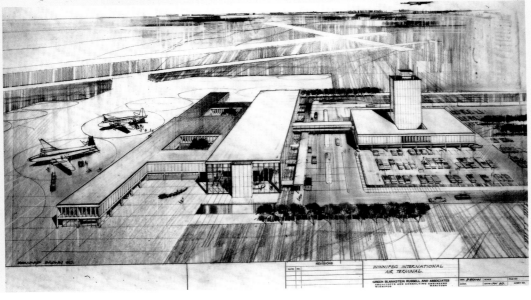

fig. 7.8
Scheme 13R (December 4, 1959)
Winnipeg International Airport
Photograph of original perspectival drawing by
Bernard Brown (1960)
Green, Blankstein, Russell, and Associates
Bernard Brown and David Thordarson
principal design
Photograph: Henry Kalen (c. 1960–61)
217K3.2–2

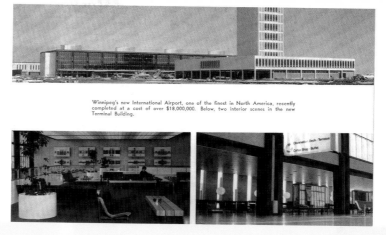

Winnipeg's new International Airport, one of the finest in North America, recently completed at a cost of over $18,000,000. Below, two interior scenes in the new Terminal Building.

fig. 7.9
From Winnipeg International Airport
Winnipeg, the Capital City of Manitoba
City of Winnipeg Archives and Records Control

administration building has been separated from the terminal and takes the axial position of the deleted hotel and carpark.

The completed terminal was a complex of three buildings: the administration building with an office tower capped by a control tower; the concourse building where the check-in counters, waiting area, shops, and luggage carousels were located; and the arrival and departure lounges, connected to the concourse with a series of fingers separated by open courtyards. (fig. 7.9) The administration building and the lounges on the airside were both clad in Tyndall stone and connected the Modernist design to the building traditions of the Winnipeg area. The most memorable part of the terminal, however, was the concourse building, a rectangular pavilion with a clear-span steel structure, glazed on the east and west sides, with solid walls on the north and south ends. The check-in counters occupied the centre section, flanked by the arrival areas and luggage carousels. A vast mezzanine level, which provided a waiting area to seat 400 people, appeared to float beneath the clear span of the concourse. It was planned as a future departures level, anticipating the construction of a second-level roadway. Natural light entering through the glazed walls was augmented by diffused light of the back-lit ceiling system incorporating translucent plastic panels. (fig. 7.10)

fig. 7.10
Winnipeg International Airport (1964)
Green, Blankstein, Russell, and Associates
Bernard Brown and David Thordarson principal design
Photograph: Henry Kalen (1964)
217K3.2–23

The Winnipeg terminal was shaped by the involvement of Bernard Brown and David Thordarson, both architects working in the office of Green, Blankstein, and Russell. Thordarson's interest in developing a form of Modernism that incorporated local influences and materials explains the combination of a glass and steel International Style architecture with traditional Tyndall stone cladding and a sensitivity to the light and landscape of the prairie, which served as regionalizing forces.[9] However, the ordered and minimalist nature of the concourse building and its clear-span structure displays an overriding influence of the work of Ludwig Mies van der Rohe, and when Bernard Brown was asked where the inspiration for the design concept came from, his answer was one word: "Mies."[10] This influence also explains the symmetrical composition

189

Bernard Flaman

fig. 7.11
Winnipeg International Airport
Photograph of original graphite drawing by
Bernard Brown (1960)
Photograph: Henry Kalen (1960)
217K3.2-1

fig. 7.12
Winnipeg International Airport (1964)
Green, Blankstein, Russell, and Associates
Bernard Brown and David Thordarson
principal design
Photograph: Henry Kalen (1964)
217K3.2–47

of major elements and a rigidly ordered structural expression that illustrates van der Rohe's interest in Neo-classicism.[11] Brown explained the design team's concern for scale, which is illustrated by the division of the large east-facing windows, within the structural bays, into smaller sections to exhibit a human scale.[12] (fig. 7.11, 7.12) The apparent influence of the work of Mies van der Rohe also illustrates the possible guidance of federal officials and an unofficial consensus in favour of an architecture of "cautious internationalism," which resulted in a vague similarity among all the terminals built during this period. The "elegance of proportion and of articulation" that distinguishes the Winnipeg terminal confirms the intentions of the design team, as explained by Bernard Brown, and also suggests somewhat less federal intervention than with the other terminals.[13]

The prairie landscape surrounding Winnipeg served as inspiration for the design of spaces within the terminal and also as a subject matter for several of the artworks. This inspiration was, however, processed through a rigorous International Style Modernism, bringing with it a high level of abstraction. The mezzanine, for example, vast and awaiting its future function as a departures level, evoked a feeling linked to the landscape of the Winnipeg area. Floating above the main level, it was as expansive and filled with light as the prairie itself, and framed on the north and south ends by large-scale structurist murals by Eli Bornstein and John Graham, which engage the space both literally and with colour. It was an example of a new type of interior public space that was no longer related to a particular city, but possessed a national stature marked by carefully composed spaces that combined fine art, Modernist architecture, and elegant furnishings.[14]

Six artworks were commissioned for the Winnipeg airport and arranged within the terminal, according to a master plan created by the architects.[15] Eli Bornstein's structurist piece on the south wall proved to be one of the most challenging—startling for its level of abstraction. (fig. 7.13) The inspiration came from nature, interpreted as a cool, pristine, and controlled composition

fig. 7.13
Structurist Relief in Fifteen Parts (1962)
Eli Bornstein
Metal relief sculpture
Winnipeg International Airport (1964)
Green, Blankstein, Russell, and Associates
Bernard Brown and David Thordarson principal design
Photograph (detail): Henry Kalen (1964)
217k3.2–24

190

fig. 7.14
The Prairie (c. 1963)
Alfred Pellan
Oil on canvas
Winnipeg International Airport
Photograph: Henry Kalen (1964)
217K3.2–28

fig. 7.15
Northern Lights (1964)
John Graham
Mosaic on metal armature
Winnipeg International Airport
Photograph: Henry Kalen (1964)
217K3.2 series

fig. 7.16
*Frederick Stevenson walking across the field
to his plane...* (1962)
Anne Kahane
Mahogany
Winnipeg International Airport
Photograph: Henry Kalen (c.1963)
217K3.2–14

of coloured enamel metal cubes arranged on a series of white "fields."[16] It relied on colour to engage the space of the terminal when viewed straight-on from the mezzanine level, appearing to be flat from this viewpoint. Viewed from the main level, the cubes seem to physically stretch out into the space, creating a dynamic terrain. Another major artwork based on the idea of abstracting the regional landscape was Alfred Pellan's large-scale oil on canvas mural that graced a curved wall in the foyer of the airport's restaurant. (fig. 7.14) Entitled *The Prairie*, it combined Pellan's surrealist style with a vibrant colour scheme that conveys a personal interpretation of the prairie colour palette. Both these artworks complemented the light and view of the actual prairie landscape available through the large areas of glass in the terminal concourse.

Several other artworks exhibited a variety of personal artistic visions, with abstraction being the common denominator. John Graham's structurist composition of mosaic tile, coloured Plexiglas, and vertical aluminum bars caught the late afternoon sunlight in the fall and glowed with yet another interpretation of prairie light and colour. (fig. 7.15) Perhaps the prettiest of all the pieces, the combination of pastel and primary colours evoked memories of early sixties style in cars, fashion, and product design. Anne Kahane's abstracted bust of pioneer aviator Frederick Stevenson, rendered in solid mahogany, stood at the end of the footbridge that connects the concourse with the administration building. (fig. 7.16)

Two large-scale metal sculptures by Walter Yarwood and Gerald Gladstone decorated the courtyards between the concourse and departure/arrival lounges. Yarwood, a member of the Toronto group Painters Eleven, created a vertical totem that appeared to engage both earth and sky. (fig. 7.17) Gladstone's fantastical piece incorporated a fountain and was consistent with his personal style that suggested a science-fiction inspiration. (fig. 7.18)

191

Bernard Flaman

fig. 7.17
Untitled (c. 1963)
Walter Yarwood
Metal
Winnipeg International Airport
Photograph: Henry Kalen (1964)

fig. 7.18
Solar Cone, Fountain (c. 1963)
Gerald Gladstone
Metal
Winnipeg International Airport
Photograph: Henry Kalen (1964)
217K3.1

fig. 7. 19
Sprung Steel Seat (c.1960)
Walter Nugent
Winnipeg International Airport
Photograph: Herbert Enns (2006)
Western Aviation Museum Collection

The furniture chosen for the airport terminals showcased Canadian design, with the Toronto and Edmonton terminals receiving several examples, particularly by Canadian designer Robin Bush. In Winnipeg, however, his only design was a monumental yellow birch bench, used in the arrivals area, that featured circular seating pads related to Bush's "lollipop" seating system designed for the Toronto Airport. The only other Canadian furniture was a seating system designed by Walter Nugent—a ganged, metal version used in the departure lounge and individual chairs with teak frames in the dining room. (fig. 7.19) The mezzanine space at Winnipeg featured American furniture designs; elegant settees in mauve and magenta by William Katavolos, Ross Littell, and Douglas Kelley (fig. 7.20 [p.197]), and metal basket chairs by Harry Bertoia were arrayed around a surfboard table by Charles and Ray Eames.[17] Three-legged leather sling chairs by Katavolos, Littell, and Kelley were featured in the VIP lounge. (fig. 7.21) The interest in American furniture design could be explained by the many architectural graduates from the University of Manitoba School of Architecture who pursued graduate studies in the United States. The director of the school, John Russell, himself an American, fostered a close relationship with academic institutions in the United States.[18] Department of Transport architect Stanley White explained the selection process for the artworks. "There was no catering to popular taste. . . . We were trying to achieve for Canada the most sophisticated image we possibly could." He promoted an idea where regional favouritism was set aside and, instead, a Vancouver artist was commissioned for a mural in Edmonton, a Montreal artist in Toronto, and a Toronto artist in Winnipeg.[19]

Unfortunately, the nationalistic goals and the abstract nature of the artworks were perhaps too far in advance of public taste and understanding. The popular press described the pieces as modernistic blobs, paint smears, welder's experiments, and carpenter's leftovers. At Winnipeg, one of the immediate effects of the criticism was the commissioning of a representational bronze bust of aviator Frederick Stevenson to help deflect criticism of Kahane's interpretation. Indeed, the carefully coordinated interiors did not endure well as the nature

193

Bernard Flaman

of air travel changed quickly, especially during the 1970s, driven by swelling passenger volumes and increased security concerns. The Winnipeg terminal has been the subject of many alterations and expansions since it was constructed. The courtyards have been filled in, resulting in the removal and disappearance of the sculptures by Yarwood and Gladstone. Kahane's version of Frederick Stevenson's image, after coexisting with the representational bronze version, was eventually removed. Pellan's mural was moved to the Mirabel terminal north of Montreal in the 1970s. Graham's and Bornstein's large-scale murals still exist in their original locations, but are now almost obscured by a small aircraft suspended from the ceiling and a clutter of real-estate company advertising. While ownership of the artworks still rests with the Crown, the private authorities that now run the airports list a series of concerns with the remaining murals.[20] These range from a difficulty in properly maintaining the pieces in an airport environment, to their size, causing constraints on expansion plans.

Canada is experiencing another airport building boom, caused by ever increasing passenger volume and the shift from government to private ownership of airport facilities. The incorporation of shops and advertising has become a prime concern of airport authorities as most modern airports derive a substantial portion of their income from retail sales. Obsolescence is perhaps one of the major threats to Modernist heritage in general, with airports being most notable examples. The 1964 terminal at Toronto's Pearson Airport was demolished in 2004, coinciding with its fortieth anniversary. Architect Eero Saarinen's expressionist masterpiece, the Trans World Airways (TWA) terminal at Kennedy Airport in New York, was closed in 2002, also on its fortieth anniversary, its future viability as a meaningful part of an airport terminal in question.

The precedents for a heritage conservation approach to airport expansion are extremely rare. Aside from heritage-designated airports in Europe—Speke in Liverpool, Le Bourget in Paris, Ferihegy 1, Budapest, and Templehof in Berlin, and ongoing design efforts to preserve and integrate Kennedy's TWA

fig.7.21
VIP Lounge
Winnipeg International Airport (1964)
Green, Blankstein, Russell, and Associates
Bernard Brown and David Thordarson principal design
Photograph: Henry Kalen (1964)
217K3.2–49

terminal—the most compelling example may be the Winnipeg airport itself.[21] Between 1986 and 1994, the Winnipeg architectural firm IKOY completed an extremely sympathetic renovation that respected the intent of the original design. Since then, advertising and retail additions have degraded and cluttered the atmosphere of the mezzanine and concourse. A heritage conservation approach need not turn back the hands of time or compromise viability, but rather ensure that expansion efforts spring from a thorough understanding of the important design aspects of the terminal.

As renovation, construction, and demolition continue at airports across Canada, the Winnipeg airport is quickly becoming one of the last recognizable examples of the 1960s-era terminal expansion program.[22] The concourse element of the terminal and the nature of the space that it houses may be worthy of a conservation approach to serve as a reminder of a unique time in Canadian history, one where cultural and nationalistic aspirations intersected with a special moment in architectural design and technological advances in air travel. It was on this level that the design work at the Winnipeg terminal was most successful, by illustrating the surprising confluence of government policy articulated in the *Massey Report* that called for an expression of "true Canadianism" with the stylistic movement of International Style Modernism.

This confluence is suprising, because it is unlikely that the authors of the *Massey Report* anticipated that Modernism would be used in the creation of a design statement that could convey Canadianism or that it could be shaped to include Canadian concerns for materials, colour, seasons, climate, and light. The result was a powerful interior public space at the Winnipeg airport, which symbolized the aspirations and cultural production of Canada in the post-Second World War era.

The avant-garde nature of these spaces, which we still admire today, would also contribute to their dismantling, stemming from the imperatives of unanticipated change in the air transportation industry coupled with a lack of

195

Bernard Flaman

understanding of their value, rarity, and fragility. As new airports are being designed and constructed, it is clear that their anticipated role no longer springs from a utopian idea of serving as a form of cultural institution, but has shifted to a much more pragmatic idea driven by revenue generation, efficiency, and image. New airports and, indeed, most current architectural design, must also grapple with issues of past and future that raise the difficult issue of accelerated obsolescence already apparent in the airport projects of the sixties. Within the space of forty years, the terminal buildings at Winnipeg, Edmonton, and Toronto have either been demolished or are no longer recognizable, suggesting that they were designed for a future that no one anticipated would be temporary.

fig. 7.20
Mezzanine
Winnipeg International Airport (1964)
Green, Blankstein, Russell, and Associates
Bernard Brown and David Thordarson principal design
Photograph: Henry Kalen (1964)
217K3.2–26

WINNIPEG MODERN
Architecture: 1945-1975

ENDNOTES

1   Val Werier, "Most Exciting Building in Town," *Winnipeg Tribune*, 21 November 1964: "It's a tonic for anyone who sweeps in across the prairie. It has space, color, light in proportions that stimulate the visitor and inspire a feeling of pride among the natives. It has the atmosphere of being built for people, an elementary concept often forgotten by those who plan public buildings. It has more than 30 times the space of the old airport terminal, yet it has something of the feeling of a living room. This is accomplished by airiness, soft diffused light, handsome furniture and the use of art and color with taste and imagination."

2   P. Lucas, "On Wings of Commerce," *Fortune* 149, 6 (22 March 2004): 120. "The era it ushered in promised to be suave and cultured—think about that the next time you're walking through security in your socks or standing in line at Pretzel Time. But if the Jet Age never fully delivered on that promise, that's not because it failed—it's because it succeeded too well, generating a public demand that has constantly outstripped the industry's capacity. It's also because travelers craved an unattainably romantic notion of what air travel could represent, . . ."

3   Frank Rasky, "Canada's New Temples of Travel," *Canadian Weekly* (2–8 May 1964): 12.

4   Ken Lum, "Canadian Cultural Policy," *Canadian Art* 16, 3 (Fall 1999): 76.

5   Vincent Massey, chairman, "Introduction," *Royal Commission on National Development in the Arts, Letters and Sciences*, part II (Ottawa: King's Printer, 1951), 271.

6   Frank Lowe, "Art in the New Airports Gives Canada a Sophisticated Image," *Canadian Art* 21 (1964): 147.

7   Frank Rasky, "The Agony and Ecstasy of Our Airport Art," *Canadian Weekly* (9–15 May 1964): 10.

8   Lydia Ferrabee, "Toronto Airport: Interior Design," *Canadian Architect* (February 1964): 63.

9   Kelly Crossman, "North by Northwest: Manitoba Modernism, c. 1950," *Journal of the Society for the Study of Architecture in Canada* 24, 2 (1999): 66–68.

10 Bernard Brown, interview at offices of GBR, Winnipeg, February 2000.

11 George Baird, *The Space of Appearance* (Cambridge: MIT Press, 1995), 149. Canadian architect and theorist George Baird describes the link between certain streams of Modernism and Neo-classicism in his 1995 book. Baird references Colin Rowe's 1947 essay, "The Mathematics of the Ideal Villa," which suggests Le Corbusier's Villa at Garches as an example of a Modernist building that is based on Neo-classical proportions.

12 Brown, interview, February 2000.

13 Rhodri Windsor-Liscombe, "Grounding the New Perspectives of Modernism: Canadian Airports and the Reconfiguration of the Cultural and Political Territory," *Journal of the Society for the Study of Architecture in Canada* 28, 1 and 2 (2003): 10.

14 Deyan Sudjic, *The 100 Mile City* (London: HarperCollins, 1992), 159. "There are precedents for the role that the airport has adopted. The railway terminus was an essential part of the Victorian metropolis. It was a new kind of civic space, and called for the creation of a new building type to accommodate it."

15 Green, Blankstein, Russell, Associates, "Fine Art Program, Winnipeg International Airport," National Gallery of Canada Library, Ottawa.

16 Eli Bornstein, interview at his office, University of Saskatchewan, Saskatoon, January 1999.

17 Klaus Jurgen Sembach, *Modern Furniture Designs 1950–80* (Atglen, Pennsylvania: Shiffer Publishing, 1997).

18 Crossman, "North by Northwest," 63.

19 Frank Lowe, "Art in the New Airports Gives Canada a Sophisticated Image," *Canadian Art* 21 (1964): 147.

20 E-mail correspondence, 23 June 2000, between the author and Claude Corbin, CGA, Manager, Financial Analysis, Airport Programs & Divestiture, Government of Canada, clarifying the ownership of artwork at Canadian airports in relation to the transfer of the airport properties from the Government of Canada to private airport authorities.

21 P. Smith and B. Toulier, *Airport Architecture of the Thirties* (Paris: Caisse nationale des monuments historiques et des sites editions du patrimoine, 2000), 24; Bronwen Ledger, ed., "The Ageing Modern 3: Prairie Phoenix," *Canadian Architect* 40, 5 (May 1995): 35.

22 The concourse at Winnipeg airport and the international waiting room at Gander airport are the only relatively intact examples of the terminal building program that spanned the 1950s and 1960s.

Bernard Flaman

MANITOBA MOD

THE WORK OF GUSTAVO DA ROZA II

Terri Fuglem

There is little scholarship that analyzes the period of Modernist architecture in Canada that bridges the gap between "high" International Modernism and Post-Modernism. The projects designed by Gustavo da Roza from 1961 to 1971 characterize the last phase of Modernism before the self-conscious, radically anti-Modernist precepts of "Po-Mo" took hold. During this period, dubbed "Supermannerist" by C. Ray Smith, artists emulated contemporary art movements, such as Fluxus, Happenings, and Pop Art. In keeping with these art movements, Smith argues, architects strove to close the gap between art and life, became more entrepreneurial and less elitist, and built "real buildings for real people."[1] Although the architecture of da Roza does not fit into the more extreme or radical categories of Supermannerism, it exhibits some of its salient traits. As Smith notes, Supermannerism's initial manifestations were an "at first gentle, sometimes witty revolution—more in the realm of whimsical disobedience than of combat."[2] Accordingly, for the first time in the history of Modern architecture, architects such as da Roza blended humour, irony, and overt references to popular culture with the more sober Modernist principles that included the influences of Le Corbusier, functionalism, Scandinavian design, and minimalism.

fig. 8.26
Main Entry and Door
Winnipeg Art Gallery (1971)
Associated Architects: The Number Ten Architectural Group and
Gustavo da Roza
Isadore Coop principal-in-charge
Gustavo da Roza principal design
Photograph: Ernest Mayer (1971)
Gustavo da Roza Collection

On 18 December 1967, the results of the national Winnipeg Art Gallery Competition were announced, and the outcome was mildly surprising. Out of 109 entries, many of them by the pre-eminent firms from across Canada, the winner was Gustavo Uriel da Roza Jr., principal, and only, architect of a tiny practice run out of his home. Yet, even as a relative newcomer to the Canadian scene, da Roza had already made headlines at the national level.

Da Roza had arrived in Canada only seven years earlier to accept a full-time appointment at the University of Manitoba, after teaching a year at the University of California at Berkeley. He opened a practice in Winnipeg in 1961 and, in 1963, with University of Manitoba colleagues Radoslav Zuk, Claude de Forest, and Tad Janowski, won a national competition for the design of the 1968 Winter Olympic Project at Banff, Alberta. (The project was not realized because the International Olympic Committee awarded the games to Grenoble, France.) This was the beginning of a sensational streak in da Roza's Canadian career that would compel him to stay in the country. Two years later, da Roza won three prizes in the National Housing Design Competition for the Canadian Lumberman's Association, including the first prize. The winning scheme was built and exhibited at Expo '67 in Montreal as the *Chatelaine* magazine demonstration house. In 1966 da Roza's work and life were part of the subject of the CTV series *This Land Is People* and, in 1967, da Roza, at age thirty-four, won the competition for the Winnipeg Art Gallery (WAG), the most prestigious award of his career. Da Roza proved that as a "one-man show," working out of his home with the help of a few students, he could compete against the largest and best firms across the country.

Gustavo da Roza endowed Manitoba with a considerable body of work during his thirty-year tenure as a full-time professor at the University of Manitoba. During his first decade here, he designed twenty-six single-family homes, seven house renovations, five commercial properties, the Winnipeg Art Gallery (including its furniture), and a forty-five-unit apartment dwelling at 727 Nassau Street. The designs after 1966, and particularly the houses, are characterized by an astonishing formal clarity, overstatement, understatement, and economy. In many of his projects, an undercurrent of humour informs the work. Perhaps this is a reflection of da Roza's personality, his largesse and humility. As an émigré whose culture of origin was itself a hybrid of Asian and European sensibilities, da Roza was adroit in negotiating disparities and contradictions.

Da Roza was born in Macau in 1933, and can trace his Portuguese lineage eight generations back to the colony's first chief justice in the early eighteenth century. Da Roza Senior sent his son to Hong Kong at age fourteen to learn English, but da Roza Junior was equally keen to master Cantonese. In 1950, he enrolled in the first year of the new School of Architecture at the University of Hong Kong. In his fourth and final year, da Roza worked for the dean of the faculty, R. Gordon Brown, who was a Modernist of Bauhaus influence, and who was designing superb buildings for the university and various colleges in Hong Kong. After graduating (First Class Honours) in 1955, da Roza taught at his alma mater while also working at Brown's private architectural firm, and in 1956 he started his own practice. That year, and again two years later, da Roza's work was exhibited in the Royal Academy in London, England. William Wurster, then dean at the University of California at Berkeley, met da Roza during student reviews in Hong Kong in 1958, and was so impressed that he invited the young architect to California to teach. It is worth noting here that Wurster, dubbed "the modest modernist," or, more pejoratively, "that shanty architect" by Frank Lloyd Wright, designed hundreds of affordable Modernist houses in California during the 1920s through the 1960s.[3] Wurster's claim that architecture is the "picture frame, and not the picture" might have been da Roza's.[4]

Da Roza remained at Berkeley until 1960, at which point John A. Russell invited him to the University of Manitoba. While in the United States, Gustavo spent the summer of 1959 working at the Architect's Collaborative in Cambridge, organizing Walter Gropius's portfolio for his application for membership in

Terri Fuglem

fig. 8.1
G. Scalena House (1963)
Gustavo da Roza, Architect
Photograph: Gustavo da Roza (1963)
Gustavo da Roza Collection

the American Institute of Architects. Da Roza claims that this encounter with Gropius in North America was a major influence on his work. He recounts that he was convinced to move to Manitoba when John Russell mailed him a black and white photograph of the freshly minted School of Architecture building designed by Smith, Carter, and Katelnikoff Architects, modelled after Mies van der Rohe's Crown Hall. Russell probably also apprised da Roza of the vigorous Modernists teaching there and of a progressive curriculum influenced by Mies van der Rohe and Gropius.[5] Gustavo was not impressed by Wurster's direction at Berkeley and reasoned that a year or two spent in the centre of the North American continent would not be detrimental.[6]

From the design of his first house in 1961 to the period of the late 1960s and early 1970s, a consolidated approach to house design in Winnipeg seems to emerge in da Roza's work, culminating in a series of wood-frame stucco houses and cementing his reputation as a Manitoban architect. The houses of this period share a cluster of unique characteristics: foremost, the houses are economical and lack pretension; spatial qualities are privileged over expensive materials; the designs are playful, even humorous in their use of geometries, colour, and graphics—offsetting the limited palette of materials; finally, the planning of each house is intricately attuned to the activities of everyday domestic life. All the houses maximize views of nature and make innovative use of topographical conditions. Despite da Roza's upper-middle-class background and his role as Consul to Portugal while he was in Winnipeg, his clients ranged from investment bankers, engineers, and doctors, to working-class railway workers and schoolteachers. His ability to engage multiple points of view was further reinforced by the fact that he was unusually attentive to the needs of families and clients with disabilities. Windows and electrical switches are set low for children and people in wheelchairs; exterior ramps are provided for wheelchairs and prams, evidence of "an architecture of inclusion" so admired by the Supermannerist architects.[7]

204

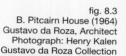

fig. 8.2
G. Kalef House (1964)
Gustavo da Roza, Architect
Photograph: Gustavo da Roza
Gustavo da Roza Collection

fig. 8.3
B. Pitcairn House (1964)
Gustavo da Roza, Architect
Photograph: Henry Kalen
Gustavo da Roza Collection

Da Roza claims that his first houses in Winnipeg, done between 1961 and 1964, were still under the influence of his residency in California. These comprise a series of modest wood-frame houses with mixed exterior finishes. The first, his own house on Waterford Bay, completed in 1962, was finished with grey stucco and chocolate brown wood trim. Similarly, the 1963 houses for Ted Speers and G. Scalena (Assiniboine Avenue), both on the Assiniboine River, are multi-levelled with vertical wood siding. (fig. 8.1) Both appear as bungalows to the road, but are two-storeyed from the river. The Speers house is distinguished by wall planes in stucco, and a flat roof outlined by a heavy brown overhang. The Scalena house, the first of two commissions for railway worker clients, is unpretentious but refined in its use of vertical siding, low-gabled roof, and deep overhangs with exposed wood rafters. The Kalef house on Laidlaw Boulevard (1964) is another modest bungalow; its exterior is treated in a culturally hybrid manner that da Roza mischievously dubs "Japanese Tudor"—whereby corners and windows are articulated by stained cedar frames, contrasting the roughly worked white stucco wall finish.[8] (fig. 8.2) A three-foot overhang and spare Modernist interior distinguish the house. The last of this group of houses, and possibly the most successful, is the Pitcairn House on Laidlaw Boulevard. (fig. 8.3, 8.4) Also a bungalow with a gable roof, the house is largely clad in white stucco contrasted with stained-wood window trim and cedar siding on eaves and bay window sections. Features include rough-sawn cedar treated with Danish oil on the exterior soffits and the interior sloped ceiling, hardwood floors, a sunken living room to accommodate built-in furniture, and accents in primary colours on cupboards and the garage door.

Although the early Winnipeg houses bear little stylistic resemblance to those of William Wurster, they are similarly modest. *House Beautiful* might have been describing da Roza's houses when it lauded Wurster's designs as having "convenience of plan but charm of composition in no small degree."[9] Like da Roza, Wurster utilized local species in landscaping and plain local materials for modest, inexpensive designs. The client's desires were pre-eminent to the design; Wurster rarely gave decorating advice and he accepted a wide range of

205

commissions. Despite da Roza's dissatisfaction with Wurster as dean at Berkeley, his own claim that "my taste is completely irrelevant; the client's is the one that matters" betrays his affinity with Wurster's ethic.[10] This remarkable humility also might stem, in part at least, from the influence of Scandinavian design, which, da Roza maintains, profoundly affected his work. Indeed, he was taught by Scandinavian architects in the first, second, and third years at the University of Hong Kong.[11] Da Roza studied the work of Arne Jacobson while at university, and later travelled to Scandinavia on a Special Arts Award from the Canada Council in the winter of 1968.[12] His slides from this trip show the buildings of Sigurd Lewerenz, Gunnar Asplund, and Arne Jacobson under blankets of freshly fallen snow, and various photographs depict the forested landscapes of Sweden, Denmark, and Finland. It seems that da Roza's interest in Scandinavian architecture stems in part from the similarities to natural landscape, climate, and light qualities found in Manitoba. The Scandinavian architects' deferential treatment of nature—their tendency to work with and around existing flora and topography—is clearly influential on da Roza.[13]

The Sokolov House on Shaftesbury Boulevard (1964) maintains many of the features of the earlier houses, but marks a transition to more boldly Modern and contextually derived design. The design was initiated by architect and colleague James Donahue, who recommended da Roza complete the contract.[14] It is difficult to know what features of Donahue's preliminary design remain in the project, except that the original proposal was for a two-storey residence, for which the ground floor was set two feet below grade to achieve the visual effect of horizontality. Da Roza's first move was to reposition the main floor to ground level. The resulting stucco "box" is punctuated on the street façade by two vertical elements that contain the formal entry and service doors, and floor-to-ceiling glazing. (fig. 8.5) The rather curious inclusion of separate formal and service entries on the front façade—repeated in several later houses—is reminiscent of the adjacent front doors on Villa Snellman (at Djursholm, Sweden) by Gunnar Asplund. (fig. 8.6) The rear façade is entirely framed by a six-foot projection of the side walls and flat roof. (fig. 8.7) The

fig. 8.4
B. Pitcairn House (1964)
Gustavo da Roza, Architect
Photograph: Henry Kalen
Gustavo da Roza Collection

207

Terri Fuglem

house's orientation to the back yard to the east and the mature oak trees—the remains of an old forest—is accentuated by floor-to-ceiling window-walls and patio doors. Significantly, da Roza went to great lengths to retain the existing woodlands on the property, which developers on adjacent lots razed. The floors on the main storey are finished with brown Vermont slate, including the two-storey living space, and the balustrades' built-in cabinetry is African mahogany. The exterior trim is painted brown, except for two vertical panels of rough-sawn cedar on the east façade. The colour palette, inside and out, is otherwise entirely restricted to white. (fig. 8.8) The Sokolov house exhibits many characteristics featured in subsequent designs: generous and well-proportioned, but plainly finished, rooms; the separation of children's quarters from the master bedroom; built-in cabinetry and furniture; orientation of living spaces toward the garden and nature; exterior overhangs; and high-quality construction secured at prices comparable to developers'. The Sokolov house is significantly more restrained than the earlier houses in its use of materials, but bolder in its formal simplicity.

The houses that follow the Sokolov house exhibit many affinities with Supermannerist architecture. These include the use of super-graphic and psychedelic signage, bold geometries, including angled walls and polygonic shapes, inverted structural logic, "camp" features such as oversized doors, and the use of textured materials such as stucco. A house designed for the Walders on Shaftesbury Avenue (1968) is one of the most playful. The street façade of white stucco is almost completely plain, save for a service door screened by five-foot-high, free-standing, "super-graphic" numbers. (fig. 8.9) The formal entrance, a preposterously tall, narrow door, fourteen feet high, is painted the same brilliant orange as the numbers, and its correspondingly tall side-light is likewise concealed by a porch and a two-storey wall parallel to the house. (fig. 8.10) In contrast to the coy blankness of the front, the rear façade is richly articulated with a second-storey strip window that extends the entire length of the fifty-two-foot building, and a brick chimney mass penetrating the six-foot projection of the flat roof and end walls. (fig. 8.11) Just as,

fig. 8.5
Watercolour Rendering on Paper (1964)
D. Sokolov House
Gustavo da Roza, Architect
Gustavo da Roza Collection

fig. 8.7
D. Sokolov House (1964)
Gustavo da Roza, Architect
Photograph: Gustavo da Roza
Gustavo da Roza Collection

WINNIPEG MODERN
Architecture: 1945–1975

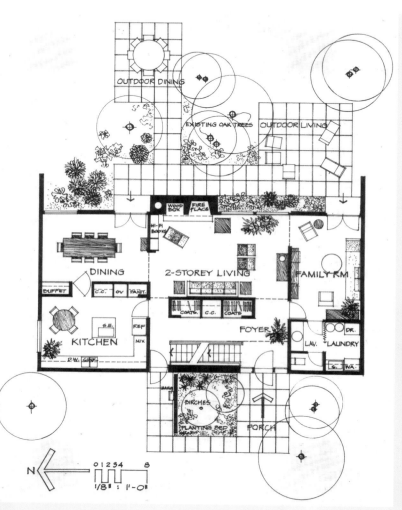

fig. 8.6
D. Sokolov House Floor Plan (1964)
Gustavo da Roza, Architect
Gustavo da Roza Collection

fig. 8.8
D. Sokolov House (1964)
Gustavo da Roza, Architect
Photograph: Office staff of Gustavo da Roza, Architect (1964)
Gustavo da Roza Collection

fig. 8.9
L. Walder House (1968)
Gustavo da Roza, Architect
Photograph:
Terri Fuglem (2005)

fig. 8.10
L. Walder House (1968)
Gustavo da Roza, Architect
Photograph: Terri Fuglem (2005)

according to Colin Rowe, "the mannerist architect . . . inverts the natural logic of its implied structural function," the continuous strip window on the Walder house belies the fact that the rear wall is a wood-frame construction bearing wall.[15] Inside, the Alice in Wonderland scenario continues to play with scale; a "tall" storey-and-a-half family room contrasts the "low" eight-foot-high living room and its picture window, set low at floor level, to view the ground and the remaining tree trunks of an old-growth forest.

Two other houses on Shaftesbury Boulevard show notable characteristics. A recessed portico, with a bright yellow panel wall, relieves the austere, horizontal façade of the Bihler house completed in 1969. Super-graphic, psychedelic house numbers transform the main door into a signboard. (fig. 8.12) More boldly, the front and rear faces of the Nitikman residence (1969) incline outwards; windows are recessed and hung vertically, giving the façade sculptural depth. (fig. 8.13, 8.14) The main entrance is on the raised first level, being accessed by a ramp. The exterior is white, save for cedar panelling on the soffit over the entrance, light grey stucco on vertical walls, and bright blue and red wall panels on the rear façade. Artisanal features also distinguish the house: a textured metal door, a hanging fireplace, and ceiling dining light fixture. The Burshtein residence (1969) on Park Boulevard is extremely daring in its stark minimalism, consisting of a low-lying, massive rectangular box, a recessed entry portico, a projected volume, and the garage door. Ironically, the Burshtein residence is notable for the absence of a discernable street address on such a huge expanse of wall. (fig. 8.15) Three houses designed in 1970 experiment with geometric forms along similar lines. The house for Mr. and Mrs. Robert Smith on Southboine Drive plays with angled volumes (fig. 8.16, 8.17); the Standing House on Kilkenny Drive works from a triangular volume (a quarter pyramid) whose large cedar-shake roof dominates its street presence (fig. 8.18); and angled projections define the Vincent Weekend Retreat House (fig. 8.19). These later experimental, polygonic-shaped buildings, including the triangular Winnipeg Art Gallery, could fit into what Smith describes as

210

fig. 8.11
L. Walder House Back Yard (1968)
Gustavo da Roza, Architect
Gustavo da Roza Collection

fig. 8.12
I. Bihler House (1969)
Gustavo da Roza, Architect
Gustavo da Roza Collection

fig. 8.13
Perspective Drawing (1968)
B. Nitikman House
Gustavo da Roza, Architect
Gustavo da Roza Collection

fig. 8.14
B. Nitikman House (1968)
Gustavo da Roza, Architect
Photograph: Gustavo da Roza (1968)
Gustavo da Roza Collection

the "decade of the diagonal"—the "raging diagonalism" that spawned designs "that resemble origami."[16]

Da Roza's houses of the latter sixties are clearly the progeny of those early purist and functionalist designs of the 1920s and 1930s, for which limited accents of colour and textured materials offset predominantly white walls, and which were notable for their investigations into modern form. Da Roza had a Modernist education, and so considered his work, given his admiration for Le Corbusier, Gropius, Neutra, and, notably, Arne Jacobson. However, there is a levity in da Roza's work that contrasts pointedly with the earlier Modernists' sober aspirations to notions of universalism and truth. Unlike the dogmatic anti-fashion stance held by early followers of Adolf Loos, who deployed white surfaces to denude architecture of ornament, da Roza's use of white has subtly absorbed the trend toward inclusivity and plurality adopted by counterculture movements of the sixties. This trend, according to C. Ray Smith, was "not (about) rejecting purification entirely, just adding liveliness and cleanliness."[17] Liveliness is achieved with "clarity and regularity, whimsy, and humour, puns and witticisms, not merely the high seriousness of a monumental order," although, as Smith contends, monumentalism is good too.[18]

This impression of levity is reinforced by the jocular way in which da Roza describes many aspects of his work, both in the press and in conversation. With characteristic good humour, he fondly recalls his moniker as the "white stucco madman" of Manitoba, and claims, not without irony, he used stucco for its "expressive" capability.[19] Stucco not only suits Manitoba's dry winter climate; it resembles snow. (Da Roza was fascinated by Manitoba's winters, and it is noteworthy how many times he photographed his buildings in snow.) Like the white canvas of a Kenneth Lochhead painting, stucco foregrounds other figures, materials, and colours. Of course, white in the sixties has been co-opted by popular culture as being "Mod." White, as Smith observes, dematerializes; da Roza's white stucco camouflages and even subverts structural expression (and Modernist principles). Da Roza's mischievous deployment of

fig. 8.15
F. Burshtein House (1969)
Gustavo da Roza, Architect
Photograph: Gustavo da Roza (1969)
Gustavo da Roza Collection

fig. 8.16
R. Smith House Perspective Drawing (1970)
Gustavo da Roza, Architect
Gustavo da Roza Collection

fig. 8.17
R. Smith House Plan Drawing (1970)
Gustavo da Roza, Architect
Gustavo da Roza Collection

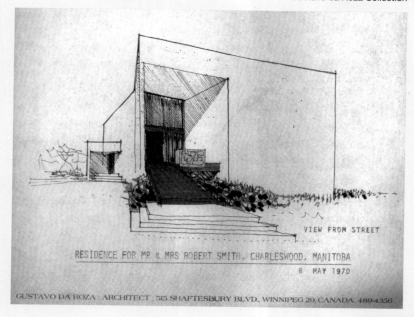

VIEW FROM STREET

RESIDENCE FOR MR. & MRS ROBERT SMITH, CHARLESWOOD, MANITOBA

8 MAY 1970

GUSTAVO DA ROZA : ARCHITECT : 515 SHAFTESBURY BLVD, WINNIPEG 29, CANADA. 489-4356

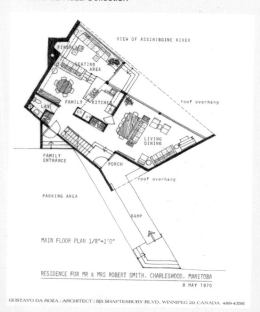

VIEW OF ASSINIBOINE RIVER

FIREPLACE

SEATING AREA

FAMILY KITCHEN

LAV

LIVING DINING

roof overhang

FAMILY ENTRANCE

PORCH

roof overhang

PARKING AREA

RAMP

MAIN FLOOR PLAN 1/8"=1'0"

RESIDENCE FOR MR & MRS ROBERT SMITH, CHARLESWOOD, MANITOBA

8 MAY 1970

GUSTAVO DA ROZA : ARCHITECT : 515 SHAFTESBURY BLVD, WINNIPEG 29, CANADA. 489-4356

SOUTH-WEST ELEVATION 1/8" = 1'-0"

fig. 8.18
K. Standing House Southwest Elevation Drawing (1970)
Gustavo da Roza, Architect
Gustavo da Roza Collection

fig. 8.19
A. Vincent Weekend House, Victoria Beach (1971)
Gustavo da Roza, Architect
Gustavo da Roza Collection

strip windows in wood construction cloaked in stucco evokes a concrete slab-and-column system. Likewise, although it reads as a massive concrete structure, the rough-texture stucco skin *à la béton brut* on the Burshtein house masks a frame structure comprised of laboriously recycled antique lumber. But, most importantly, stucco draws attention away from the building itself and foregrounds nature and everyday life. In da Roza's hands, stucco, with its working-class connotations, achieves a remarkable elegance and yet maintains its humility. One reporter wrote of the Sokolov house, "its exterior is both modest and enigmatic . . . nothing elaborate and showy."[20] As a Winnipeg real estate agent put it, "the home has a very serene and solid sort of feel. It is earthy and contemporary at the same time. The integrity of the structure is very special. I don't know how else to put it."[21] Even aspirations to pretense in the toniest of homes are playfully inverted: da Roza describes the tall door of the Walder house as the "arrogant" door and the stucco portico wall as the "arrogant wall that hides the arrogant door."[22]

fig. 8.20
Winnipeg Art Gallery Wood Model
Gustavo da Roza
Photograph: Office staff of Gustavo da Roza (1967)
Gustavo da Roza Collection

Da Roza's house designs of the late sixties coalesce into a remarkable oeuvre, built with an economy of expression and means that competes directly, and consciously, against the developer market. Da Roza was impatient with academic theorizing; instead, he espoused an entrepreneurial spirit in his pledge to beat developers at their own game: to make houses for the same price. Da Roza claimed, "If a builder can build a house for $15,000.00, so can I."[23] This is where da Roza's practice most closely aligns with the Supermannerists, whose proponents claimed that "only by assuming an active role in construction and real estate will the architect be capable of assuming the position of leadership. . . ."[24] This attitude accords with that of David Sellers at Yale in 1965:

> Architects who don't know how things are paid for, and who don't know why things have got to make money, I think, are irresponsible to their field. . . . Any half-wit speculator seems to be able to make something that doesn't leak, stays warm, and you can see out of, and he usually does it so that people can afford it—and he gets rich. That seems out of the scope of most architects.[25]

214

Da Roza was well versed in land values, frequently chose property for clients, and familiarized himself with construction by knowing the builders: "I learned everything I know from the stucco man, the tile man, the duct man."[26] Da Roza even streamlined the productivity of his own small practice: all drawings were 8.5 inches wide, in order to fit into an IBM Selectric typewriter, to save on the labour of hand lettering and the costs of blueprinting. He copied the strategies of developers to standardize components such as windows, and judiciously chose materials based on cost and availability. Local construction techniques and materials were used wherever possible. Stucco, for example, was ideal for its low cost and maintenance. Essential components such as structure, even if hidden under finishes, were never compromised. Unlike developers, da Roza specified piles instead of footings for the unstable Winnipeg gumbo, and the best, and often most expensive, materials were used for framing and masonry.

The single greatest achievement of da Roza's career, the design and realization of the Winnipeg Art Gallery (WAG), also occurred during this fertile period. (fig. 8.20, 8.21) A comparison with the far more famous National Gallery of Art in Washington, DC, and with avant-garde work at Expo '67 will uncover some of the outstanding features of this extraordinary accomplishment. Da Roza's scheme for the Winnipeg Art Gallery was stunning for its originality and its apparent simplicity. The jurors included H. Harvard Arnason, Vice-President of the Guggenheim Museum in New York; John C. Parkin, of John B. Parkin Associates, Toronto; C.E. Pratt, of Thompson, Berwick, and Pratt, Vancouver; Harry Weese, of Harry Weese and Associates, Chicago; and Raph Rapson, architect, of Minneapolis. They wrote:

> The winning entry brilliantly and sensitively satisfies the requirements of the program and the Conditions of the Competition, expressing with dignity and monumentality the objectives of the Gallery. It exemplifies excellent town planning in its relationship to the site and demonstrates sensitive character and scale within the framework of a highly functional

fig. 8.21
Winnipeg Art Gallery Wood Model
Gustavo da Roza
Photograph: Office staff of Gustavo da Roza (1967)
Gustavo da Roza Collection

Terri Fuglem

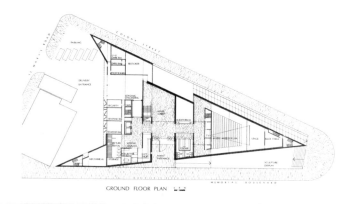

GROUND FLOOR PLAN

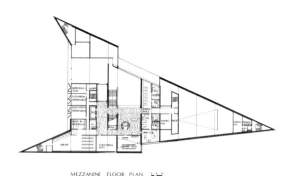

MEZZANINE FLOOR PLAN

and dynamic plan. It is the Jurors' unanimous conviction that this building will stand as a brilliant symbolization of a progressive Winnipeg.[27]

It is noteworthy that two of the jurors, Harry Weese and Ralph Rapson, are cited as "second generation modernists," or "proto-Supermannerists" by Smith.[28] The competition drawings (which differ very little from the completed building) depict a bold chevron plan, in the stark shape of a delta wing or an arrow, oriented north. (fig. 8.22, 8.23) The building derives its cuneiform outline from its triangular site, while leaving a residual space on the east side in the form of a wedge-shaped Tyndall stone plinth on Memorial Boulevard for the display of sculpture. The three corners of the triangular edifice each terminate in a sharp-edged blade. (fig. 8.24) A sketch of the east façade shows a massive ceremonial stone door, eight feet high by sixteen wide (which would weigh 13,700 pounds), inconspicuously flanking the glass entrance doors. (fig. 8.25, 8.26 [p. 200]) Stark, massive, stone-clad walls with limited window area define an imposing mass, yet the building is equally unobtrusive in its minimalism. A south-looking perspective from Memorial Boulevard demonstrates the gallery's deference to Manitoba's Legislative Building; the converging lines of the gallery's east façade terminate with the vanishing point on the Legislative Building's portico. (fig. 8.27) Paradoxically, the project abounds with remarkable features, yet retains humility. The use of Tyndall stone, locally quarried, enables the gallery to blend in with the adjacent buildings, including the Hudson's Bay department store and the Civic Auditorium (now Archives of Manitoba) across the street, and the massive Legislative Building.

Da Roza's triangular art gallery certainly does appear to anticipate, as Harold Kalman suggests, the much-touted extension to the National Gallery of Art in Washington by I.M. Pei (1968 to 1978), another "diagonalist" building.[29] (fig. 8.28, 8.29, 8.30) The East Building of the National Gallery also had the constraint of an irregular site—a trapezium bounded by the diagonal of Pennsylvania Avenue to the north. Both architects admit that the sites' geometry was the main generator of their designs. Pei's response was to divide the site

fig. 8.22
Floor Plan Drawings (c. 1967)
22.a Ground Floor
22.b Mezzanine
22.c Gallery Floor
22.d Roof Plan
Winnipeg Art Gallery
Gustavo da Roza
Gustavo da Roza Collection

fig. 8.23
Winnipeg Art Gallery Site Plan Drawing (c. 1967)
Winnipeg Art Gallery (1971)
Gustavo da Roza
Gustavo da Roza Collection

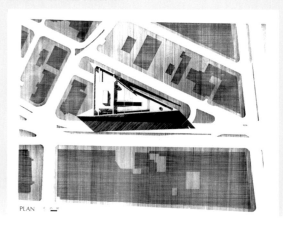

PLAN

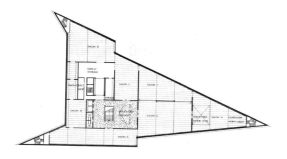

GALLERY FLOOR PLAN

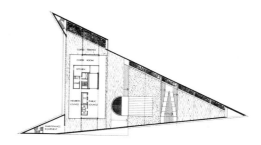

ROOF LEVEL PLAN

fig. 8.24
Winnipeg Art Gallery (1971)
Associated Architects: Number Ten Architectural Group and
Gustavo da Roza
Isadore Coop principal-in-charge
Gustavo da Roza principal design
Photograph: Ernest Mayer (c. 1971)
Gustavo da Roza Collection

fig. 8.28
East Building
National Gallery of Art
Washington, DC
I.M. Pei and Partners
Photograph: Oliver Botar (2006)

fig. 8.29
Atrium Stair East Building
National Gallery of Art
Washington, DC
I.M. Pei and Partners
Photograph: Oliver Botar (2006)

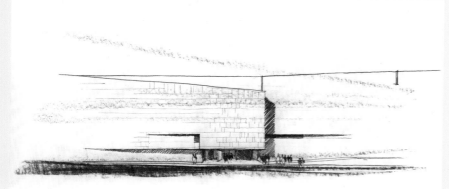

fig. 8.25
Sketch of East Elevation (1968)
Winnipeg Art Gallery
Associated Architects: Number Ten Architectural Group and
Gustavo da Roza
Isadore Coop principal-in-charge
Gustavo da Roza principal design
Gustavo da Roza Collection

fig. 8.27
Perspective Drawing (1968)
Winnipeg Art Gallery
Associated Architects: Number Ten Architectural Group and
Gustavo da Roza
Isadore Coop principal-in-charge
Gustavo da Roza principal design
Gustavo da Roza Collection

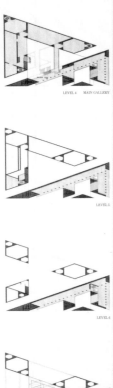

NGA PLAN

into two triangles: an isosceles and a right-angle triangle. Like da Roza's, Pei's much larger triangular mass turns its acute nineteen-degree corner with a knife's edge, and is precisely faced, both inside and out, with smoothly dressed Tennessee marble. The atrium, similar to the much smaller entry court of da Roza's scheme, also had a grand stair leading to a mezzanine along an angled wall. Both galleries achieve an austere, simple, and dignified monumentality. At the time of their openings in 1971 and 1978, respectively, members of the press applied similar metaphors to both galleries. The WAG was compared to an iceberg, an arrowhead, and the bow of a ship: "the (Winnipeg) gallery plows resolutely, and symbolically northward . . . like a brutish prairie frigate."[30] Likewise, the East Building of the National Gallery was a "reckless glacier," celebrated for its "knives of stone" and "pink prows."[31]

But perhaps the comparisons end here. The Winnipeg Art Gallery is very finely detailed; however, Pei's building achieves a fastidiousness unparalleled in Modernist architecture for the jewel-like precision of its craftsmanship. This discrepancy between the two buildings is evident in the disparity in the building budgets; the Winnipeg Art Gallery cost $27 (Canadian) per square foot ($2.50 under budget); the East Building cost $158 (American).[32] Pei's budget, for instance, allowed him to hire cabinetmakers to make the formwork for the exposed concrete out of clear-grain fir. By contrast, da Roza specified standard components wherever possible to save money and expedite construction.

The contemporary criticism underscores more major differences. Da Roza's building was lambasted by Macy DuBois for its inconsistency: "After taking the triangular site as a starting point . . . da Roza decided to stick to an almost entirely rectangular interior wall layout. Thus the dynamic quality of the exterior is not carried into the project. It is as if his exterior walls were chopped down onto an existing rectangular plan. Because of this, the building loses vitality."[33] In contrast, critics chided the National Gallery of Art in Washington for the very opposite attribute: "The endless restatement of a single theme throughout one building is tiresome enough: it becomes distasteful when it is

fig. 8.30
East and West Building Plans (ca. 1976)
National Gallery of Art
Washington, DC
I.M. Pei and Partners
Gallery Archives

219

Terri Fuglem

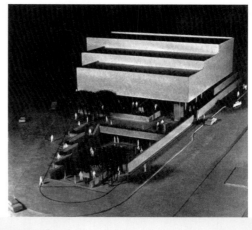

passed off as 'total design.'"[34] In the same roundtable discussion, *Progressive Architecture* editor John Morris Dixon recounted, "As Pei has pointed out, the triangular motif in plan ceases to be a choice, once the geometry starts to work. That was the problem for Wright, with both triangles and circles, and is clearly a problem here."[35]

Pei's schema rigorously and systematically employs its triangular geometry at many levels of design—from its overall planning, to the structural space frame, to the triangular pattern of the four-foot-deep concrete coffered slabs. In contrast, da Roza's building is far less systematic and much more idiosyncratic. Instead of systematizing the triangular geometry as a basis for structural and planning geometries, da Roza's building plays against, inflects, and erodes this geometry. As DuBois suggests, almost nothing in plan, except for the exterior walls and the fire escapes, follows a regularized triangular geometry. The divisions in plan are either parallel with, or perpendicular to, Memorial Boulevard. The skylight is a half-circle in plan. Even the overall triangle employs irregular angles. Each corner where the fire exits terminate employs an eccentric angle: thirty-two degrees on the north edge, twenty-five degrees on the east edge, and thirty-four degrees on the west edge. In the façades, the exterior walls are cut at the top according to a myriad of shallow angles so that the building's upper profile is never level. Although barely discernable, no exterior wall is vertical, but all subtly cant inward at a slope of 1:48 in order to, as da Roza claimed, better reflect the horizontal prairie sunlight. The Winnipeg Art Gallery is an intricate work of "origami" indeed.

In contrast to other contemporary Canadian buildings, da Roza's design for the Winnipeg Art Gallery appears to be on a radical course. A quick study of the other entries in the competition reveals their more fundamental similarity to Pei's scheme than to da Roza's. The second-place scheme, by Gordon S. Adamson and Associates, places a large atrium, covered by a large truss system, between two multi-storeyed halves of a trapezium. (fig. 8.31) The

third-place scheme, by Manitoba's Libling, Michener, and Associates, nests three rectangular boxes within each other. (fig. 8.32) Both schemes are very straightforward, presenting, without nuance, clear, simple volumes. Similarly, the highly influential cadre of Canadian experimental designs for Expo '67 demonstrates an overwhelming predilection for object-making, geometries that are generative of formal and structural systems, as well as for the expression and celebration of those systems. Parkin Associates' design for the CNR pavilion (fig. 8.33), Affleck, Desbarats's "Man the Producer" pavilion (fig. 8.34) and the Canadian pavilion by Ashworth, Robie, Vaughan, and Williams all loudly proclaim their geometric prowess. Even the more "organic" pavilions, such as Arthur Erickson's "Man in the Community" pavilion (fig. 8.35), or Ron Thom's polymer pavilion (fig. 8.36), overtly express their geometry in their structural systems.

In contrast, everything about the design of the Winnipeg Art Gallery resists a totalizing sense of consistency and regularity. The geometry is site-determined, localized, and inflected. The parapet of the east wall is cut into in a variety of ways: first, by a large opening on the north end that allows light into a clerestory skylight over one of the main galleries; second, by a narrow vertical cut at the "valley" of two slopes. A cantilevered plane, protruding on an angle to the main face and overhanging the entrance, adds depth and shadow to the east elevation, but also plays against, and in front of, the singularity of the wall's angle. The gap created at the end of the cantilever provides an opportunity for a north-facing window, and gaps for administrative offices allow for chamfered strip windows in the horizontal bands of stone. On the east and west façades, shallow folds in the taut plane of limestone accommodate features such as the door of a fire exit, or narrow bands of windows. The straight line of the east façade is broken on the ground floor at the south end, weakening and nuancing the mass of the wall. Unlike the stone facing of Pei's building, which is cut into uniform rectangular sizes, the Tyndall limestone on the WAG subtly varies in its coursing; as reported by

fig. 8.38
Gallery Installation (1971)
Winnipeg Art Gallery
Associated Architects:
Number Ten Architectural Group and
Gustavo da Roza
Isadore Coop principal-in-charge
Gustavo da Roza principal design
Photograph: Ernest Mayer (1971)
Gustavo da Roza Collection

fig. 8.37
Stairway
Winnipeg Art Gallery (1971)
Associated Architects:
Number Ten Architectural Group and
Gustavo da Roza
Isadore Coop principal-in-charge
Gustavo da Roza principal design
Photograph: Ernest Mayer (1971)
Gustavo da Roza Collection

the *Winnipeg Tribune*, "Da Roza had a draftsman lay out scores of drawings with random patterns of different sizes."[36]

Structure in the Winnipeg Art Gallery is subordinate and invisible. There is a predominant emphasis on walls, which are, for the most part, load-bearing, poured-in-place, reinforced concrete. Walls are variations of planar compositions and layering, whose masses appear visually light because of the precision and tautness of the saw-cut, four-inch-thick stone facing. The reinforced, profiled, concrete floor slabs and beams are not exposed; and, throughout the entire structure, there is not a single free-standing column. Attention is instead called to planes and surface materials, emphasizing space and surface, and giving the building a quiet monumentality. In the galleries themselves, the triangular geometries disappear almost completely. In the lobby and lounge spaces, the soft tones and fossil patterns of Tyndall stone prevail. (fig. 8.37) With the exception of the large entrance lobby and the third-floor lounge, the interiors are subdued in the service of displaying art. (fig. 8.38)

With characteristic humour, da Roza describes his building as "slightly schizophrenic"; the outside is "bold, strong and dynamic—yes, arrogant—because it is a challenge. The inside—neutral, with no personality . . . so you go away remembering the pre-Columbian gold, or the Renaissance art exhibition, not the carved rosewood doors, or the solid granite ashtrays."[37] As with the houses, da Roza embraces the interpretations of the popular media and even claims that "the iceberg, characteristic of Manitoba's winter environment," was the original inspiration for the design.[38] He would later recant: "They say that I was influenced by an iceberg—the nearest I've been to one is the ice in my Scotch."[39] Journalists were consistently impressed with da Roza's "great charm and keen sense of humour" and noticed its effects in the gallery. According to a local journalist, "Mr. da Roza's fey humour . . . is discernable throughout"; and the same journalist observes, for example, that da Roza's triangular chimney "appear(s) more like a monument, like Cleopatra's Needle, than an outlet for smoke."[40] (fig. 8.39) This sometimes reckless humour

223

belies a deep sense of responsibility and commitment; the final report of the chairman of the Winnipeg Art Gallery Building Committee recorded that "Professor da Roza . . . has left no stone unturned to ensure that the building in every respect will live up to the high promise with which the original sketches were endowed."[41]

It is difficult to imagine a Modernist of the 1950s or earlier admitting to designing a "schizophrenic" building, or a "Japanese Tudor" house. Da Roza's work appears at a time when deeply held Modernist precepts were loosening their grip—precepts such as notions of universality and sobriety, the need for constructional "truth" and stylistic consistency, and the authorial pre-eminence of the architect. The Winnipeg Art Gallery's "origami" geometry is familial with, but even subtler than, the "diagonalism" of the Supermannerists. Furthermore, the effects of da Roza's humour run very deep to an uncanny ability to navigate and celebrate the contradictions and extremes of site constraints, climate, budget, culture, and class in a single building. The real strength of da Roza's work stems from the geographic context within which he worked. Gustavo relished living in Manitoba; he counted himself as one of their citizens. He revered and defended Manitobans, their landscape, their plucky resolve, and their absurdist acceptance of their regional condition. He photographed and painted extensively the prairies and its horizons, embraced all aspects of the harsh winters, and blended the very soul of Manitoba into his pluralist works.

fig. 8.39
Photo of Chimney
Winnipeg Art Gallery (1971)
Associated Architects:
Number Ten Architectural Group and
Gustavo da Roza
Isadore Coop principal-in-charge
Gustavo da Roza principal design
Photograph: Ernest Mayer (1972)

WINNIPEG MODERN
Architecture: 1945–1975

ENDNOTES

This article was written with the asssistance of a grant awarded by the University of Manitoba SSHRC Research Grants Program. Jonathan Trenholm, Ken Borton, Liv Valmestad, Aldona Dziedziejko, Serena Keshavjee, Oliver Botar, and Herb Enns helped immeasurably with research, editing, and production of the final layout. The author is deeply indebted to Gustavo da Roza for the munificent allotment of his time, his Vancouver office, and his archive, and his permission to reproduce the images in this essay, which are taken from his collection.

1   C. Ray Smith, *Supermannerism: New Attitudes in Post Modern Architecture* (New York: E.P. Dutton, 1977), 25.

2   Ibid., 68.

3   Eve M. Kahn, "The Modest Architect," *House Beautiful* 137, 11 (November 1995): 68.

4   John Knox Shear, "Competition for U.S. Chancery Building, London," *Architectural Record* 118 (April 1956): 220.

5   Kelly Crossman, "North by Northwest: Manitoba Modernism, c. 1950," *JSSAC* 24, 2 (1999): 63.

6   Gustavo da Roza in conversations with the author, 14 and 15 May 2003, Winnipeg, and 20 December 2003, Vancouver.

7   Smith credits Charles Moore with the notion of the architecture of "inclusion," *Supermannerism*, 55.

8   Da Roza in conversation with the author, 15 May 2003 in Winnipeg.

9   Kahn, "The Modest Architect," 68.

10 Da Roza in conversation with the author, 20 December 2003 in Vancouver.

11 Da Roza mentioned these architects in passing, but could not recall their names. These might have also been the three architects who worked at the office of Professor Brown: his associate Lars Myrenberg, Kell Astrom, and Folke Bjork. See Gordon R. Brown, "Buildings in Hong Kong," *Architectural Review* 119 (June 1956): 316.

12 Kent Hurley, *Contemporary Architects* (New York: St. Martin's Press, 1980), 189.

13 Moreover, the earthy vernacular houses of Norway also appear in many of da Roza's lecture slides, and the humble reverence for family life that is evident in the slides of modern Scandinavian housing projects matched da Roza's.

14 Da Roza claims that Donahue was his closest friend at the Faculty of Architecture.

15 Colin Rowe, quoted by Smith, *Supermannerism*, 98.

16 Smith, *Supermannerism*, 103.

17 Ibid., 49.

18 Ibid., 48.

19 "Da Roza Suggests Stucco All Around and Some Expression," *Winnipeg Free Press*, 17 April 1968.

20 Michele LeTourneau, "A Modest Enigma: Home Designed by da Roza Both Earthy and Contemporary," *Winnipeg Free Press*, n.d.

21 Realtor Richard Mikucki quoted by LeTourneau, "A Modest Enigma," n.d.

22 Da Roza in conversation with the author, 15 May 2003 in Winnipeg.

23 Da Roza in conversation with the author, 20 December 2003 in Vancouver.

24 Paul Farrell, quoted by Smith, *Supermannerism*, 20.

25 Smith, *Supermannerism*, 23.

26 Da Roza in conversation with the author, 15 May 2003 in Winnipeg.

27 From the "Announcements of Awards," 18 December 1967, issued by Ralph Rapson, Professional Advisor to the Winnipeg
   Art Gallery. Courtesy: Personal Archive of Gustavo da Roza.

28 Smith, *Supermannerism*, xxv.

29 Harold Kalman, *A History of Canadian Architecture* (Don Mills: Oxford University Press, 2000), 578.

30 Ted Allan, "The Art Centre: A Building of Contradiction," *Winnipeg Tribune*, 1 May 1971. Another journalist writes,
   "The triangular structure's apex juts northward like a ship's bow from a downtown berth." See "Premier to Set Art Gallery's
   Datestone Today," *Winnipeg Free Press*, 6 May 1971.

31 The poet William Meredith, 1979, quoted by Andrea Oppenheimer Dean, "The National East: An Evaluation,"
   Architecture (October 1984): 74.

32 Calculated from a final cost of $95.4 million US (1978) for a total of a 604,000-square-foot building area. "P/A on
   Pei: Round Table on a Trapezoid," *Progressive Architecture* (October 1978): 58.

33 Macy DuBois, "Competition: Winnipeg Art Gallery," *Canadian Architect* (February 1968): 38.

34 Martin Filler, "P/A on Pei: Round Table on a Trapezoid," *Progressive Architecture* (October 1978): 52.

35 John Morris Dixon, "P/A on Pei: Round Table on a Trapezoid," *Progressive Architecture* (October 1978): 52.

36 Val Werier, "Our Latest Building for Culture," *Winnipeg Tribune*, 10 August 1971.

37 "Architect Leads Tour," *Winnipeg Tribune*, 28 October 1971.

38 Arlene Billinkoff, "New Art Gallery Designed to Resemble an Iceberg," *Winnipeg Free Press*, 19 December 1968.

39 Quoted by Lorraine Smith in an untitled Hong Kong newspaper article. Courtesy: WAG Archives.

40 Allan, "The Art Center."

41 J. Hoogstraten, Chairman of the Winnipeg Art Gallery Building Committee, Report for the Annual Meeting, June 1969.
   Courtesy: Personal Archive of Gustavo da Roza.

Terri Fuglem

ÉTIENNE GABOURY

MANITOBA MODERNIST

Faye Hellner

Étienne Gaboury began his practice in the early 1960s when designers were reacting to the Miesian ideals of universal space and the resulting glass and steel box. The austerity of the Bauhaus was giving way to a less rigid approach as architects began to critically explore technology, the environment, and the human spirit. Like his colleague Gustavo da Roza, Gaboury rejected some elements of the International Style, believing that "architecture is of necessity anthropocentric," and defining it as "space structured to serve human needs."[1] He can be placed within the Modernist movement as a fusion architect, a man with multiple interests who produces a variety of forms. His spirituality, his integrity, his concern for the environment, and his passion for the inherent logic of structure have produced a unique body of work on the Canadian prairies.

fig. 9.8
Precious Blood Church (1968)
Gaboury, Lussier, and Sigurdson
Étienne Gaboury principal design
Photograph: Henry Kalen (1968)
1071N1.1–15

Gaboury was educated at the University of Manitoba and received his Bachelor of Architecture in 1958. Among his professors at the Faculty of Architecture, James Donahue was an important mentor and influence. Throughout his years as a student, Gaboury's flamboyant nature and style were curtailed in a respectful manner by Donahue, who was adamant about order, clarity, and integrity in the expression of structure and materials. Gaboury recalled, "He was a true Miesian minimalist. I clearly remember his emphasis on the proper sequencing of space and his persistent, almost obsessive remonstrations that space must have a clear order, and that structure was an integral, essential part of it. Donahue also had a propensity for formality, for podium buildings, preferably cantilevered with clear articulation of base and body, of structure and fenestration, as best seen in the John. A. Russell Building [1959, School of Architecture] at the University of Manitoba."[2] (fig. 9.1)

After returning from a year in Paris in August 1959, Gaboury joined the firm of Libling, Michener, and Associates, who had just been hired by the Province of Manitoba to provide a new health services facility. Under the supervision of Melvin Michener, Gaboury practised architecture for the first time. The Manitoba Health Service Building on Empress Street (1959) is a classic Modernist building, cantilevered on two floating slabs, and clearly paralleling Donahue's architectural advice and his School of Architecture Building. (fig. 9.2) The elegant *brise soleil*, which controls the effects of the sun by the use of natural aluminum mullions or fins, was inspired by Corbusier, another important early influence on Gaboury. Libling and Michener had wanted a prize-winning building and they got it when, in 1962, the Health Service Building was awarded the Massey Gold Medal, reinforcing Gaboury's early efforts in experimenting with regional climate demands.[3] It is interesting to compare the Manitoba Health Service Building to the Civic Centre buildings in St. Boniface, designed by Gaboury a few years later in 1963, which use the same building vocabulary. (fig. 9.3) The Civic Centre buildings of St. Boniface are seminal buildings in that they embody the Mies/Donahue formality and the Bauhaus functionalism. Yet, Gaboury sees these buildings as marking the beginning of his evolution away

230

fig. 9.1
School of Architecture (1959)
(John A. Russell Building)
The University of Manitoba
Smith, Carter, and Katelnikoff
Ernest Smith partner-in-charge
James Donahue principal design with Doug Gillmor
Grant Marshall interior design
Photograph: Henry Kalen (1962)
249D4.2–32

fig. 9.2
Manitoba Health Service Building (1959)
Libling, Michener, and Associates
Gerald Libling principal-in-charge
Étienne Gaboury principal design
Photograph: Henry Kalen (1959)
265F1.1

from his Bauhaus training and of his turn towards environmental concerns. The Health Unit, in particular, has a strong overlay of regional expressionism, using a directional north-south axiality as a sun control, with the north facing wall closed and the south facing side open. (fig. 9.4) It appears to burst into space to reach the sun, suggesting traces of Corbusier.

Gaboury's earliest work shows a fundamental relationship between function and space, and an honesty of expression of building construction, form, and materials. Technological advances over the years eventually allowed Gaboury to change his priorities: "Space can be done well without celebration of the structure itself," he said.[4] But technology was only part of the reason that his work began to deviate from Bauhaus principles; within the first decade of his practice, metaphysical concerns became part of his design process. In his paper on "Metaphors and Metamorphosis" (1991), Gaboury states:

> Contrary to the impression one might have of an architect's role, the act of drawing plans and juxtaposing rooms is the easy part; imposing an order, structuring spaces to give them meaningful expression, is quite another matter. Creativity is not merely putting rooms, materials and techniques together; it really blossoms when the work takes on a new reality, when the spaces stir up emotions, when the materials themselves are transcended. Truly valid architecture, like all other arts, lays claim to the metaphysical through the intellectual, emotional, even spiritual experiences that it must provide, along with the message it must convey to us.[5]

Following graduation from the University of Manitoba in 1958, Gaboury continued his studies at the École nationale supérieure des Beaux-Arts in Paris (August 1958 to July 1959), where he visited a number of famous European buildings. In his search for architectural identity, Gaboury was influenced early in his career by the French Modernist architect Le Corbusier. Gaboury was fascinated by Corbusier's "indescribable space" as well as the way in which he was able to structure space by using light. Gaboury's focus on spirituality,

fig. 9.4
St. Boniface Health Unit, Civic Centre (1963)
Étienne J. Gaboury
Photograph: Henry Kalen (1963)
462M2 series

the emotional quality of his architecture, and the complexity of his buildings in relation to their site owe much to an understanding of Le Corbusier's later works, especially the Chapel at Ronchamp. Gaboury describes his first visit to Corbusier's church (fig. 9.5):

> My epiphany occurred during a visit to the Notre Dame du Haut chapel at Ronchamp, designed by Le Corbusier. This tiny chapel was devoid of any reference point, measure or scale. Classical orders of architecture, rational plans, structural integrity had all vanished as if the very rules of architectural composition had been tossed aside. Yet this miniscule chapel was every bit as powerful as the cathedral at Chartres! Even more than its unusual, immeasurable form, the true wonder of Ronchamp was the extraordinary quality of space and light, or, to be more accurate, of space created by light. Le Corbusier gives us the key to Ronchamp and to all his work when he states that architecture is the quest for "indescribable space."[6]

fig. 9.5
Notre Dame du Haut (1955)
Ronchamp, France
Le Corbusier
Photograph: Oliver Botar (2003)

The opportunity to see Corbusier's work gave meaning to the spirituality already imbued in Gaboury during his youth. His mother was a devout Catholic and poetically inclined. From her he learned the value of the human dimension and that mere physicality in architecture is not enough. Over the years, this knowledge translated into a spiritual awareness that is apparent in both his religious and secular work.

Gaboury's professional career was perfectly timed with Catholic reform throughout the Western world. During the Second Vatican Council (1962 to 1965), when Catholic symbology was being revisited, Gaboury's talent for novelty and experimentation found its expression in the design of many churches, as architects and artists were freed by an 1963 edict from the Pope that granted them permission to explore spiritual expression beyond dogma:

> The canons and ecclesiastical statutes which govern the provision of external things which pertain to sacred worship should be revised as soon as possible, together with the liturgical books, as laid down in Article 25.

233

Faye Hellner

fig. 9.6
St. Louis le Roi Chapel (1959)
Libling, Michener, and Associates
Étienne Gaboury principal design
Photograph: Henry Kalen (1961)
278N1.1–10

fig. 9.7
St. Louis le Roi Chapel (1959)
Libling, Michener, and Associates
Étienne Gaboury principal design
Photograph: Henry Kalen (1961)
278N1.1–19

These laws refer especially to the worthy and well-planned construction of sacred buildings, the shape and construction of altars, the nobility, placing, and security of the eucharist tabernacle, the suitability and dignity of the baptistry, the proper ordering of sacred images, and the scheme of decoration and embellishment. Laws which seem less suited to the reformed liturgy should be amended or abolished. Those which are helpful are to be retained, or introduced if lacking.[7]

Pope John XXIII reassessed the symbolism in Catholic religious practice, simplifying the cacophony of messages and iconographic clutter that had attached itself to the Church over two millennia. He wanted a sense of community to return to the Church, and thus gave priority to the significance of the sacraments. This *circumventes* offered opportunity for reform in church design; the congregation became part of liturgical function and moved closer to the sanctuary. The Pope ended the separation of the Holy Reserve from the common people. Instead of small boxes for confession, public confession offered opportunities for communal acceptance and openness. At the same time, the Pope abandoned Latin for the language of the people.

After conceptually designing a church for his thesis/practicum, Gaboury had the opportunity to actually design a small chapel, St. Louis le Roi in 1959, while working at Libling, Michener. (fig. 9.6, 9.7) Gaboury utilized the building vocabulary of wood beams and canopy entrance from the seminary in front, and used a systematic organization of planar forms, rather than three-dimensional volumes, to create the chapel. This marked the beginning of a new type of spatial organization that Gaboury adopted for many of his subsequent works, creating a perception of movement as a result of carefully articulated composition and the use of light. Playing with planes and using light and form are consistent motifs in his work. It was at St. Louis le Roi that Gaboury first broke the pattern of traditional church design, rejecting the familiar Gothic A-frame church type. The chapel won a Massey Medal in 1961.

Faye Hellner

Following that, Gaboury further explored spatial reorganization based on the new policies of Vatican II at Église Precieux-Sang (Precious Blood, 1968). (fig. 9.8 [p. 228], 9.9) The Stations of the Cross are found in a circular path around the inner circumference of the sanctum. It is not only the circulation change here that causes the spiritual impact, but also the quality of the deep red light penetrating the space from an opening in the spiralling roof, which intensifies along the path as the sun moves around the building, day by day and season by season. (fig. 9.10) The culmination of Gaboury's novel circulation and light, abstraction and representation, is in St. Anne's Church and Rectory, Regina, Saskatchewan (1967). Here, Gaboury carries the liturgical innovations to their zenith:

> There was an existing parochial hall/gymnasium; the new church, rectory and hall are merged and the hall thus becomes an extension of the narthex, in effect, the traditional hall of the catechumen, and the liturgical action begins here and progresses in a cadence of sacramental movements culminating at the altar. All sacraments, including Penance (confession), are in the sanctuary; a radical return to the roots of early Christianity in a modern, regional architectural vocabulary.[8]

Étienne Gaboury designs buildings that respond to the conditions and qualities of the prairies. Raised on his family's farm 100 kilometres west of Winnipeg in the area historically known as La Montagne, Gaboury learned early about the patterns of the seasons and the impact of the forces of nature upon the environment.

> I did not have to search long to unearth the mysteries of regional architecture; I needed only rediscover the wisdom of our forebears. The family farm was imbued with this wisdom. Its layout, centred around the sun and the northwest winds and drawn from sections of land that seen from above look like a patchwork quilt, provided a basic lesson in regional urbanism. The north and west flanks of the farm were lined with rows of poplar, elm and spruce, forming windbreaks that were as effective as they were beautiful. Poplars grow quickly but are short-lived; elms are slow but majestic; spruces provide a lovely deep green colour year round and

fig. 9.10
Interior Ceiling
Precious Blood Church (1968)
Gaboury, Lussier, and Sigurdson
Étienne Gaboury principal design
Photograph: Henry Kalen (1968)
1071N1.1–8

fig. 9.9
Precious Blood Church (1968)
Gaboury, Lussier, and Sigurdson
Étienne Gaboury principal design
Proof Print: Henry Kalen (1968)
1071N1.1–1

236

1071 N1.1-1

create shelter at ground level. All was in balance: aesthetics and practicality. The barn, granaries, house, garage, garden and orchard were laid out according to their respective functions but were always dependent on direction, terrain and landscape. The family home was a microcosm of the farm, with the north and west façades being as closed off as possible, and the south and east sides featuring huge windows and a veranda for those stifling July and August Sunday afternoons. To me, prairie architecture is one that should be proud, majestic, heliocentric. It should be strongly oriented with a symmetry limited to the north-south axis. And, since natural light is the element that is essential to the transcendence of space, it follows that the interplay of the fenestration will be crucial.[9]

To live on the prairies is to experience space and light. Gaboury takes full advantage of the subtleties of the natural landscape, the brutality of the changing seasons, the clarity of the prairie light, and the spirituality of the prairie's cultural history. One cannot make good architecture on a flat plane without acknowledging the sun, wind, snow, ice, and open expanse of land against sky. Blessed Sacrament Church (1966) (fig. 9.11 [p. 243], 9.12), his own house on River Road (1968) (fig. 9.13), and the Royal Canadian Mint (1975) (fig. 9.14) are excellent examples of how he creates strong, asymmetrical forms in response to these elements, resulting in copious openings for light, and vertical elements, roofs, and slopes. The forms are bold to take advantage of the high contrast that results from the prairie sun.

Gaboury has strong convictions about the role of the architect in society. He believes it is his obligation to propose alternative visions to the existing social order. He applies the notions of functional planning and the delight of dreaming to buildings, public spaces, towns, and cities. His plans for experimental housing projects, Domicil (1968-74) (fig. 9.15) and Stelco (1969) (fig. 9.16), demonstrate his commitment to using architecture for sociological change. Each of these projects is an attempt to rethink human comfort in a domestic environment in terms of interaction, density, spatial organization, technology, and sustainability. As Gaboury describes it, Domicil is "the ultimate

fig. 9.12
Blessed Sacrament Church
Étienne J. Gaboury
Photograph: Henry Kalen (1967)
905N1.1 series

fig. 9.13
Gaboury Residence (1969)
Gaboury, Lussier, and Sigurdson
Étienne Gaboury principal design
Canadian Architect (March 1969)
Neil Minuk Collection

fig. 9.14
Royal Canadian Mint (1975)
Gaboury, Lussier, and Sigurdson
Number Ten Architectural Group
Étienne Gaboury principal design
Photograph: Henry Kalen (1975)
1781H–1

made-to-measure prefabricated factory home, designed to meet all needs, all means and all eclectic tastes."[10] Stelco, a prairie city of the future, is a "linear city of glass and light, cutting through the plain like a railroad track or hydro towers; heliocentric and braced against the winter winds. It defies earth's gravity and releases the ground from stifling agglomeration and hideous urban thoroughfares."[11]

If there is a correlation between effective design solutions and the enhancement of the human condition, Gaboury's architecture offers many examples. During his prolific career, he has provided social service and created environments for education, health and wellness, worship, and residential comfort. The variation of scale and complexity, of private and public spaces, of built and conceived works, demonstrates his adaptability and energy. His projects exude optimism and determinism, and respond to aesthetic, technical, social, and psychological needs:

> Like all other art forms, architecture is both the mirror of a society and a subtle filter of its thinking, customs and socio-cultural values. Since architecture is so ubiquitous, its conditioning power runs deep and affects our well-being as well as our behaviour. If it is harsh, closed-in and dark, it will make us more predisposed to depression or aggressiveness, to physical and mental degeneration. If, on the other hand, it is open, bright, vibrant and peaceful, it will make us more joyful and serene. But to ensure psychological well-being, matter must be transcended. To achieve this transcendence, the concept of functionalism needs to be broadened to encompass psychological and spiritual needs.[12]

When St. Isadore of Seville wrote the *Etymologies* (the origins of words) in the seventh century AD, he traced the word "city" back to its roots. One root is *urbs*, the "stones of a city." The stones were laid for practical reasons of shelter, commerce, and warfare. The other root is *civitas*, a word relating to emotions, rituals, and convictions. This division in meaning reflects a persistent dichotomy. Too much of one causes imposed order and sterility; too much of the other, chaos and confusion. Gaboury always attempts to strike a balance between the two, creating a complementary union of function and emotion. His work transcends the mundane to attain the sublime, seeking as he does to house the human spirit and intellect.

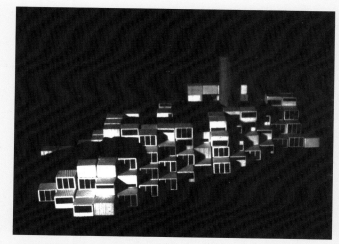

fig. 9.15
Domicil (1968–74)
Gaboury, Lussier, and Sigurdson
Étienne Gaboury principal design
Photograph: Henry Kalen
Étienne Gaboury Collection

fig. 9.16
Competition Entry (1969)
Trend Stelco
Gaboury, Lussier, and Sigurdson
Étienne Gaboury principal design
Étienne Gaboury Collection

241

Faye Hellner

ENDNOTES

This essay is a modified version of my introduction written for the book *Étienne Gaboury* (Winnipeg: Éditions du Blé, 2005).

1 Étienne Gaboury, "Métaphores et Métamorphoses en architecture," *Cahiers franco-canadiens de l'Ouest* 3, 2 (Automne 1991): 184, also in Faye Hellner, ed., *Étienne Gaboury* (Winnipeg: Éditions de Blé, 2005), 23–34.

2 Conversations between Étienne Gaboury and Faye Hellner, Winnipeg, 2004, 2005.

3 On the basis of projected calculations for cost reduction in heating and cooling over a ten-year period, the Province agreed to an increased construction budget. As Gerald Libling had wanted, the Manitoba Health Service Building did win a Massey Gold Medal in 1961. Conversations between Leslie Stechesen and Faye Hellner, Winnipeg, 2005.

4 Conversations between Étienne Gaboury and Faye Hellner, Winnipeg, 2004, 2005.

5 Gaboury, "Métaphores et Métamorphoses," 188.

6 Ibid., 181.

7 Excerpt from the text of his holiness Pope John XXIII, "Constitution of the Sacred Liturgy," 4 December 1963, of the Second Vatican Council following three years of profound examination of modern conditions of faith and religious practice, and of Christian and especially Catholic vitality. See Documents of Vatican II, URL www.rc.net/rcchurch/vatican2/.

8 Conversations between Étienne Gaboury and Faye Hellner, Winnipeg, April 2005.

9 Gaboury, "Métaphores et Métamorphoses," 195.

10 Hellner, *Étienne Gaboury*, 166.

11 Ibid., 168.

12 Gaboury, "Métaphores et Métamorphoses," 192.

fig. 9.11
Blessed Sacrament Church
Étienne J. Gaboury
Photograph: Henry Kalen (1967)
905N1.1–1

BIOGRAPHIES OF MANITOBA ARCHITECTS AND DESIGNERS 1945–1975

Aldona Dziedziejko

ALERS, Valdis Martins, B.Arch., M.Arch., MAA

(1924-1988) Born in Latvia; immigrated from England to Canada, 1949. B.Arch. (Gold Medal), University of Manitoba; MA, Massachusetts Institute of Technology, 1959. Design architect, Smith, Carter Associates, eleven years. Professor, North Dakota State University and University of Manitoba, 1970-76. Registered member, MAA, 1965. Government of Canada Public Works to 1988. Works represented: Manitoba Wheat Board (1962); University of Manitoba School of Fine Arts and School of Music (1964); Royal Bank Bldg., Portage Avenue (1965); Richardson Bldg. (former Lombard Place Development, 1967); Canadian Grain Commission Bldg. (1972); Manitoba Telephone Bldg. (1983); Concert Hall of the Manitoba Centennial Arts Centre (Design Architect under Partner-in-Charge Ernest Smith, 1967).

BLANKSTEIN, Cecil N., B.Arch, FRAIC, MAA

(1908-1989) Born in Winnipeg. B.Arch, University of Manitoba, 1929. With L.J. Green, formed Green and Blankstein (later Green, Blankstein, Russell, and Ham, 1932; then Green, Blankstein, Russell, and Associates [GBR]). President, MAA, 1955; Fellow, RAIC. Works represented: Winnipeg Art Gallery Studio Bldg. (former Mall Medical Bldg., 1947-48); Shaarey Zedek Synagogue, Principal-in-Charge (with Charles Faurer, 1949); Winnipeg International Airport (with David Thordarson and Bernard Brown, 1964); Winnipeg City Hall (with Thordarson and Brown, 1962-65); Cecil Blankstein House (1948).

BLANKSTEIN, Morley, B.Arch, M.Sc. (Arch.), FRAIC, MAA, OAA, RCA

(1924-) Born in Winnipeg, younger brother of architect Cecil N. Blankstein. B.Arch, University of Manitoba, 1949. Intern, Green, Blankstein, and Russell Architects. M.Arch., Illinois Institute of Technology, 1952, studied under Mies van der Rohe and Ludwig Hilberseimer. College of Fellows, 1966. Life member, MAA, 2002. Partners: Cecil Blankstein with Green, Blankstein, and Russell; with Isadore Coop (1955-58); with Coop, joined with Gillmor and Hanna as BCGH (1959), which later joined Waisman and Ross as Number Ten Architectural Group (1964); Isadore Coop as design critic, University of Manitoba (1955-56). Works represented: Continental Travel Group (formerly GBR Architects' Offices, 1951); Winnipeg General Post Office (1953); award-winning entry for National Gallery of Canada, Ottawa (with Coop, 1953-54); Kildonan Park Pavilion (1964); Sharon Home (1970-74); Blankstein residence (1956).

BROWN, Bernard Peter, MRAIC, MAA

(1931-) Born in England. Attended bldg. trades school; Design Diploma, South East Essex School of Architecture, 1953. Admitted to RAIC on basis of external examinations. Immigrated to Canada, 1953. Designer, John B. Parkin Associates (Toronto), then with principal designers Grierson, Walker, and Warren. Art editor, *Canadian Architect* magazine (1954-55). Worked with Green, Blankstein, and Russell Associates, Winnipeg, 1958 and 1959, to illustrate proposal and then design Winnipeg International Airport and Power House, developed by Senior Designer Jim Weller and David Thordarson (Max Herst Architect, Production Assistant). Registered member, MAA, 1969; life member, 2004. Works represented: Winnipeg City Hall (National Design Winning Competition with Principal Designer Donald Bittoff and D. Thordarson, 1964); Winnipeg International Airport (with D. Thordarson, 1964); Air Canada Powerhouse and Cargo (with D. Thordarson, 1964); St. Nicholas Ukrainian Catholic Church (1969); Holy Family Nursing Home (1970-77); Assiniboine Community College, Brandon (phase one).

CARTER, Dennis H., B.Arch., FRAIC, MAA, MOAA

(1920-) Born in Montreal. Early education in England, then returned to Canada, 1938. B.Arch. (Hons), University of Manitoba, 1945. RAIC Gold Medal, 1945. Founding partner, Smith, Carter Architects with Ernest J. Smith, 1947 (first Smith, Carter, Munn; then Smith, Carter, and Katelnikoff, 1948-59; then Smith, Carter, Searle, and Associates 1959-69; Smith, Carter, and Parkin 1969-70; Smith, Carter Partners, 1970; Smith, Carter Architects and Engineers Inc., 1986). Founding member, Western Canada Aviation Museum (1970). Works represented as Principal-in-Charge: Central Housing and Mortgage Corporation (1954); Rae and Jerry's Steak House (1957); Vincent Massey Collegiate (1957); J.A. Russell Bldg. (with James Donahue, 1959); Monarch Life Bldg. (with J. Donahue, 1959-61); Royal Bank Bldg., Portage Avenue (with Valdis Alers in 1965).

CHRISTIE, James H., FRAIC, MAA, RIBA, IABC

(1929-) Born in Glasgow. Glasgow School of Architecture, 1946-52. Gillespie Kidd & Coia Architects, Glasgow, 1947-54; Moody, Moore Partners, Manitoba, 1954-74. Partner and Senior Architectural Designer: Whiteshell Nuclear Research Establishment, Pinawa (1961-62); University College, University of Manitoba (1964); Manitoba Centennial Arts Centre—Manitoba Museum (former Manitoba Museum of Man and Nature, 1967-70). Partner-in-Charge and Design Coordinator, University of Winnipeg (with design team of Lewis Morse, Centennial Hall; and John Davidson, Lockhart Hall, 1968-72). President, MAA, 1968; Elected Fellow, RAIC, 1969; Elected Fellow, Royal Society of Arts UK, 1975; President, Social Planning Council of Winnipeg, 1970.

CHRISTIE, Jean Stuart Campbell (neé Wallace), B.Sc. (Arch.), MAA

(1932-) Born in Cardiff, Wales. University of Strathclyde, Scotland, 1954. Member, Royal Institute of British Architects. Moody, Moore Partners, Winnipeg, 1974; Libling, Michener, 1959. Member, MAA. Canadian Wood Design Council Award (Honourable Mention) for Andison House in St. Agathe, Manitoba (1966, including interior and landscape design, and furnishings).

COOP, Cynthia Lauren (neé Bookbinder) BID, PIDIM, IDC, IDCF

(1929-) Born in St. Boniface. BA Interior Design (Gold Medal), University of Manitoba, 1950. Lecturer, University of Minnesota, 1950-51. Draughtsperson, Illinois Institute of Technology, Chicago (1951-53). Associate Professor, Faculty of Architecture, Interior Design Department, University of Manitoba (1963-83, 1986-89). Professional interior designer, 1954-2004. Interior design, Provincial Law Courts (1983-86, with Number Ten Architectural Group).

COOP, Isadore, B.Arch., M.Sc. (Arch.), FRAIC, MAA, OAA

(1926-2003) Born in Winnipeg. B.Arch., University of Manitoba, 1948; M.Arch., Illinois Institute of Technology. Studied under Mies van der Rohe, 1951-53. Associates: Green, Blankstein, and Russell; Morley Blankstein (1955-58); with M. Blankstein, Douglas Gillmor and Alan Hanna, BCGH in 1959 and amalgamation, 1964, with Jack Ross and Allan Waisman, Number Ten Architectural Group, 1966. President, MAA, 1963; life member, MAA, 2002. Works represented as Partner-in-Charge of Design and Production: Clifford's Clothing (former Man with an Axe, Principal Designer, 1958); University of Manitoba Pharmacy Bldg. (Principal Designer, 1962); University of Manitoba Swimming Pool Bldg. (1964-65); University Centre, University of Manitoba (Number Ten Architectural Group; Doug Gillmor and Carl R. Nelson, 1969); Manitoba Theatre Centre (with Allan Waisman and Michael Kirby, 1970); Winnipeg Art Gallery (with Gustavo da Roza, 1969-71); Winnipeg Convention Centre (with Number Ten and Libling and Michener, 1974); private residence, Lanark Street (1958).

CRAM, Jack, B.Arch., Res. Des.

(1945-) Born in St. John's. B.Arch., University of Manitoba, 1969. Design Architect: Libling, Michener, and Associates, 1967-70; Stechesen, Katz Architects, 1972-75. Reno Negrin Architects, Vancouver, 1971-72; Roseisle Design & Consulting, 1976-present. Works represented, Libling, Michener: working drawings, Red River Community College (1967); St. John Cantius Church (Winnipeg, 1968); Sturgeon Creek High School (Winnipeg, 1969-71). Works represented, Stechesen and Katz: Seniors' Home on Elizabeth Rd. (Winnipeg, 1974-75).

DAVIDSON, John B., B.Arch., M.Arch., MAIBC, FRAIC

(1944-) Born in St. Thomas, ON. B.Arch., University of Toronto, 1967. M.Arch., Massachusetts Institute of Technology, 1971. Compton and Canadian Mortgage and Housing Corporation fellowships, 1969, 1970. Certified Professional Program, Vancouver, 1984. Moody, Moore Partners, Winnipeg, 1967-69. Eduardo Catalano, Cambridge MA, 1969-71; Dunlop, Farrow & Aitken, Toronto, 1972-74; IBI Group/Beinhaker/Irwin Associates, Toronto and Vancouver, 1975-82. Principal, Davidson Yuen Simpson Architects (formerly Davidson Yuen Partners), 1982-present. RAIC Gold Medal, 1967; Raymore Medal, Ontario Association of Architects, 1973. Design of master plan: Winnipeg Medical Centre, 1968 (Winnipeg General Hospital complex: Children's Hospital, Manitoba Rehab Centre, schools of Medicine and Dentistry); Lockhardt Hall (1969).

DA ROZA II, Gustavo, B.Arch., MAIBC, RCA

(1933-) Born in Hong Kong -Macau. B.Arch., Hong Kong-Macau, 1955. Partner: Gordon Brown Architects (Hong Kong). Lecturer: University of Hong Kong; University of California at Berkeley, 1958. Architect's Collaborative, Cambridge, 1959, organizing W. Gropius's portfolio for application for membership, American Institute of Architects. Immigrated to Canada, 1960. Professor, University of Manitoba, 1971; head of School of Architecture, 1984-89. Active architectural practice since 1962, specializing in cultural and residential developments. Honorary Consul of Portugal, Winnipeg, 1970; Commander of the Order of Prince Henry (international recognition in architecture, 1985); Officer of the Order of Canada (distinction in the architectural profession and contribution). Works represented: Winnipeg Art Gallery (with Isadore Coop, 1969-71); Manitoba Housing Project, Nassau St. (1975); Lochhead residence; residences on Shaftsbury Blvd. (1960s). Appointed, RCA.

DONAHUE, James, B.Arch.

(1918-1996) Born in Regina. Associate of Arts Degree, Regina College, 1937; B.Arch. (Hons), University of Minnesota, 1941. First Canadian graduate, Harvard School of Design, 1942, studied under Marcel Breuer, Walter Gropius, and Konrad Wachsmann. Studied science and arts, McGill University. National Housing Authority, Ottawa (city planning and housing research, 1942-43). With Douglas Simpson, developed the world's first, one-piece, moulded plastic stacking chair, 1945-46, which predates Charles Eames's fibreglass chair. Designed Canadian Coconut Chair (1950). Associate Professor of Architectural Design, University of Manitoba, 1946-63. Guest professor, industrial and architectural design, Institute of Design in Chicago, University of Minnesota, and Notre Dame University. Works include twenty houses, two apartment buildings, and three warehouses, 1946-63. Designed his residences, Fulham Avenue (1950), and Hosmer Boulevard (1955), Winnipeg. Works represented with Smith, Carter, Katelnikoff, and Searle: Monarch Life Bldg. (1959-61); J.A. Russell Bldg. (with Ernest Smith, 1959) and Animal Science Bldg., University of Manitoba (1962). Other works represented: Welgrove Apartments (1955); Medical Arts Parkade (1959).

FAURER, Charles, B.Arch, MRAIC, MAA

(?-1975) B.Arch., University of Manitoba. Registered member, MAA, 1936. Specialized in church and synagogue designs. Works represented: Shaarey Zedek Synagogue (with Cecil Blankstein, 1948); Rosh Pina Synagogue (1952); Northern Sales Bldg. (Principal Designer Allan H. Waisman, 1952-53).

FINCH, Lloyd H., B.Arch., MRAIC, MAA

(1904-1967) B.Arch., University of Manitoba, 1926. Architect, Chicago, six years. Returned to Winnipeg, 1932. Officer, RCAF, WWII. Lloyd Finch and Associates, affiliated with realty company L.A. MacDonald Ltd., 1956. Works represented for L.A. MacDonald Ltd.: preliminary plans for East Kildonan Industrial Site; Northern Electric Co. Ltd.; Eastman Photographic Materials Ltd.; Nash Motors of Canada Ltd.; Sidney Roofing and Paper Co. Ltd.; National Carbon Ltd.; RCA, Victor Limited; Western Plywood Ltd.; Tidewater Associated Oil Co. of Canada Ltd.; Addison Ltd. Design projects: Addictions Research Foundation (formerly Accountants Offices -Apex Bldg., 1947); Somerville Ltd. milk carton factory, St. James (1956).

GABOURY, Étienne, BA (Arch.), FRAIC, MAA, RCA

(1930-) Born in Bruxelles, MB. BA, Latin Philosophy, 1953; B.Arch., 1958, University of Manitoba; École des Beaux-Arts, Paris, 1959. Adjunct professorship, School of Architecture, University of Manitoba, 1989-90. MAA awards: St. Boniface Police Station, County Court and Health Unit (1963); Gaboury Architectural Office (1965); St. Claude Roman Catholic Church (Canadian Architect Yearbook Significant Bldg. Award, St. Claude, Manitoba, 1964). Manitoba Historical Society Centennial Medal of Honour, 1970. Principal: Gaboury and Associates Inc., 1960-98; Partner: Gaboury, Préfointaine, and Perry Architects. Works represented: Manitoba Health Service Bldg. (with Libling, Michener, 1959, Massey Medal, 1961); St Louis le Roi (with Libling, Michener, 1959, Massey Medal, 1961); Blessed Sacrament Church (1966); Messiah Lutheran Church (1968); Precious Blood Church (1968), the latter two with Gaboury, Lussier, and Sigurdson; Gilbert Plains and Pierre Radisson schools (1969); Royal Canadian Mint with Number Ten Architectural Group (1975); Gaboury residence on River Road (1968).

GERSON, Wolfgang, MAIBC, FRAIC, RCA

(1916-1991) Born in Hamburg, Germany. School of Architecture, West of England Academy, Bristol, 1935-36; Architectural Association in London, 1937-40. Relocated, Montreal, 1940. Interned, Montreal, 1940-43. Private practice 1943-47. Professor of Architecture, University of Manitoba, 1947-56; Professor of Architecture, University of British Columbia, 1956-81. Fellow, RAIC, 1976. Works represented: Gerson residence on South Drive (1947); Triangle Gardens housing project, Elmwood (Supervising Architects: Allan H. Waisman, Jack M. Ross, 1957).

GILLMOR, Douglas R., B.Arch., M.Arch., FRAIC

(1930-) Born in Fort Frances. B.Arch. (Gold Medal), University of Manitoba, 1954. MA, Massachusetts Institute of Technology, 1955 (studied with Eero Saarinen and Buckminster Fuller). Sessional appointment, University of Manitoba, while with Smith, Carter Architects, 1955-58. Associate Professor, Faculty of Architecture, University of Manitoba, 1959. Entered partnership of Blankstein, Coop, Gillmor, and Hanna, 1959, which amalgamated with Waisman and Ross to form Number Ten Architectural Group, 1964. College of Fellows, 1969. Founding Director, Architecture Program, University of Calgary, 1971, and Professor Emeritus, 1992.

Works represented: Peace Chapel, International Peace Gardens, Manitoba/North Dakota (1963); J.A. Russell Bldg. (Smith, Carter, and Katelnikoff with James Donahue, 1959); University Centre, University of Manitoba (Number Ten Architectural Group; Isadore Coop and Carl R. Nelson Jr. [1969]); Winnipeg Art Gallery (Associate Architects: Number Ten Architectural Group and Gustavo da Roza, Architect, with I. Coop, 1971).

GREEN, Lawrence J., B.Arch., MAA

(1899-1969) Born in Winnipeg. B.Arch., University of Manitoba, 1926. Practice with Cecil N. Blankstein, 1932. Joined by G. Leslie Russell, Ralph Ham, Herbert Moody, and Sherman Wright, 1934, to design public housing projects on McPhillips Street (1938 and 1939). Green, Blankstein, Russell, and Ham, civilian architects, Royal Canadian Navy, 1942 (Green stayed in Winnipeg as District Engineer). Green, Blankstein, and Russell Associates (GBR), 1944 (Green in charge of construction). President, MAA, 1935 and 1946. GBR awarded National Design Competition for new Winnipeg City Hall. Works represented as specifications and construction supervisor with GBR: Wildwood Park (1946); Winnipeg City Hall (1962-65).

HAM, Ralph Carl, B.Arch.

(1902-1942) Born in Winnipeg. B.Arch., University of Manitoba, 1928. Partnership with Green, Blankstein, and Russell, 1933. Registered architect, Manitoba (1932), British Columbia. Technical adviser, Wartime Housing, 1941. With GBR, civilian architect, Royal Canadian Navy, 1942. Member, Housing and Town Planning Division, Committee on Post-War Reconstruction, Dominion government, until 1942.

HANNA, Alan H., B.Arch., M.Arch., FRAIC

(1931-) Born in Regina. B.Arch., University of Manitoba, 1955; M.Arch., Massachusettes Institute of Technology, 1956 (lectures by Eero Saarinen and Louis Kahn). Design department, Smith, Carter, and Katelnikoff, 1958. With Coop, Blankstein, and Gillmor, formed BCGH, 1959, which amalgamated with Waisman and Ross to form Number Ten Architectural Group, 1964; with Isadore Coop, designed University of Manitoba Pharmacy Bldg., 1962, and Isbister Bldg. Design and management of Town Centre and Hospital Bldg. in Churchill, MB. President, MAA, 1969; member, council of RAIC, 1969-70. Honorary Doctorate, University of Winnipeg, 1989.

HARLAND, Joan M., B.Arch, MA, FIDEC, FIDC, FPIDIM

(1914-) Born in Leeds, England. Immigrated to Winnipeg in 1915. B.Arch. (Gold Medal), University of Manitoba, 1938; MA, Teacher's College, Columbia University, New York, 1948. Lecturer, Assistant, Associate Professor, Full Professor, University of Manitoba Department of Interior Design, 1939-80; Interior Design Department, 1953-76. Writings: *The History of Interior Decoration/Design at the University of Manitoba 1938-1997* (1998), *St. George's Church Architecture* (2006). Church Design Committee, St. George's Anglican Church, 1955-58. Professor Emeritus, University of Manitoba, 1981.

KATELNIKOFF, Walter L., B.Arch., MAA

(?-1974) B.Arch. 1944. Registered member, MAA, 1947. Partner with Smith, Carter, 1948-59. Works represented, design projects as junior architect, with Smith, Carter: Klinic Community Health Centre (former Central Mortgage and Housing Corporation, 1954); J.A. Russell Bldg. (with Ernest Smith Partner-in-Charge, James Donahue, Douglas Gillmor, and Grant Marshall interior design, 1959).

LIBLING, Gerald A., B.Arch., MAA

(1930-) B.Arch., University of Manitoba, 1952. Private practice at 100B-149 Portage Ave. West, 1954. Partnership with Mel P. Michener to form Libling, Michener, and Associates, 1955 (now LM Architects, recipient of three Massey medals, ten Canadian Housing Design Council awards, and Honour Award of MAA). President, MAA, 1970. RAIC College of Fellows, 1971. First Jewish member admitted to the Manitoba Club (1972). With Libling, Michener, and Associates, built Manitoba's first high-rise public housing project, 1971, also head office, Manitoba Housing and Urban Renewal Corporation. Works represented with Libling, Michener, and Associates, design project as Principal-in-Charge: Manitoba Health Service Building (Principal Designer Étienne Gaboury, 1959, Massey Medal, 1961); Public Safety Bldg. (Principal Designer Leslie Stechesen, 1965).

MACDONALD, Gerald Doull, B.Arch., FRAIC, MAA

(1930-) Born in Winnipeg. B.Arch., University of Manitoba. Principal, Ward and Macdonald (now MCM Architects), 1958; Senior Partner, Macdonald, Cockburn, and McFeeters Architects (completed over 500 school projects in several school divisions). Member of council, MAA; councillor, RAIC (1976-77); member, RAIC Public Relations Committee and RAIC Documents Committee. Works represented: Faculty of Law Bldg., University of Manitoba (1954-64); Centennial Auditorium, University of Brandon; Brandon Correctional Facility Keystone Sports and Exhibition Centre, Brandon; own residence on Roch St. (1962); Lutheran Church of the Cross (1965); Centennial Library (with John Turner, 1975-77).

MARSHALL, Grant C., MA, BID

(1931-) Born in Winnipeg. BA, Interior Design, University of Manitoba, 1955; MA, San Diego State University, 1973; Advanced Painting Studies, University of Manitoba School of Art, 1979-80, 1994-95. Professor, Department of Interior Design, University of Manitoba, 1974; Head, 1989-94. Member, Professional Interior Designers Institute of Manitoba, 1956-97, and Interior Designers Educators' Council, 1973-96. Works represented: *Canadian Interiors*—featured Matas residence, Winnipeg (1960); *Homemakers Magazine*—featured eight residential interiors (1973-76). Professional creative works: design of decorations for Greater Winnipeg—The Royal Tour (with Jack Graham in 1959); theatre design, Royal Winnipeg Ballet (costumes and settings, 1950-89); Winnipeg Contemporary Dancers (costumes, 1964, 1972); Rainbow Stage (settings, 1955, 1956); University of Manitoba School of Music (settings, 1967). Interior design: School of Architecture (1959), Monarch Life Building (1959-61) and Manitoba Health Service Building (1959). Grant Marshall Interiors imported international designed furniture into Winnipeg during 1960s and 1970s.

MICHENER, Mel P., B.Arch., FRAIC, MAA

(1930-) Born in Winnipeg. B.Arch., University of Manitoba, 1952. Design Architect, John B. Parkin Associates, Toronto. Senior Design Architect, Smith, Carter, and Katelnikoff Architects (Winnipeg). Senior Partner, 1954, with Gerald A. Libling, to form Libling, Michener, and Associates in 1955 (now LM Architects). Design critic, University of Manitoba School of Architecture, 1958. President, MAA; Vice-President, RAIC. Works represented as Principal Architect and Principal-in-Charge for Libling and Michener: Executive House Apartments (Principal Designer Leslie Stechesen, 1959, Massey Medal 1961); St Louis le Roi (Principal Designer É. Gaboury, 1959, Massey Medal 1961); St. Paul's College High School and Chapel (Principal Designer L. Stechesen, 1964, Massey Medal, 1964); St. Mary's Academy (1962); St. John Brebeuf Church (Principal Designer L. Stechesen, 1965); Boeing Canada, Winnipeg (1972, 1979); Manulife House (1977); Manitoba Teacher's Society Bldg. (Principal Designer L. Stechesen, 1966, MAA Award of Excellence, 1968).

250

McGARVA, Gordon W., B.Arch., FRAIC, MAA, OAA, SAA, MAIBC, RA MINN.

(1935-) Born in Winnipeg. B.Arch., University of Manitoba, 1958. Began practice with Kurnarski and Weinberg Architects. Project Architect, Waisman and Ross Architects, 1959. With Waisman and Ross, amalgamated with Blankstein, Coop, Gillmor, and Hanna, 1964, to form Number Ten Architectural Group (named after original office address). Partner, Number Ten Architectural Group, 1976. President, MAA, 1977. Stelco Design Award (Air Canada Maintenance Hangar, Winnipeg), and Massey Award (IBM Bldg., Winnipeg, 1961, and Britannia House, 1964). Works represented: "Gull Wing" Safeway Stores at Portage Ave., Ellice Ave., and Main St. (1963); Broadway office buildings including Britannia House, Imperial House, MEPC, IBM Bldg. (1960-75); Misericordia Nurses' Residence (1960).

MOODY, Herbert Henry Gatenby, B.Arch., FRAIC, RAA, MAA

(1903-1991) Born in Winnipeg. Attended Royal Military College in Kingston, ON. B.Arch., University of Manitoba, 1926. Derby and Robinson Architects, Boston, 1926-28. Sproatt & Rolph, Toronto, 1928-34. Partnership, Robert Moore, 1936. Senior Partner, Moody, Moore Partners, Architects and Engineers (Moody, Moore Partners, at 295 Broadway; practised here for forty years). President, Winnipeg Art Gallery Association; Chancellor, College of Fellows, RAIC, 1961-64; Academician, Royal Canadian Academy of the Arts. Works represented as Senior Partner: Women's Hospital Maternity Pavilion, Winnipeg General Hospital (with George W. Northwood, 1949); Churchill Secondary School (1955-63); Manitoba Hydro Electric Board (1956); University College Bldg. (Arts College), University of Manitoba (Principal Designer James Christie, 1964); Centennial Hall (Principal Designer Lewis Morse), University of Winnipeg (1970-72); Manitoba Centennial Arts Centre (Principal-in-Charge, 1967).

MOORE, Robert, B.Arch., FRAIC, MAA, OAA

(1909-?) Born in Winnipeg. B.Arch., University of Manitoba, 1932. Registered member, MAA, 1934; Fellow, RAIC, 1953; President, MAA, 1937. Senior Partner of Moody, Moore Partners, Architects and Engineers. Member, Advanced Committee on Art, Standing Committee, University of Manitoba. Works represented as Senior Partner: Women's Hospital Maternity Pavilion, Winnipeg General Hospital (with George W. Northwood, 1949); Churchill Secondary School (1955-63); Manitoba Hydro Electric Board (1956); University College Bldg. (Arts College), University of Manitoba (Principal Designer James Christie, 1964); Centennial Hall (Principal Designer Lewis Morse), University of Winnipeg (1970-72).

MORSE, Lewis, B.Arch.

(1944-) B.Arch. (Pilkington Traveling Scholarship), University of Manitoba, 1967. Arup and Associates, London, England, 1968 (Biochemistry building system at Cambridge). Number Ten Architectural Group, Winnipeg, 1969. Canadian Architect Project Award for Riverside Elementary School, Thompson, 1969. Partner, ADAPT (industrial design firm, Winnipeg); Design Consultant, University of Athabasca, Conceptual Design Phase, Edmonton, 1971. Affiliations: John C. Parkin Architects, Toronto, 1972; ARCOP Associates, Montreal, 1974; IKOY Partnership, Winnipeg, 1976-77. Lecturer, McGill University, 1974, and University of Manitoba, 1975. Works represented: Riverside Elementary School, Thompson (1969); renovations, Billinkoff residence on Lamont Blvd.; Centennial Hall, University of Winnipeg (Principal Designer with Mike Rattery and Sam Sorel) under James Christie at Moody, Moore, Duncan, Rattray, Peters, Searle, and Christie (1970-72).

NORTHWOOD, George W.
(1876-1959) Came to Winnipeg from Montreal in 1905; former member, Northwood and Chivers. With Northwood and Chivers (with Moody, Moore Partners), some design for Women's Hospital Maternity Pavilion, Winnipeg General Hospital (1949); Manitoba Medical Service Bldg. (1952).

PRATT, Kenneth Reginald Dixon, B.Arch., MAA, FRAIC
(1926-1980) Born in Russell. Served in Canadian army, WWII. B.Arch., University of Manitoba, 1949. Principal in architectural firms with associates Lindgren, Snider, and Tomcej. Design critic, University of Manitoba. Permanent member, MAA Registration Board; Fellow, RAIC, 1972. Major project as Partner in Pratt and Lindgren: St Vital Municipal Office (1959).

ROSS, Jack M., B.Arch., MRAIC, MAA, OAA, RA Minn.
(1929-2003) Born in Winnipeg. B.Arch., University of Manitoba, 1951. Principal (Founding) Partner of Waisman, Ross Associates, 1953-64; Number Ten Architectural Group (Waisman, Ross, with BCGH: Blankstein, Coop, Gillmor, and Hanna), 1964-72; own practice, Jack M. Ross Architect, 1972-78. Lecturer, University of Manitoba, 1951-59. Fellow, RAIC, 1974. With Waisman, Ross and Number Ten Architectural Group, Massey Medal and International Stainless Steel Design Award for Thompson Municipal Bldg., 1960. Works represented: J.M. Ross residence on Cloutier Drive (1963); Mary Speechly Hall, University of Manitoba (1964); Kensington Bldg. (1975).

RUSSELL, John Alonzo, B.Arch., M.Arch., FRAIC
(1907-1966) Born in Hinsdale, NH. B.Sc. (Arch.), Massachusetts Institute of Technology, 1928; M.Arch.,1932; Diploma d'Architecture, Fontainbleu School of Fine Arts, 1932. Assistant Professor of Architecture, Faculty of Engineering and Architecture, University of Manitoba, 1928-38; Professor of Architecture and first Dean, School of Architecture, 1946-66. Member, Winnipeg Town Planning Commission, 1944-48. Designer, Wartime Housing Ltd., 1944. Associate, Moody, Moore Partners, two summers. Instructor, Stage-craft, Banff School of Fine Arts, 1952. Author, "The Auditorium and Stage in Your Community Centre," 1945; regular contributor, *The Journal (Royal Architectural Institute of Canada)*, 1954-58. Key proponent of regional Modernism, linking the University of Manitoba School of Architecture with the Massachusetts Institute of Technology and Harvard University. Contributed to founding of Canada Council, 1957. Involved in completion of new School of Architecture Bldg., 1959 (J.A. Russell Bldg.). Organized national competitions for Winnipeg City Hall and Winnipeg Art Gallery. Designed John Alonzo Russell residence on South Drive (with Roy Sellors), 1957, and a house on Deer Lodge Place.

RUSSELL, G. Leslie, B.Arch., FRAIC
(1901-1977) Born in Winnipeg, B.Arch., University of Manitoba, 1925. Associate, Childs & Smith Architects, Chicago, 1925-27, with whom he designed buildings for North Western University. Associate, G.H.G. Russell, Winnipeg, 1927-32. Partnership, Lawrence G. Green, Cecil M. Blankstein, and R.C. Ham in Green, Blankstein, Russell, and Ham Associates, 1934 (in 1944, Green, Blankstein, and Russell). Designed buildings during naval service at Cornwallis Naval Base, NS, 1942-44. Works represented (with Green, Blankstein, Russell Associates): St. George's Anglican Church (Design Architect of present version with David Thordarson, 1956-57); winning

competition for Winnipeg's City Hall, 1959 (built 1962-65); Government of Manitoba Administration Bldg. (Advisory Architect Gilbert Parfitt, design in 1960), Science Bldgs., University of Manitoba (Allen Bldg., Parker Bldg., and Armes Lecture Hall, 1960); Winnipeg International Airport (with Bernard Brown and D. Thordarson, 1964).

SEARLE, James Elmhurst, B.Arch.

(1929-) Born in Winnipeg. B.Arch., University of Manitoba, 1951. Associate Partner, Smith, Carter, and Katelnikoff, Winnipeg, 1951; Partner, 1959. Managing Partner, Eastern Canada Parkin Engineers Planners, 1969; Managing Partner, Searle, Wilbee, Rowland, 1969 (John B. Parkin Associates, Toronto, merged with Smith, Carter of Western Canada, formed Searle, Wilbee, Rowland in eastern Canada and Smith, Carter [Parkin] in western Canada, simultaneously in 1969; provided architectural, engineering, and planning services). Works represented as Partner-in-Charge with Smith, Carter, Searle, Winnipeg: Pan-American Games Pool (1966); Richardson Bldg. (1967); Centennial Concert Hall (1967).

SECTER, Lloyd William, B.Arch., MAA, MRAIC

(1939-) Born in Winnipeg. B.Arch., University of Manitoba, 1965. Architectural Designer, Smith, Carter, and Searle Architects, 1965-68. Architectural Designer, Ram Karmi Architects, Tel Aviv, 1968-69. Winner of National Competition for Fountain Sculpture, University of Saskatchewan, 1971. Established architectural practice, 1972, in partnership with wife Marcia Ellen Secter (B.Arch. 1968). Since 1972, most projects and commissions in private residential design. Works represented with Smith, Carter, and Searle, as part of design team: Concert Hall (1967); Winnipeg Inn; Bank of Canada; Richardson Bldg. (1967-69). Designed corporate graphics for Smith, Carter, and Searle (1966). Individual projects in Winnipeg include Tower Drugs Bldg. (1965); joint projects with Marcia Ellen Secter include: renovation and addition, Fleisher residence, West Kildonan (1971); dental offices for Dr. Sydney Fleisher (1971); home office of Dr. Philip Katz (1975-76).

SECTER, Marcia Ellen (neé Moscovitch), B.Arch

(1944-) Born in Kingston, ON. B.Arch. (RAIC Bronze Medal), University of Manitoba, 1968. Architectural critic, *The Canadian Architect*, 1971-72. Began architectural practice with husband Lloyd W. Secter in 1972. Specialized in renovation projects, then expanded and specialized in single-family residential design, including architecture, interior design, furniture design, and landscape design, in 1970-80s and continuing. Joint projects in Winnipeg with Lloyd W. Secter include: renovation and addition, Fleisher family home, West Kildonan (1971); dental offices for Dr. Sydney Fleisher (1971); home office of Dr. Philip Katz (1975-76).

SELLORS, Roy, B.Arch., M.Arch., FRAIC, MAA, AIA

(1913-2005) Born in Winnipeg. B.Arch., University of Manitoba, 1936; M.Arch., Massachusetts Institute of Technology, 1939 (among the first graduates). Worked in Chicago, West Virginia, and Texas. Associate, Wyatt Hedrick (Texas); Thorshov Czerny, Minneapolis. Lecturer, Faculty of Architecture, University of Manitoba, 1946. Private practice, Winnipeg, 1939. Member, MAA, 1939. Acting Dean, School of Architecture, University of Manitoba (replacing John A. Russell), 1967. Education Committee, RAIC. College of Fellows, RAIC, 1960; member, Architectural Advisory Committee, University of Manitoba, 1960. Specialized in church architecture, residences, and schools. Works represented: J.A. Russell residence on South Drive (with John A. Russell, 1957); St. Vital Church (1958); St. Morris School (1958); Our Lady of Perpetual Help Church, Roblin Boulevard (1962); own residence, South Drive (1954).

SMITH, Ernest John, B.Arch., M.Arch., RCA

(1919-2003) Born in Winnipeg. B.Arch. (RAIC Medal), University of Manitoba, 1944; M.Arch., Massachusetts Institute of Technology, 1947. With Dennis Carter, founded Smith, Carter, and Munn, 1947 (then Smith, Carter, and Katelnikoff 1948-59; Smith, Carter, Searle, and Associates 1959-69; Smith, Carter, and Parkin 1969-70; Smith, Carter Partners 1970; Smith, Carter, and Partners 1972). Canadian Chancery in Warsaw, Poland (1965), under Smith's direction. Dean and Chancellor, College of Fellows, RAIC; member, MAA and Ontario Association of Architects. Designed and built own retirement home at Hillside Beach on Lake Winnipeg, 1985. Works represented with Smith, Carter: Winnipeg Square (1980); Woodsworth Bldg. (1973); Monarch Insurance Bldg. (with James Donahue, 1959-61); J.A. Russell Bldg. (with Dennis Carter and J. Donahue, 1959); own residence on Kildonan Drive (1959).

SNIDER, Kenneth R., B.Arch., M.Arch., MAA

(1928-) Born in Winnipeg. B.Arch., 1951, M.Arch., 1953, University of Manitoba. Affiliations: Moody, Moore Partners (1953-54); Waisman, Ross Architects (1955-64); Pratt, Lindgren, Snider, and Tomcej Architects (Partner, 1965-78); Pratt, Snider, Tomcej (Partner, 1978-84); Tomcej Architects (1985-95). Played Bassoon First, Winnipeg Symphony Orchestra (1948-53) and CBC Concert Orchestra. Design instructor, University of Manitoba (1964-65). Design awards (shared with Waisman, Ross Architects): Massey Silver Medal (Thompson Municipal Offices); International Stainless Steel Award, 1961 (Curtain Wall, Thompson Hospital). Works represented: Assiniboine Christian Centre (1968); Snider residence (1957); Thompson Hospital (1961); Assiniboine Park Conservatory (prior to 1976). Involved in design presentation for Winnipeg Arena at Polo Park (1955).

STECHESEN, Leslie J., B.Arch., MAA, FRAIC

(1934-) Born in Fort William. B.Arch., University of Manitoba, 1957. Graduate studies, Planning and Urban Design, Architectural Association, London, England, 1965-66. Head of Design, Libling, Michener, and Associates, 1957-71. Private practice, Leslie J. Stechesen Architect, 1971; then Stechesen, Frederickson, and Katz Architects, 1975 (Stechesen and Katz, 1980-present). Member, RAIC, 1959, and MAA, 1959; Fellow, RAIC, 1978. Vincent Massey Award for Excellence in the Urban Environment, 1975. Fifteen Massey awards for architecture, 1957-64 (with Libling, Michener, and Associates). Works represented as Head of Design, Libling, Michener, and Associates: Executive House Apartments (1959, Massey Medal, 1961); St. Paul's College High School (1964, Massey Medal, 1964); Grosvenor House (1961, Massey Medal, 1964); Public Safety Bldg. (1965); Manitoba Teachers' Society Bldg. (1966).

STEWART, George A., B.Arch., MAA Hon., FRAIC

(1922-1994) Born in Boissevain. BA (Arch.), University of Manitoba, 1948. Own practice in Fort Garry until 1970. Director, University of Manitoba Planning Office, 1970-82. University architect in charge of major projects (part time) to 1987. President, MAA, 1958; Fellow, RAIC; Honorary member of the MAA in 1986; Chairman, MAA Registration Board; member, RAIC National Certification Board. Works represented: St. Vital Library and Community Centre (1963); Fort Garry Library (1955).

THORDARSON, David F., B.Arch.

(1926-2003) Born in Winnipeg. Canadian Army, 1945. BA (Arch.), University of Manitoba, 1949 (first graduate of Icelandic descent). Member, RAIC and MAA, 1951-91. Green, Blankstein, and Russell (GBR), 1949-91. Works represented as Design Architect, GBR: Elizabeth Dafoe Library, University of Manitoba (1953); St. George's Anglican Church (1957); Norquay Bldg. (1959); St. Andrew's

College, University of Manitoba (1964); Winnipeg International Airport (with Bernard Brown, 1964). Principal Designer, Winnipeg City Hall and Administration Bldg. (with B. Brown, 1964).

TURNER, John Robert Davenall, B.Arch., MRAIC

(1937-1990) Born in Edmonton. B.Arch., University of Manitoba, 1960. Travelling scholarship, RAIC, to research post-war housing in Europe. Own practice, 1967. RAIC Medal, 1960; designs won three of the five categories in the Winnipeg Infill Housing Competition. President, MAA and MBSA. Accomplished watercolourist. Works represented: Centennial Concert Hall (1967); Manitoba Cultural Centre-proposed Art Gallery (1966-70); Winnipeg Centennial Library (1976); Pembina Trail Library (1986-87); Duff Roblin Bldg., University of Manitoba.

WAISMAN, Allan, B.Arch., FRAIC, ARIBA, AICP, MAIBC, OAA, MAA, APA

(1928-) Born in Winnipeg. B.Arch., University of Manitoba, 1950. Draughtsman with Charles Faurer, Winnipeg, 1945 (subsequently Chief Architect). Formed Waisman, Ross, and Associates, 1953 which joined BCGH to become Waisman, Ross, Blankstein, Coop, Gillmor, and Hanna, Architects/Engineers/Planners, 1964, later renamed Number Ten Architectural Group. Fellow, RAIC, 1968. International Steel Design Award, 1960. Massey medals for architecture, 1961, for Thompson Municipal Office, Manitoba (1961); Crop Research Centre, University of Manitoba (with J. Bargh, 1961). Principal Designer: Northern Sales Bldg. (with Charles Faurer, 1952-53). Works represented as architect with Number Ten: Manitoba Theater Centre (with Isadore Coop, Michael Kirby, and MTC Artistic Director Brian Dewar, 1970). Founding partner, Waisman, Dewar, Grout, and Carter, Vancouver (renamed Architectura in 1995).

WARD, James Thomas Laurence, B.Arch., MAA

(1925-1985) Born in Winnipeg. Governor General's Medal, Centennial School. B.Arch., University of 1947 (Thesis Prize). Moody, Moore Partners, 1948; Edgar Prain, 1949 (Junior Partner, 1951, firm renamed Prain Ward; joined by Gerald Doull Macdonald, 1958, firm renamed Ward and Macdonald; renamed Ward, Macdonald, Cockburn, McLeod and McFeetors, 1969 [Ward Macdonald and Partners]). MAA, 1949. Private practice, 1974. Chairman, School Buildings Projects Committee, Government of Manitoba Department of Education, 1985. Works represented as Principal-in-Charge, Ward and Macdonald: Brandon College Residence (1963); Law Society Bldg. (former North American Life, 1960).

WOOKEY, Donald, B.Arch., MAA

(1929-2002) Born in Winnipeg. B.Arch., University of Manitoba, 1951. Registered member, MAA, 1958. While at school, interned with Moody, Moore, and Partners, 1951; joined firm, 1954; Partner, 1958. With Moody, Moore, designed educational and institutional projects, 1951-70. Pratt, Lindgren (Pratt, Lindgren, Tomjec, and Snider), 1970. Specialized in industrial buildings and motor inns. Works represented with Moody, Moore, and Partners: Winnipeg Arena (Supervising Arch. J. Graham; Design Presentation Ken Snider, 1955); Charleswood Motor Inn (1955-64); Harrow School (1957); Manitoba Hydro Head Office (1957); initial studies, Atomic Energy Plant, Pinawa (final conceptual plan and detail design James H. Christie, 1963).

YAMASHITA, James, B.Arch., FRAIC, CFM, MAA, SAA, OAA, NSAA

(1940-) Born in Vancouver. B.Arch., University of Manitoba, 1963. Principal, IKOY Partnership, 1968-92. Works represented with IKOY: Deer Lodge Centre, 1986; expansion to the Terminal Bldg., Winnipeg International Airport. Principal, Smith, Carter Architects and Engineers Incorporated, 1993. Partners Program Advisory Board, Faculty of Architecture, University of Manitoba, 1994-present; Advisory Committee, Master and Certificate Program in Facilities Management, University of Manitoba, 1995-97; Jury, RAIC Awards of Excellence and Contract Documentation, 2001. Lecturer, University of Manitoba, 1986-98. Works represented: Crescent Drive Golf Course, Club House (1964); Fort Garry Fire Hall (1965); residence on Parkwood Place (1975).

ZUK, Radoslav, B.Arch., M.Arch., FRAIC

(1931-) Born in Lubacziw, Ukraine. B.Arch., McGill University, 1956; M.Arch., Massachusetts Institute of Technology. Honorary doctorate, Ukrainian Academy of Art, Kyiv, 1992. Lecturer, University of Manitoba, University of Toronto, McGill University (professor, 1979). Affiliated, Zunic and Sobkowich, 1963; Number Ten Architectural Group, and Smith, Carter, and Searle, 1963-68. Fellow, RAIC and Royal Society of Arts; Honorary Fellow, Ukrainian Academy of Architecture. Co-recipient, RAIC Governor General's Medal for Architecture, 1986. Dunlop Traveling Scholarship and Pilkington Traveling Scholarship, 1956. Nine Ukrainian churches first exhibited at Architekturgalerie in Munich, Germany, 1996. Ukrainian Catholic churches, Manitoba (with Associated Architects, Number Ten Architectural Group): St. Joseph's (1964); St. Michael's (Transcona, 1966). Works represented with Associated Architect Gustavo da Roza: St. Michael's Ukrainian Catholic Church, Tyndall, Manitoba (1963); as Consulting Architect for design with Zunic and Sobkowich, Architects: Holy Family Ukrainian Catholic Church (1963). Massey medals for Architecture 1964 Exposition: St. Michael's and Holy Family.

256

ACKNOWLEDGEMENTS

I wish to give special thanks to Jenny Western, who provided a starting point in researching Manitoba Modernist architects in April 2002. I am also indebted to sources (again by way of Ms Western) such as *The Canadian Who's Who*, 1964-1971 (Toronto: University of Toronto Press); the Property Assessment Department, City of Winnipeg; William Thompson, *Winnipeg Architecture 1975* (Winnipeg: Faculty of Architecture, University of Manitoba, 2002); and the *Winnipeg Building Index* (Architecture and Fine Arts Library, University of Manitoba). Credit also goes to the Winnipeg Architectural Foundation, and the Manitoba Association of Architects. I owe much to the last generation of Modernist architects: Allan Waisman, Douglas Gillmor, James Christie, Mel Michener, and Morley Blankstein. This project would not have been possible without the energy and commitment of Professor Serena Keshavjee. I thank the University of Winnipeg Work Study Program, and the Undergraduate Student Research Awards (Natural Sciences and Engineering Research Council) for funding this project. Personal thanks and dedication to Romi, David, and Sylvia Topper. These biographies were researched over a period of two years. I made every effort to contact the architects or their families on this list. I gave each architect and his/her family members the opportunity to review these entries. However, more research remains to be done.

Aldona Dziedziejko

257

BIBLIOGRAPHY

Jenny Western

Archival Materials

Architecture and Fine Arts Library, University of Manitoba. Building Vertical Files and Winnipeg Building Index

Canadian Centre for Architecture (CCA), Montreal

Canadian Architectural Archives (CAA), Calgary

City of Winnipeg Planning, Property and Development Department. Downtown Area Modern Buildings Binder

City of Winnipeg Archives and Records Centre

    City Hall, Old and New File

    Letter from Gordon Chown to Eric Thrift, 17 May 1954, File 4195

    Letters between Dufferin Roblin and Steven Juba, 4 May 1960 and 30 May 1960

    Letter from Nathan Philips to Steven Juba, 12 November 1957

    Rahkin. F.A. "Do We Need a New City Hall?" Speech, 4 October 1957

    Simpson, E.G. "Winnipeg's New City Hall and Urban Renewal"

    Speech by Major Steven Juba. "The Sod Turning Ceremony for the New City Hall," 12 June 1962

Jewish Heritage Centre Archives, Winnipeg,

    Blankstein Fonds, JHS 20 1997–34, Files 1–6

    Green Blankstein and Russell Portfolio directly under Blankstein

National Archives of Canada (NAC)

Provincial Archives of Manitoba

    Green, Blankstein and Russell Fonds

    Moody, Moore and Partners Fonds

    Aronovitch and Leipsic Limited. "A City's Despair." *Winnipeg Views*, 115: "Slum areas, Dufferin Ave," 1964

Winnipeg Art Gallery Archives

    Winnipeg Art Gallery Building Files

Winnipeg Architecture Foundation, Historical Buildings Committee, the City of Winnipeg

    Winnipeg Building Files, 2001

University of Manitoba, Department of Archives & Special Collections, Elizabeth Dafoe Library.

    Winnipeg Tribune Clipping Files and Henry Kalen Archives

University of Winnipeg Archives

    Anonymous. *Some Important Historical Facts about United College*. Winnipeg, c. 1950, AC–38–1, file 1

    Bedford, Gerald. "One Hundred Years of History." *The University of Winnipeg: The Commemorative Journal 1888–1988* 4, 2 (Summer 1988)

    Christie, James. "University of Winnipeg Expansion '70 programme." 23 April 1971. UW–3–1, file 4

    Duckworth, Henry. "Address by Dr. Henry Edmison Duckworth on the Occasion of His Installation as President and Vice–Chancellor." *A Souvenir of the 100th Birthday*. Ed. Joy S. McDiarmid. Winnipeg: University of Winnipeg, 1971. AC–18–1, file 4

Lockhart, Wilfred C. "The Sixteen Years." University of Winnipeg, 1971. AC–37–1, file 3

McDiarmid, Joy. "The University of Winnipeg Announces University at Noon." Public Service Announcement, 8 October 1971. WW–3–1, file 1

McDiarmid, Joy. "University of Winnipeg opens Centennial Hall." News Release, 14 September 1972. AC–37–1, file 4

Reid, Crowther and Partners. *An Interim Report of the Examination of Potential Role, Size and Campus Development for the University of Winnipeg.* Parts 1 and 2. Winnipeg, Manitoba, 1967, AC–22–2, files 1 and 2

Private Archives

James Christie, Calgary, Alberta

Étienne Gaboury, Winnipeg, Manitoba

Henry Kalen, Winnipeg, Manitoba

Gerald Macdonald, Winnipeg, Manitoba

Ernest Mayer, Manitoba

Lewis Morse, Vancouver, British Columbia

Gustavo da Roza II, Vancouver, British Columbia

Stantec Architecture/GBR, Manitoba

Glenn Tinley, Winnipeg, Manitoba

Allan Waisman, Manitoba

Published Sources
Author Unknown

"A Case When More Means Less." *Winnipeg Tribune*, May 1965 [file 7128]. University of Manitoba, Archives & Special Collections, Winnipeg Tribune Clipping Files.

"Advice Given to Architects: 'Get With It.'" *Winnipeg Tribune*, 22 January 1966.

"Advisory Committee to Aid Slum Redevelopment Planning." *Winnipeg Tribune*, 3 August 1956.

"A Gong and a Concrete Tree." *Winnipeg Tribune*, 18 November 1958.

"ALCAN District Sales Office Results of Competition." *The Journal (Royal Architectural Institute of Canada)* 34 (August 1957): 318.

"Alderman & Awards." *Canadian Architect* 3 (January 1958): 16.

"Ald. Seeks Report on Expropriation." *Winnipeg Tribune*, 4 January 1967.

"All the Same But What to Do?" *Winnipeg Tribune*, 10 August 1961.

"A Multi–million Dollar Transplant of the City's Heart?" *Winnipeg Tribune*, 24 January 1968.

"A New 'Old Chinatown' Would Ban Vehicles." *Winnipeg Tribune*, 24 January 1968.

"Annual Report of the School of Architecture and Fine Arts." *University of Manitoba Calendar.* Winnipeg: University of Manitoba, 1946–1953.

"A Profit in Subsidy Housing." *Winnipeg Tribune*, 15 September 1960.

"Archigram: Architects (1961–1974)." *Design in Britain*. [Available on-line <http://www.designmuseum.org/design/index.
php?1d=87> [accessed 11 February 2005].

"Architect Leads Tour." *Winnipeg Tribune*, 28 October 1971.

"Architect Leaves Partnership to Start Own Practice in East." *Winnipeg Tribune*, 5 February 1971.

"Architect Says Cities in the Future to Be Tiered." *Winnipeg Tribune*, 21 January 1966.

"Architect Says People Select Location First." *Winnipeg Tribune*, 29 October 1959.

"Architects Aim to Combine Needs." *Winnipeg Tribune*, 21 July 1966.

"Architects Needed By Gov't: Steinkopf." *Winnipeg Tribune*, 18 January 1965.

"Architect's Own Houses." *The Journal (Royal Architectural Institute of Canada)* 36 (February 1959): 42–43.

"Architects President Pleads for Core Plan." *Winnipeg Tribune*, 9 May 1970.

"Architects' Profit Secondary." *Winnipeg Tribune*, 3 June 1960.

"Architects Report: 'Drab' Life in Suburbia." *Winnipeg Tribune*, 9 February 1960.

"Architects Told Fight Bad Design: Better Town Plans Urged." *Winnipeg Tribune*, 2 June 1960.

"Architectural Firm Announces Merger." *Winnipeg Tribune*, 5 March 1969.

"Architectural Stethoscope: They'll Study Sick Spots." *Winnipeg Tribune*, 26 September 1959.

"Architecture in the Winnipeg Area." *Canadian Architect* 15 (May 1970): 45–48.

"Beautiful Shop Centre a Challenge to Artists." *Winnipeg Tribune*, 12 November 1958.

"Big Shopping Centre Planned in Transcona." *Winnipeg Tribune*, 4 April 1964.

"Blankstein, Cecil Nat." *The Canadian Who's Who*. Volume X. Toronto: Trans-Canada Press, 1964–1966.

"Blight in City Centre Price of Suburban Sprawl." *Winnipeg Tribune*, 1 June 1960.

"Board of 6 Citizens for Slum Clearance." *Winnipeg Tribune*, 5 September 1958).

"Building at Near-Record Level in '60," *Winnipeg Tribune,* December 1960 [file 1777]. University of Manitoba, Archives & Special
Collections, Winnipeg Tribune Clipping Files.

"Building Exceeds Pre–War Demand," *Winnipeg Tribune,* 18 February 1950.

"Building Permits Increase." *Winnipeg Tribune*, 20 April 1968.

"Building Permits Nearly Double of 1953." *Winnipeg Tribune*, 23 December 1954.

"Building Permits Top Old Record by $14,000,000." *Winnipeg Tribune*, 6 January 1955.

"Building Permits up 55% in Value." *Winnipeg Tribune*, 22 November 1968.

"Building Trade Trends Termed Uncertain." *Winnipeg Tribune*, 13 October 1972.

"Burglar Proof Bank?" *Architecture Canada* 48 (12 July 1971): 3.

"Campus Planning." *Architecture Canada* 45 (November 1968): 78.

"Canada Council Appointment." *The Journal (Royal Architectural Institute of Canada)* 34 (May 1957): 190.

"Canadian Housing Design Council Award 1964." *Canadian Architect* 9 (December 1964): 78, 86, 88.

"Central Section Outlined." *Winnipeg Tribune*, February 1960 [file 3581]. University of Manitoba, Archives &
Special Collections, Winnipeg Tribune Clipping Files.

"Centre Georges Pompidou Piano and Rogers: A Statement." *Architectural Design* 47, 2 (1977): 87–147.

"Chamber Opposes City Low Rent Housing." *Winnipeg Tribune*, 23 October 1953.

"Chamber Supports Assault on Slums." *Winnipeg Tribune*, 15 September 1960.

"Changing Face of Winnipeg: New Wheat Board Building." *Winnipeg Tribune*, 1963 [file 7128]. University of Manitoba, Archives & Special Collections, Winnipeg Tribune Clipping Files.

"Changing Face of Winnipeg: Our 'Donut' Loses its Hole." *Winnipeg Tribune*. December 1963 [file 7128]. University of Manitoba, Archives & Special Collections, Winnipeg Tribune Clipping Files.

"Chapel St. Louis Le Roi." *The Journal (Royal Architectural Institute of Canada)* 38 (November 1961): 55.

"Chapel St. Louis Le Roi." *The Journal (Royal Architectural Institute of Canada)* 38 (December 1961): 52.

"Chapel St. Louis Le Roi, St. Boniface, Man." *Canadian Architect* 7 (February 1962): 57.

"Church of St. John Brebeuf, Winnipeg." *Canadian Architect* 11 (April 1966): 45–49.

"Church of St. Rose of Lima, St. Rose du Lac, Man." *Canadian Architect* 7 (February 1962): 54–57.

"Citizens to Have No Say in Scheme." *Winnipeg Tribune*, 3 September 1962.

"City Architects Criticized for Not Acting on Housing." *Winnipeg Tribune*, 29 October 1959.

"City Builder Takes Award Once Again." *Winnipeg Tribune*, 6 April 1967.

"City Building Figures Zoom by $20 Million." *Winnipeg Tribune,* 2 July 1957.

"City Centre No Longer Hub of Metro Area." *Winnipeg Tribune,* 24 June 1967.

"City Core Facelift Proposed." *Winnipeg Tribune*, 13 February 1969.

"City Council Seeks Housing Authority." *Winnipeg Tribune*, 2 May 1950.

"City Expropriation Policy 'Unfair, Ridiculous' Zuken." *Winnipeg Tribune*, 16 December 1966.

"City Hall Blamed for Renewal Drag." *Winnipeg Tribune*, 7 June 1962.

"City of Winnipeg Hydro Electric Sub–Station No. 21." *The Journal (Royal Architectural Institute of Canada)* 38 (November 1961): 57.

"City Renewal Scheme Started Roblin Dream." *Winnipeg Tribune*, 3 June 1967.

"City Seeks More Aid for Housing Survey." *Winnipeg Tribune*, 10 April 1957.

"City Through as Wallflower?" *Winnipeg Tribune*, 24 August 1967.

"City's 1948 Building Tops All Marks but 1912 Boom." *Winnipeg Tribune,* 4 January 1949.

"Close to 1,000 Families in Blighted Home Areas." *Winnipeg Tribune*, 17 September 1957.

"CMHC Calls Suite Plan 'Ghetto,' Refuses Funds." *Winnipeg Tribune,* 26 November 1969.

"A Comment by the Editors: Winnipeg, the City Hall Competition." *Canadian Architect* 5 (January 1960): 35–42.

"Committee Design Blocks Urban Beautification: Reid." *Winnipeg Tribune*, 15 June 1965.

"Competition: Winnipeg Art Gallery." *Canadian Architect* 13 (February 1968): 37–44.

"Conference in Winnipeg on Implementation of Environment Report in Western Canada." *The Journal (Royal Architectural Institute of Canada)* 38 (February 1961): 63.

"Construction Awards, Plans." *Winnipeg Tribune*, 16 June 1959.

"Construction up by 13 Per Cent." *Winnipeg Tribune*, 16 December 1957.

"Contemporary Winnipeg Artist Wins 1970 RAIC Allied Arts Medal."*Architecture Canada* 47 (11 May 1970): 4.

"Co-op Centre Sod Turned." *Winnipeg Tribune*, 27 September 1957.

"Councils Shocked by Urban Aid Slash." *Winnipeg Tribune*, 15 August 1969.

"Crop Research Centre, University of Manitoba." *Canadian Architect* 9 (March 1964): 54–57.

"Cutback in Building Economic Indicator." *Winnipeg Tribune*, 25 August 1970.

"Danzker on the Spot over 'Pigs' Remark." *Winnipeg Tribune*, 7 October 1966.

"Dear John A. Russell, FRAIC." *Architecture Canada* 44 (January 1967): 5.

"Deaths—Cecil N. Blankstein." *Winnipeg Free Press*, 7 July 1987, p. 30.

"Deaths—G. Leslie Russell, B. Arch., FRAIC." *Winnipeg Free Press*, 31 May 1977, p. 37.

"Deaths—Herbert H. G. Moody." *Winnipeg Free Press*, 1 March 1991, p. 16.

"Decision Follows 5 Women's Briefs." *Winnipeg Tribune*, 7 March 1961.

"Decision on Housing." *Winnipeg Tribune,* 22 September 1952.

"Development Design Given to Local Firm." *Winnipeg Free* Press, 26 June 1965.

"Downtown Development Survey to Cost $200,000." *Winnipeg Tribune*, 23 August 1965.

"Eaton's Build $5 Million Store in Polo Park." *Winnipeg Tribune*, 20 May 1966.

"Ecclesiastical." *The Journal (Royal Architectural Institute of Canada)* 35 (December 1958): 472.

"Educational Park Gets Official Okay." *Winnipeg Tribune*, 24 January 1968.

"$18 Million Plan for 'Shopperville' Announced in City." *Winnipeg Tribune,* 12 November 1952.

"8,000,000 Will Visit Polo Park in '68." *Winnipeg Tribune*, 1968 [file 6111]. University of Manitoba, Archives & Special Collections, Winnipeg Tribune Clipping Files.

"81 Groups Approve Resolution." *Winnipeg Tribune*, 23 April 1958.

"11–Storey Office Building for Edmonton-York Area." *Winnipeg Tribune*, 2 July 1960.

"É.J. Gaboury Office Building, St. Boniface, Man." *Canadian Architect* 9 (June 1964): 53–58.

"Elmwood Bid Turned Down." *Winnipeg Tribune*, 28 May 1957.

"Everything Is Available for a Modern Family at Grant Park Plaza." *Winnipeg Tribune*, 26 August 1969.

"Executive House Apartments." *The Journal (Royal Architectural Institute of Canada)* 38 (November 1961): 56.

"Expansion of University of Winnipeg Building Continues in 1971." *Winnipeg Free Press*, 7 May 1971, p. 36.

"Eye-Opener for Winnipeg." *Winnipeg Tribune*, 30 May 1962.

"Facts Just Facts Reversed a Policy." *Winnipeg Tribune*, September 1960 [file 3581]. University of Manitoba, Archives & Special Collections, Winnipeg Tribune Clipping Files.

"Fall Start Is Definite on Polo Park Centre." *Winnipeg Tribune*, 29 June 1956.

"The Federal Building of Public Works." *Canadian Architect* 1 (June 1956): 64.

"Federal Income Tax Building, Winnipeg, Manitoba." *The Journal (Royal Architectural Institute of Canada)* 34 (October 1957): 406.

"Federal Spending Cutbacks Kill Urban Renewal Projects." *Winnipeg Tribune*, 20 August 1969.

"$15 Million Co–op House Project for St. Boniface." *Winnipeg Tribune*, 21 October 1955.

"Final Report of the Jury, Winnipeg City Hall Competition." *The Journal (Royal Architectural Institute of Canada)* 37 (March 1960): 111–113.

"Firm Seeks Free Land for Housing." *Winnipeg Tribune*, 4 December 1953.

"First Phase May Start this Year." *Winnipeg Tribune*, March 1960 [file 3581]. University of Manitoba, Archives & Special
     Collections, Winnipeg Tribune Clipping Files.

"Five Buildings: Waisman Ross & Associates." *Canadian Architect* 9 (April 1964): 49–60.

"$500,00 Polo Park Enclosed Mall." *Winnipeg Tribune*, 17 September 1963.

"Fortunately it Will Be up to Date." *Winnipeg Tribune*, 2 June 1960.

"Four Unitarian Churches." *Architecture Canada* 45 (February 1968): 31–34.

"Funeral Chapel, St. Boniface, Manitoba." *Canadian Architect* 8 (March 1963): 51–53.

"General Post Office Building, Winnipeg, Manitoba." *The Journal (Royal Architectural Institute of Canada)* 36 (February 1959): 33–37.

"Giant Project Will Include Homes, Shops." *Winnipeg Tribune*, 22 March 1954.

"Give Leadership Architects Told." *Winnipeg Tribune*, 16 January 1965.

"Government Precinct Near City Hall." *Winnipeg Tribune*, 24 January 1968.

"Green Blankstein Russell Associates." *Canadian Architect* 14 (April 1969): 10.

"Group Deplores Home Standards." *Winnipeg Tribune*, 1 June 1960.

"Guidebook to an Hiatus." *Canadian Architect* 5 (July 1960): 6.

"Happiness Is Sunset at Burrows-Keewatin." *Winnipeg Tribune*, 8 February 1969.

"Head Office for Smith Carter Searle Associates." *The Journal (Royal Architectural Institute of Canada)* 40 (December 1963): 43–47.

"Headquarters Building, Manitoba Teacher's Society, Winnipeg." *Canadian Architect* 13 (July 1968): 49–51.

"Health Unit, St. Boniface, Manitoba." *Canadian Architect* 10 (May 1965): 50–53.

"Henry D. Kalen." *The Journal (Royal Architectural Institute of Canada)* 38 (April 1961): 70.

"Herbert H.G. Moody." *The Journal (Royal Architectural Institute of Canada)* 28 (March 1951): 80.

"Hollinsworth Shop, Winnipeg, Manitoba." *The Journal (Royal Architectural Institute of Canada)* 25 (August 1948): 276.

"Hospitals." *The Journal (Royal Architectural Institute of Canada)* 29 (June 1952): 172.

"House of Ernest J. Smith." *The Journal (Royal Architectural Institute of Canada)* 33 (August 1956): 300–301.

"House of Mr. A.J. Donahue, Winnipeg, Manitoba." *The Journal (Royal Architectural Institute of Canada)* 27 (December 1950): 406–407.

"Houses in Manitoba." *The Journal (Royal Architectural Institute of Canada)* 16 (May 1939): 102–105.

"Housewives Start Battle of Burrows." *Winnipeg Tribune*, March 1960 [file 3581]. University of Manitoba, Archives &
     Special Collections, Winnipeg Tribune Clipping Files.

"Housing." *The Journal (Royal Architectural Institute of Canada)* 4 (April 1939): 74.

"Housing Authority." *Winnipeg Tribune*, 3 May 1950.

"Housing Decision Regretted." *Winnipeg Tribune*, 1962 [file 3581]. University of Manitoba, Archives & Special
     Collections, Winnipeg Tribune Clipping Files.

"Housing Design Awards." *Canadian Architect* 12 (April 1967): 8–9.

"Housing for All." *Winnipeg Tribune*, 8 August 1967.

"Housing Plan Corners Alderman in Living Room." *Winnipeg Tribune*, 1 October 1957.

"The Housing Project By-Law." *Winnipeg Tribune*, 22 October 1953.

"Housing: Resolutions of National Conference on Housing." *The Journal (Royal Architectural Institute of Canada)* 4 (April 1939): 78.

"Housing Study." *Winnipeg Tribune*, 16 September 1960.

"Huge Housing Scheme Studied." *Winnipeg Tribune*, 1 September 1954.

"Individuality and Housing." *Winnipeg Tribune,* 12 February 1949.

"Industrial Buildings." *The Journal (Royal Architectural Institute of Canada)* 36 (September 1959): 298, 300, 302.

"Insurance Building." *The Journal (Royal Architectural Institute of Canada)* 32 (October 1955): 375.

"Interior Design." *Architecture Canada* 50 (March/April 1973): 7. Insert, "Pilkington Scholarship—1965." *The Journal (Royal Architectural Institute of Canada)* 42 (August 1965): 33–41.

"It Was a Record Building Year." *Winnipeg Tribune*, 9 January 1970.

"Jarvis Landlords Defended by Frith." *Winnipeg Tribune*, 1962 [file 3582]. University of Manitoba, Archives & Special Collections, Winnipeg Tribune Clipping Files.

"John A. Russell." *The Journal (Royal Architectural Institute of Canada)* 32 (June 1955): 233.

"John A. Russell Perspective, '66." *Architecture Canada* 44 (August 1967): 8.

"Juba Seeks $5 Million Slum Vote." *Winnipeg Tribune*, 18 June 1958.

"Judging Housing Standards." *Winnipeg Tribune*, 28 August 1961.

"Kent Street School, Winnipeg, Manitoba." *The Journal (Royal Architectural Institute of Canada)* 31 (September 1954): 304.

"Knox United Church." *The Journal (Royal Architectural Institute of Canada)* 33 (December 1956): 463.

"Liquid Carbonic Canadian Corporation Limited." *The Journal (Royal Architectural Institute of Canada)* 30 (July 1953): 188–189.

"Low Income Families Would No Longer Be Placed in 'Ghettos' on the Outskirts of the City." *Winnipeg Tribune*, 2 August 1967.

"Low Rent Housing Planned." *Winnipeg Tribune*, 1953 [file 3581]. University of Manitoba, Archives & Special Collections, Winnipeg Tribune Clipping Files.

"Low Rental Housing Scheme Urged at Welfare Probe of Dalke Family." *Winnipeg Tribune*, 1 April 1948.

"Low–Rental Project Pronounced Success." *Winnipeg Tribune*, 17 April 1959.

"Low Rental Suites." *Winnipeg Tribune*, 1953 [file 3581]. University of Manitoba, Archives & Special Collections, Winnipeg Tribune Clipping Files.

"MAA." *Architecture Canada* 47 (16 February 1970): 8.

"MAA Annual Meeting." *The Journal (Royal Architectural Institute of Canada)* 38 (February 1961): 65.

"MAA Annual Meeting." *Architecture Canada* 44 (March 1967): 7.

"MAA First Design Awards Program." *Architecture Canada* 45 (March 1968): 9, 11.

"Manitoba." *The Journal (Royal Architectural Institute of Canada)* 40 (January 1963): 30.

"Manitoba Annual Meeting." *The Journal (Royal Architectural Institute of Canada)* 39 (February 1962): 72–73.

"Manitoba Association Annual Meeting." *Architecture Canada* 46 (March 1969): 5.

"Manitoba Association of Architects." *The Journal (Royal Architectural Institute of Canada)* IX (May 1932): 133.

"Manitoba Association of Architects." *The Journal (Royal Architectural Institute of Canada)* X (February 1933): 42.

"Manitoba Association of Architects." *The Journal (Royal Architectural Institute of Canada)* XII (February 1936): 36.

"Manitoba Association of Architects." *The Journal (Royal Architectural Institute of Canada)* XIV (February 1937): 33.

"Manitoba Association of Architects." *The Journal (Royal Architectural Institute of Canada)* XIV (June 1937): 116.

"Manitoba Association of Architects." *The Journal (Royal Architectural Institute of Canada)* 40 (April 1963): 78.

"Manitoba Association of Architects." *The Journal (Royal Architectural Institute of Canada)* 40 (June 1963): 93–94.

"The Manitoba Centennial Project Winnipeg." *Architecture Canada* 44 (October 1967): 50.

"Manitoba Discusses Public Housing." *Architecture Canada* 50 (February 1973): 8.

"Manitoba Fortieth Annual Meeting." *The Journal (Royal Architectural Institute of Canada)* 32 (May 1955): 186.

"Manitoba Power Commission Building." *The Journal (Royal Architectural Institute of Canada)* 32 (May 1955): 171–173.

"Manitoba Rehabilitation Hospital." *The Journal (Royal Architectural Institute of Canada)* 40 (October 1963): 66–67.

"Manitoba Telephone System Building, Winnipeg." *Canadian Architect* 9 (September 1964): 57–59.

"Manitoba Theatre Centre, Winnipeg." *Canadian Architect* 16 (September 1971): 62–65.

"Massey Awards." *Canadian Architect* 6 (November 1961): 6, 8.

"Massey Medals 1964." *The Journal (Royal Architectural Institute of Canada)* 42 (January 1964): 73–83.

"Massey Medal and School Award." *The Journal (Royal Architectural Institute of Canada)* 42 (January 1965): 38–39, 46–47.

"Mayor Can't Give Answer to Slums." *Winnipeg Tribune*, 12 August 1960.

"Mayor Is Anxious for Pilot Project." *Winnipeg Tribune*, 31 October 1959.

"Members of the Jury." *The Journal (Royal Architectural Institute of Canada)* 35 (December 1958): 454.

"Metro Extension Pressed." *Winnipeg Tribune*, 2 August 1967.

"Million Dollar Plant Underway." *Winnipeg Tribune*, 4 September 1959.

"The Monarch Life Building." *The Journal (Royal Architectural Institute of Canada)* 39 (July 1962): 33–40.

"Moody, Herbert H.G." *The Canadian Who's Who.* Volume X. Toronto: Trans-Canada Press: 1964–1966.

"Moore, Robert E." *The Canadian Who's Who.* Volume X. Toronto: Trans-Canada Press: 1964–1966, 789.

"More Urban Involvement Urged Among Architects." *Winnipeg Tribune*, 5 May 1970.

"Most Homes Are Neatly Kept in the Burrows–Keewatin Development." *Winnipeg Tribune*, 15 October 1966.

"MTS Building Tops Architectural Contest." *Winnipeg Tribune*, 27 January 1968.

"Name Committee on Preservation of Historic Buildings." *The Journal (Royal Architectural Institute of Canada)* 36 (December 1959): 437.

"The National Gallery Competition Results." *Canadian Architect* 22 (April 1977): 19.

"National Housing Design Competition for Canadian Lumbermen's Association: Jury Report." *Canadian Architect* 11 (January 1966): 41.

"Neighbours Want Squalor Ended." *Winnipeg Tribune*, 27 September 1966.

"New Commercial Centre Opens." *Winnipeg Tribune*, 29 October 1963.

"New, Continuing Building Promises an Active Year." *Winnipeg Tribune*, 11 January 1962.

"New Homes for 5,000 People." *Winnipeg Tribune*, 10 August 1956.

"New Members of College of Fellows." *Architecture Canada* 47 (11 May 1970): 2, 5.

"New Shopping Centre Development." *Winnipeg Tribune*, 27 February 1965.

"Nine New Fellows." *Architecture Canada* 50 (June 1973): 4.

"1966 Convocation: College of Fellows/College des Fellows." *Architecture Canada* 43 (July 1966): 7–8.

"No Great Women Architects So Far Says Marcel Breuer." *Winnipeg Tribune*, 16 April 1971.

"Northgate Plaza Offers the Ultimate in Comfort." *Winnipeg Tribune*, 24 November 1964.

"Norwood Collegiate Institute, Winnipeg." *The Journal (Royal Architectural Institute of Canada)* 32 (October 1955): 389.

"Norwood Plan for Housing Approved." *Winnipeg Tribune*, 11 May 1945.

"Number Ten Architectural Group." *Manitoba Business Magazine* (April 1993).

"Office & Warehouse for Western Grocers Ltd., Winnipeg." *Canadian Architect* 16 (March 1971): 38–39.

"Office for the Architects Libling, Michener & Associates Winnipeg." *The Journal (Royal Architectural Institute of Canada)* 40 (December 1963): 40–42.

"Office for Waisman Architectural Group, Vancouver." *Canadian Architect* 19 (July 1974): 30–31.

"Offices of Green, Blankstein, Russell and Associates." *The Journal (Royal Architectural Institute of Canada)* 25 (October 1948): 380.

"Offices of Moody, Moore, Architects, Winnipeg." *The Journal (Royal Architectural Institute of Canada)* 25 (October 1948): 366.

"Offices of Smith Carter Katelnikoff Architects Winnipeg." *The Journal (Royal Architectural Institute of Canada)* 25 (October 1948): 380.

"Only One Job Bigger in Canada." *Winnipeg Tribune*, 19 January 1956.

"150 Angry Residents Balk at Expropriation." *Winnipeg Tribune*, 21 December 1967.

"1000 in Charleswood Seek Shopping Centre." *Winnipeg Tribune*, 24 May 1960.

"1,500-Home Plan O.K.'d for Suburb." *Winnipeg Tribune*, 28 October 1952.

"Opening Seen by Sept. 1957." *Winnipeg Tribune*, 28 September 1956.

"Ottawa's Fiscal Policies Slow Down Construction." *Winnipeg Tribune*, 27 September 1969.

"Outside Is Inside in Downtown Plan." *Winnipeg Tribune*, 5 June 1969.

"Pan-Am Pool Winnipeg." *Architecture Canada* 45 (August 1968): 37.

"Park Residents to Get Answers." *Winnipeg Tribune*, 17 May 1967.

"Parkin and Smith Carter Searle Merge." *Architecture Canada* 46 (March 1969): 6.

"Partnership." *The Journal (Royal Architectural Journal of Canada)* 25 (March 1948): 98.

"People and Positions." *Manitoba Business Journal* (July/August 1972): 48.

"The Philadelphia Story." *Winnipeg Tribune*, 2 April 1962.

"Pilot Housing Backed." *Winnipeg Tribune*, 21 December 1955.

"Planning Well Advanced for the 53rd Annual Assembly at Winnipeg." *The Journal (Royal Architectural Institute of Canada)* 37 (February 1960): 81.

"Plug-in Urban Living." *Architecture Canada* 47 (8 June 1970): 6.

"Police Station & Court House, St. Boniface, Man." *Canadian Architect* 11 (April 1966): 53–56.

"Polo Park Centre Now One Year Old." *Winnipeg Tribune*, 31 August 1960.

"Polo Park Is Sold to Montreal Firm." *Winnipeg Tribune*, 11 August 1961.

"Polo Park Sale Nears Completion." *Winnipeg Tribune*, 19 June 1961.

"Polo Park Shopping Centre Winnipeg." *The Journal (Royal Architectural Institute of Canada)* 32 (October 1955): 374.

"Polo Park to Get $5 Million Store." *Winnipeg Tribune*, 20 May 1954.

"Practice Notes." *Architecture Canada* 46 (March 1969): 67.

"Prairie Architecture Examined." *Canadian Architect* (October 1979): 21–30.

"Prairie Phoenix." *Canadian Architect* 40, 5 (May 1995): 32–35.

Precieux-Sang/Precious Blood Church. St. Boniface: Paroisse du Precieux-Sang, 1980.

"Princess Elizabeth Hospital." *The Journal (Royal Architectural Institute of Canada)* 31 (November 1954): 418.

"Private, Not Public, Buildings Highlight '71 Permit Picture." *Winnipeg Tribune*, 16 January 1972.

"Proceedings of the Twenty-Fifth General Meeting of the Royal Architectural Institute of Canada." *The Journal (Royal Architectural Institute of Canada)* IX (March 1932): 71.

"Program for Architectural Design." *The Journal (Royal Architectural Institute of Canada)* 31 (March 1954): 64–65.

"Project Preview." *Canadian Architect* 13 (December 1968): 51–52.

"Projects." *Architecture Canada* 47 (9 November 1970): 4.

"Projects." *Architecture Canada* 48 (7 June 1971): 3.

"Projects." *Architecture Canada* 48 (22 November 1971): 3.

"Projects." *Canadian Architect* 5 (June 1960): 69–74.

"Projects." *The Journal (Royal Architectural Institute of Canada)* 34 (October 1957): 406.

"Projects May Cost over $136 Million." *Winnipeg Tribune*, 3 May 1969.

"Proposed Low-Cost Development." *The Journal (Royal Architectural Institute of Canada)* XI (July/August 1934): 109–112.

"Protests at No Shop Centre." *Winnipeg Tribune*, 10 March 1960.

"Provincial Page—Manitoba." *The Journal (Royal Architectural Institute of Canada)* 14 (August 1937): 170.

"Public Welfare Practices Probe Urged by Joint Civic Committees." *Winnipeg Tribune*, 1 April 1948.

"Question Sparks Council Argument." *Winnipeg Tribune,* 29 May 1962.

"RAIC Executive Committee." *The Journal (Royal Architectural Institute of Canada)* 39 (May 1962): 34.

"Red Cross, Deer Lodge Military Hospital." *The Journal (Royal Architectural Institute of Canada)* 22 (November 1945): 223–225.

"Renewal Board Proposed 4-Stage Slum Clearance." *Winnipeg Tribune*, 27 November 1958.

"Renewal Financing Approved." *Winnipeg Tribune*, 15 July 1966.

"Rent Project in Elmwood Urged to Replace Slums." *Winnipeg Tribune*, 20 October 1955.

"Rental Project Cost $5 Million." *Winnipeg Tribune*, 27 April 1966.

"Report Criticizes Architects Stand." *Winnipeg Tribune*, 28 May 1966.

"Report Follows Studies in 1966." *Winnipeg Tribune*, 24 January 1968.

"Report's History." *Winnipeg Tribune*, 17 September 1957.

"Residence of Professor and Mrs. James Donahue, Tuxedo, Winnipeg." *The Journal (Royal Architectural Institute of Canada)* 36 (February 1959): 42.

"Residence, Winnipeg, Manitoba." *Canadian Architect* 11 (November 1966): 52–54.

"Residents Aroused by Low-Rent Scheme." *Winnipeg Tribune*, 3 October 1957.

"Riverside Elementary School, Thompson, Manitoba, Number 10 Architectural Group." *Canadian Architect Yearbook* (1969): 39–40.

"Role of Architect Changing; Expert Says." *Winnipeg Tribune*, 14 January 1965.

"Ross, Jack M." *The Canadian Who's Who*. Volume X. Toronto: Trans-Canada Press, 1964–1966.

Royal Canadian Academy of Arts: Prairie Region Exhibition. Toronto: Royal Canadian Academy of Arts, 1997.

"Russell, G. Leslie." *The Canadian Who's Who.* Volume X. Toronto: Trans-Canada Press, 1964–1966.

"School of Architecture, University of Manitoba." *The Journal (Royal Architectural Institute of Canada)* 19 (February 1942): 22–23.

"School of Architecture, University of Manitoba." *The Journal (Royal Architectural Institute of Canada)* 20 (February 1943): 19.

"School of Architecture, University of Manitoba." *The Journal (Royal Architectural Institute of Canada)* 21 (April 1944): 72.

"School of Architecture, University of Manitoba." *The Journal (Royal Architectural Institute of Canada)* 35 (May 1958): 196.

"School of Architecture, University of Manitoba." *The Journal (Royal Architectural Institute of Canada)* 35 (August 1958): 315.

"Schools." *The Journal (Royal Architectural Institute of Canada)* 29 (June 1952): 179.

"Schools." *The Journal (Royal Architectural Institute of Canada)* 29 (June 1952): 181.

"Schools." *The Journal (Royal Architectural Institute of Canada)* 32 (October 1955): 390.

"Schools." *The Journal (Royal Architectural Institute of Canada)* 36 (October 1959): 336–337, 342, 346–348.

"Science Service Laboratory." *The Journal (Royal Architectural Institute of Canada)* 32 (October 1955): 393.

"Searle, James Elmhurst." *The Canadian Who's Who.* Volume XII. Toronto: Trans-Canada Press, 1970–1972.

"Separation of Pedestrians and Vehicles." *The Journal (Royal Architectural Institute of Canada)* 29 (September 1952): 4–5.

"70 Elmwood Residents at Meeting Protest Housing Project." *Winnipeg Tribune,* 8 March 1957.

"7-Up Bottling Plant, Winnipeg." *The Journal (Royal Architectural Institute of Canada)* 33 (May 1956): 173.

"Sewers Win Out over Happiness." *Winnipeg Tribune,* 30 October 1959.

"Shaarey Zedek Synagogue." *The Journal (Royal Architectural Institute of Canada)* 28 (January 1951): 5–7.

"Slum Clearance Speedup Sought." *Winnipeg Tribune,* 1 July 1958.

"Slum Dwellers Unite." *Winnipeg Tribune,* 1960 [file 3581]. University of Manitoba, Archives & Special Collections, Winnipeg Tribune Clipping Files.

"Slum Profiteers." *Winnipeg Tribune,* 15 October 1959.

"Smith Carter Partners Office, Winnipeg." *Canadian Architect* 24 (November 1979): 32–33.

"Smith Carter Shares New Venture." *Winnipeg Tribune,* 15 February 1972.

"Smith Residence." *The Journal (Royal Architectural Institute of Canada)* 39 (May 1962): 48–49.

"Some Sober Second Thoughts." *Winnipeg Tribune,* 14 June 1962.

"Southwood Green Crates New Concept in Elegant Town House Living." *Winnipeg Tribune,* 9 September 1967.

"Splitting up Poor the Cure?" *Winnipeg Tribune,* 4 October 1966.

"St. James Public Library." *The Journal (Royal Architectural Institute of Canada)* 36 (April 1959): 103.

"St. Paul's College High School, Tuxedo, Manitoba." *Canadian Architect* 9 (December 1964): 44.

"St. Paul's College High School, Winnipeg." *Canadian Architect* 11 (January 1966): 36–39.

"St. Paul's University College of Manitoba Winnipeg." *The Journal (Royal Architectural Institute of Canada)* 33 (May 1956): 170.

"Stereotypes Not True: Prof Blasts Bias against Suburbs." *Winnipeg Tribune,* 11 February 1960.

"Study Reveals Crowded Houses." *Winnipeg Tribune,* 14 March 1967.

"'Subsidized' Slums." *Winnipeg Tribune,* 17 October 1959.

"Subsidy Is Good Business." *Winnipeg Tribune,* 16 September 1960.

"Suburban Building in 1950 Tops '49 despite Floods." *Winnipeg Tribune*, 19 January 1951.

"Summer Residence at Husavick." *The Journal (Royal Architectural Institute of Canada)* 38 (November 1961): 58.

"Summer Sport for Lockhart Autumn Years: Changing Patterns Ahead." *Winnipeg Free Press*, 7 May 1971, p. 25.

"Synagogue and School, Winnipeg." *The Journal (Royal Architectural Institute of Canada)* 32 (October 1955): 373.

"Taxes Subsidize Big Landlords." *Winnipeg Tribune*, 14 October 1959.

"$10 Million Construction Drop in 1961." *Winnipeg Tribune,* 30 December 1961.

"A Terminal Building for Winnipeg." *The Journal (Royal Architectural Institute of Canada)* 37 (February 1960): 52.

"They Have Designs on Winnipeg." *Winnipeg Real Estate News* (9 January 1987): 6.

"325 Houses to be Built in Ft. Garry," *Winnipeg Tribune*, 1945 [file 3589–1]. University of Manitoba, Archives & Special Collections, Winnipeg Tribune Clipping Files.

"$30 Million Spent on New Homes Is Changing the Face of the City." *Winnipeg Tribune*, 18 June 1955.

"30-Storey Building for Graham Avenue." *Winnipeg Tribune*, 25 July 1969.

"Thompson Medical Office Building." *The Journal (Royal Architectural Institute of Canada)* 38 (November 1961): 59.

"$3 Million Building Ready in Late 1957." *Winnipeg Tribune*, 15 September 1954.

"3.5 Million Dollar Grant Plaza Shop Centre." *Winnipeg Tribune*, 4 April 1962.

"The Toronto Dominion Bank, East Kildonan, Manitoba." *The Journal (Royal Architectural Institute of Canada)* 34 (February 1957): 51.

"To Tour Jarvis Slum. " *Winnipeg Tribune*, 6 November 1966.

"20 Stores in Crossroads Centre." *Winnipeg Tribune*, 23 November 1966.

"Two Airport Projects." *The Journal (Royal Architectural Institute of Canada)* 37 (February 1960): 51.

"Two Architects' Houses in Manitoba." *The Journal (Royal Architectural Institute of Canada)* 35 (February 1958): 51–55.

"Two Firms to Plan Developments." *Winnipeg Tribune,* 15 February 1965.

"$200,000 Tab on Urban Study." *Winnipeg Tribune*, 27 May 1966.

"Two-Part Plan over 20 Years." *Winnipeg Tribune*, 5 June 1969.

"Two Winnipeg Architects Win Home Design Awards." *Winnipeg Tribune*, 30 November 1962.

"Unique Collegiate for Thompson, Manitoba." *Architecture Canada* 47 (28 September 1970): 4–5.

"University Awards." *The Journal (Royal Architectural Institute of Canada)* 31 (June 1954): 217.

"University of Manitoba." *The Journal (Royal Architectural Institute of Canada)* 24 (May 1947): 146–149.

"University of Manitoba." *The Journal (Royal Architectural Institute of Canada)* 25 (May 1948): 144–151.

"University of Manitoba." *The Journal (Royal Architectural Institute of Canada)* 30 (October 1953): 290–291.

"University of Manitoba." *Canadian Architect* 9 (May 1964): 50.

"The University of Manitoba Faculty of Architecture." *The Journal (Royal Architectural Institute of Canada)* 41 (March 1964): 56–68.

"University of Manitoba School of Architecture and Fine Arts." *The Journal (Royal Architectural Institute of Canada)* 23 (April 1946): 97–99.

"University of Manitoba—School of Architecture." *The Journal (Royal Architectural Institute of Canada)* 26 (May 1949): 160–165.

"Urban Shopping." *Winnipeg Tribune*, 18 September 1963.

"Virden Hospital, Virden, Manitoba." *The Journal (Royal Architectural Institute of Canada)* 29 (October 1952): 294–295.

"Waisman, Allan Harvie." *The Canadian Who's Who.* Volume X. Toronto: Trans–Canada Press, 1964–1966.

"We're Paying to Preserve a Blight, Expert Claims." *Winnipeg Tribune*, 25 June 1960.

"West Kildonan Approves $16 Million 'Garden City.'" *Winnipeg Tribune*, 21 December 1953.

"What's Happened to the Building Boom?" *Winnipeg Tribune*, 30 May 1970.

"Wildwood Shopping Centre Is Unique in Dominion." *Winnipeg Tribune*, 30 October 1947.

"Windsor Park Collegiate, St. Boniface, Manitoba." *The Journal (Royal Architectural Institute of Canada)* 38 (July 1961): 53.

"Winners Winnipeg Art Gallery Competition." *Architecture Canada* 45 (January 1968): 5.

"Winnipeg Architect Étienne Gaboury." *Canadian Architect* 14 (April 1969): 9.

"Winnipeg Architects Win 5 Medals." *Winnipeg Tribune*, 3 November 1961.

"Winnipeg Art Gallery." *Canadian Architect* 17 (July 1972): 24–31, 35.

"Winnipeg Art Gallery Competition." *Architecture Canada* 44 (July 1967): 5–6.

"Winnipeg Art Gallery Competition." *Architecture Canada* 44 (December 1967): 7.

"Winnipeg Art Show." *Canadian Architect* 1 (August 1956): 8.

"Winnipeg City Hall." *Canadian Architect* 10 (January 1965): 51–55.

"Winnipeg City Hall—Architects: Green Blankstein Russell Associates." *Canadian Architect* 10 (January 1965): 51–55.

"Winnipeg City Hall Competition." *Canadian Architect* 5 (January 1960): 35–42.

"Winnipeg City Hall Competition." *The Journal (Royal Architectural Institute of Canada)* 37 (January 1960): 31–34.

"Winnipeg City Hall Competition." *The Journal (Royal Architectural Institute of Canada)* 37 (March 1960): 111–113.

"Winnipeg Design (Y) by Green, Blankstein, Russell, and Associates, Winnipeg." *The Journal (Royal Architectural Institute of Canada)* 31 (April 1954): 104–107.

"Winnipeg Downtown Construction Shows Signs of Regaining Strength." *Globe and Mail* (Toronto), 3 August 1973.

"Winnipeg Free Press." *The Journal (Royal Architectural Institute of Canada)* 37 (July1960): 312.

"Winnipeg General Hospital, Maternity Pavilion, Winnipeg, Manitoba." *The Journal (Royal Architectural Institute of Canada)* 28 (April 1951): 107–109.

"Winnipeg General Hospital, New North Wing." *The Journal (Royal Architectural Institute of Canada)* 32 (October 1955): 385.

"Winnipeg Honours RAIC Committee." *The Journal (Royal Architectural Institute of Canada)* 36 (November 1959): 403–404.

"Winnipeg Lacks Face." *Winnipeg Free Press*, 6 March 1973, p. 14.

"Winnipeg Winter Club." *The Journal (Royal Architectural Institute of Canada)* 27 (June 1950): 192–193.

"Winnipegged." *Canadian Architect* 3 (July 1958): 13.

"Winnipeggers." *Canadian Architect* 4 (January 1959): 12, 14.

"'Worst Crowded' Notre Dame Area Requires Immediate Development." *Winnipeg Tribune*, 17 September 1957.

"Zuken Plan Would Free 'Trapped' Flora Residents." *Winnipeg Tribune*, 1 October 1969.

Published Sources

Attributed Sources

Aarons, Anita. "Art and Architecture—The Western Provinces." *The Journal (Royal Architectural Institute of Canada)* 42 (November 1965): 16–18.

____. "Art and Architecture—Western Tour: Part II." *The Journal (Royal Architectural Institute of Canada)* 42 (December 1965): 24A.

____. "Art for Architecture ... Any New Year's Resolutions?" *Architecture Canada* 46 (January 1969): 15.

____. "Conquering the Concrete Campus." *Architecture Canada* 46 (September 1969): 8–9.

____. "Eli Bornstein Allied Arts Medalist 1968." *Architecture Canada* 45 (May 1968): 22.

Ackerman, R.F., B.H. Green, M.R. Johnson, D.A. McQuaig, and K.R. Webber. "Red River Skyline." *Journal (Royal Architectural Institute of Canada)* 31 (March 1954): 81–85.

Akitt, Alan D. "The University Schools Architecture: University of Manitoba." *The Journal (Royal Architectural Institute of Canada)* 28 (March 1951): 49–55.

Allan, Ted. "The Art Center: A Building of Contradiction." *The Winnipeg Tribune*, 1 May 1971.

Allsopp, Robert. "Model for the Future." *Canadian Architect* 17 (January 1972): 30–31.

Aquin, Stephane, ed. *Global Village: The 1960s*. Montreal: Montreal Museum of Fine Arts, 2003.

Arnold, Cheryl. "Grant Marshall: A Life by Design." *SMART Connections* (Winter 2000): 8–9.

Arthur, Eric R. "Architecture." In *Documents in Canadian Architecture*. Peterborough: Broadview Press,1952.

____. "Editorial." *The Journal (Royal Architectural Institute of Canada)* 37 (March 1960): 87.

____. "The National Gallery of Canada Competition." *The Journal (Royal Architectural Institute of Canada)* 31 (April 1954): 104–117.

____. "School Design: A New Look at Some Old Problems." *The Journal (Royal Architectural Institute of Canada)* 37 (February 1960): 61–70.

[Arthur, Eric R.], ed. "Canada Council Appointment." *The Journal (Royal Architectural Institute of Canada)* 34 (May 1957): 190.

Artibise, Alan. *Winnipeg: An Illustrated History*. Toronto: James Lorimer & Company, 1977.

Atkinson, Don. "Architects Rearrange Sights." *Winnipeg Tribune*, 14 July 1962.

____. "Bleak Year for Construction Appears to Have Materialized." *Winnipeg Tribune*, 29 January 1971.

____. "Storefront Architects: Continued Service Planned." *Winnipeg Tribune*, 27 October 1972.

Axworthy, N. Lloyd. "The Task Force on Housing and Urban Development: A Study of Democratic Decision-making in Canada." PhD thesis. Princeton University, 1972.

Bacher, John C. *Keeping to the Marketplace: The Evolution of Canadian Housing Policy*. Montreal and Kingston: McGill-Queen's University Press, 1993.

Baird, George. *The Space of Appearance*. Cambridge: MIT Press, 1995.

Balassu, Carlo, and Jeff Bickell, et al. "A.J. Donahue." Unpublished paper for the University of Manitoba course Canadian Architecture 079.333, 23 March 2001.

Banham, Reyner. *Los Angeles: The Architecture of Four Ecologies*. London: Allen Lane, 1971.

_____. *Theory and Design in the First Machine Age*. New York: Praeger, 1960.

Baraness, Marc, et al. *Toronto Modern Architecture 1945–1965*. Toronto: Coach House Press, The Bureau of Architecture and Urbanism, 1987.

Baudelaire, Charles. *The Painter of Modern Life and Other Essays*. Trans. Jonathan Mayne. London: Phaidon, 1963.

Beamish, Robert, ed. *Dilemmas of Modern Man*. Winnipeg: Great West Life Assurance, 1975.

Bedford, Gerald Allan. "One Hundred Years of History." *The University of Winnipeg: The Commemorative Journal 1888–1988* 4, 2 (Summer 1988): 8.

_____. *The University of Winnipeg: A History of the Founding Colleges*. Toronto: University of Toronto Press, 1976.

Bellan, Ruben. *Winnipeg First Century: An Economic History*. Winnipeg: Queenston House, 1978.

Berman, Marshall. *All That Is Solid Melts into Air: The Experience of Modernity*. Harmondsworth: Penguin, 1988.

Berton, Pierre. "Heritage Preservation." Manitoba Historical Society. Transactions, Series 3 (1975–76). [Available on-line <http://www.mhs.mb.ca/docs/transactiosn/3/heritagepreservation.shtml>, accessed 1 April 2006]

Billinkoff, Arlene. "New Art Gallery Designed to Resemble an Iceberg." *Winnipeg Free Press*, 19 December, 1967.

Blanchard, Jim. *Winnipeg 1912: Diary of a City*. Winnipeg: University of Manitoba Press, 2005.

Blankstein, Cecil. "The Profession and the Package Deal." *The Journal (Royal Architectural Institute of Canada)* 37 (July 1960): 306.

_____. "Viewpoint." *The Journal (Royal Architectural Institute of Canada)* 33 (August 1956): 312.

_____, James Donahue, and H.H.G. Moody. "Syndicate Discussions." *The Journal (Royal Architectural Institute of Canada)* 37 (July 1960): 306-310.

Blankstein, Morley. "Book Reviews." *The Journal (Royal Architectural Institute of Canada)* 36 (August 1959): 292–293.

_____. "Closed Shop Trend in Manitoba." *Canadian Architect* 18 (March 1973): 90, 92.

_____. "Viewpoint." *The Journal (Royal Architectural Institute of Canada)* 34 (February 1957): 62.

_____. "Viewpoint." *The Journal (Royal Architectural Institute of Canada)* 36 (January 1959): 26.

Bothwell, Robert, Ian Drummond, and John English. *Canada since 1945: Power, Politics and Provincialism*. Toronto: University of Toronto Press, 1989.

Boux, Pierre. "Architecture in the Winnipeg Area." *Canadian Architect* 15 (May 1970): 45–48.

Bowser, Sara. "Shoemaker's Children." *Canadian Architect* 3 (April 1958): 41, 53–55.

Broddy, Trevor. "Compliments to Mies, or Emoluments to Phillip?" *Canadian Architect* 43 (June 1998): 12–13.

_____. *Modern Architecture in Alberta*. Regina: Alberta Culture and Multiculturalism and the Canadian Plains Research Center, 1987.

Brown, Bernard Peter. "City Hall Introduction: Brief History." Winnipeg: Winnipeg Architecture Foundation, Historical Buildings Committee, City of Winnipeg, 2001.

Brown, Gordon. "Buildings in Hong Kong." *Architectural Review* 119 (June 1956).

Brown, Ian M. "Institute News." *The Journal (Royal Architectural Institute of Canada)* 35 (April 1958): 151.

Brushett, Kevin. "Blots on the Face of the City: The Politics of Slum Housing and Urban Renewal in Toronto, 1940–1970." PhD thesis, Queen's University, 2001.

Buchanan, Donald. "Design in Industry: The Canadian Picture." *The Journal (Royal Architectural Institute of Canada)* 24 (July 1947): 234–239.

273

Bumsted, J.M. "Blankstein, Cecil." In *Dictionary of Manitoba Biography*. Winnipeg: University of Manitoba Press, 1999.

_____. "Russell, John Alonso." In *Dictionary of Manitoba Biography*. Winnipeg: University of Manitoba Press, 1999.

_____. *The University of Manitoba: An Illustrated History*. Winnipeg: University of Manitoba Press, 2001.

Byfield, T. "Building Soars over '56 Peak." *Winnipeg Tribune*, 2 November 1957.

Canada Task Force on Housing and Urban Development. *Report of the Federal Task Force on Housing and Urban Development*. Ottawa: Queen's Printer, 1969.

Came, Barry. "May Offer Lure to Developers." *Winnipeg Tribune*, 23 April 1966.

Carter, Dennis H. "Viewpoint." *The Journal (Royal Architectural Institute of Canada)* 31 (December 1954): 459.

Cawker, Ruth, and William Bernstein. *Contemporary Canadian Architecture: The Mainstream and Beyond*. Markham: Fitzhenry and Whiteside, 1988.

Chambers, Merton. "Formation of a National Crafts Council." *The Journal (Royal Architectural Institute of Canada)* 42 (June 1965): 26, 28.

Charter of The Hudson's Bay Company, 2 May 1670. *The Royal Charter for Incorporating The Hudson's Bay Company, A.D. 1670*.

Chermayeff, Serge. *Design and the Public Good: Selected Writings 1930–1980*. Ed. Richard A. Plunz. Cambridge: MIT Press, 1983.

_____. *Oral History of Serge Chermayeff*. Interviewed by Betty J. Blum. Chicago Architects Oral History Project. Chicago: The Art Institute of Chicago, 1986. [Available on-line: <http://www.artic.edu/aic/libraries/ caohp/chermayeff.pdf>]

_____, and Christopher Alexander. *Community and Privacy: Toward a New Architecture of Humanism*. Garden City: Doubleday, 2001.

Chivers, John. "Manitoba." *The Journal (Royal Architectural Institute of Canada)* 25 (May 1948): 179–180.

Christensen, E.M. "Student Participation." *Canadian Architect* 17 (January 1972): 32–33.

Christie, James. "Centennial Hall University of Winnipeg." *Design in Steel* (January 1975).

_____. "University of Winnipeg." *Western Construction and Industry* (August–September 1972): 5.

Clark, S.D. *The Suburban Society*. Toronto: University of Toronto Press, 1966.

City of Winnipeg. *Urban Renewal and Rehabilitation Board. South Point Douglas*. Winnipeg: The Author, 1959.

Collins, Peter. *Changing Ideals in Modern Architecture*. London: Faber and Faber 1965.

_____. "Three New International Air Terminals." *The Journal (Royal Architectural Institute of Canada)* 41 (February 1964): 44–68.

Colquhuon, Alan. "Critique: Pompidou." *Architectural Design* 47, 2 (1977): 96–103.

Conrad, Margaret, and Alvin Finkel. *Canada: A National History*. Toronto: Pearson Educational Publishing, 2003.

Coop, Isadore. "Manitoba." *The Journal (Royal Architectural Institute of Canada)* 32 (December 1955): 477–478.

_____. "The Sixties: A Decade of Innovation?" *Canadian Architect* 16 (July 1971): 50–51.

_____. "Viewpoint." *The Journal (Royal Architectural Institute of Canada)* 33 (July 1956): 270.

_____. "Viewpoint." *The Journal (Royal Architectural Institute of Canada)* 35 (April 1958): 150.

_____. "Voice." *Canadian Architect* 16 (July 1971): 47–51, 57.

_____, H.H.G. Moody, and J.A. Russell. "Annual Reports to RAIC Council Standing an Special Committees." *The Journal (Royal Architectural Institute of Canada)* 41 (May 1964): 58–61.

Cross. "Creating Domestic Space in 1950s Canada." *Architecture and Arts* 1 (1996): 90–99.

Crossman, Kelly. "North by Northwest: Manitoba Modernism, c. 1950." *Journal of the Society for the Study of Architecture in Canada* 24, 2 (1999): 61–69.

Currie, Marion G. "Light as a Design Element." *The Journal (Royal Architectural Institute of Canada)* 41 (March 1964): 45–50.

Curtis, William J.R. *Modern Architecture since 1900*. London: Phaidon Press Limited, 1982.

Davidson-Hunt, I., and F. Berkes. "Learning as You Journey: Anishinaabe Perception of Social-Ecological Environments and Adaptive Learning." *Conservation Ecology* 8, 1 (2003): 5. [Available on-line: <http://www.consecol.org/vol8/iss/art5/>, accessed 2 April 2006]

Davis, J.L. "Editorial." *The Journal (Royal Architectural Institute of Canada)* 37 (July 1960): 275.

Dean, Andrea Oppenheimer. "The National East: An Evaluation." *Architecture* (October 1984).

Dixon, John Morris, and Joyce Reback. "Canada: A View from the South." *Progressive Architecture* 53 (September 1972).

_____, Martin Filler, and James A. Murphy. Roundtable Discussion. "P/A on Pei: Round Table on a Trapezoid," *Progressive Architecture* 59 (October 1978).

Donahue, A.J. "News from the Institute: Manitoba." *The Journal (Royal Architectural Institute of Canada)* 34 (September 1957): 365.

_____. "Viewpoint." *The Journal (Royal Architectural Institute of Canada)* 32 (September 1955): 355.

_____. "Viewpoint." *The Journal (Royal Architectural Institute of Canada)* 37 (February 1960): 76–77.

_____, and W. Gerson. "Structure: A Technique in its Instruction." *The Journal (Royal Architectural Institute of Canada)* 31 (March 1954): 77–79.

_____, Cecil Blankstein, and H.H.G. Moody. "Syndicate Discussions." *The Journal (Royal Architectural Institute of Canada)* 37 (July 1960): 306–310.

Doucet, Michael, and John Weaver. *Housing the North American City*. Montreal and Kingston: McGill-Queen's University Press, 1991.

Duckworth, Henry E. *One Version of the Facts: My Life in the Ivory Tower*. Winnipeg: University of Manitoba Press, 2000.

DuBois, Macy. "Competition: Winnipeg Art Gallery." *Canadian Architect* 13 (February 1968): 39–44.

Eckhardt, Ferdinand. "21 Years of the Winnipeg Art Gallery." Unpublished manuscript, 1986.

Elder, Alan, ed. *Made in Canada: Craft and Design in the Sixties*. Montreal and Kingston: McGill-Queen's University Press, 2005.

Elte, Hans. "Architecture of the Prairies." *The Journal (Royal Architectural Institute of Canada)* 42 (June 1965): 33–41.

Epp, Edward. "City Profile: Winnipeg: Agrarian Metropolis." *Canadian Architect* 40 (September 1995): 18–27.

Faculty of Architecture, University of Manitoba. "A Study of Wildwood Park." Unpublished research report, 1972.

Fairbairn, Clarence. "Things Looking Up at City Centre." *Winnipeg Tribune*, 1965 [file 1778]. University of Manitoba, Archives & Special Collections, Winnipeg Tribune Clipping Files.

Farquharson, Duart. "Winnipeg Has Failed its Citizens." *Winnipeg Tribune*, 28 April 1970, pp. 1–2.

Fenske, Gail, and Deryck Holdsworth. "Corporate Identity and the New York Office Building: 1895–1915." In *The Landscape of Modernity: New York City, 1900–1940*. Ed. David Ward and Olivier Zunz. Baltimore: Johns Hopkins University Press, 1992.

Ferrabee, Lydia. "Toronto Airport: Interior Design." *Canadian Architect* (February 1964): 63–64.

Flaman, Bernard. "When 'la Dolce Vita' Met 'True Canadianism': Canadian Airports in the Sixties." In *Made in Canada: Craft and Design in the Sixties*. Ed. Alan Elder. Montreal and Kingston: McGill-Queen's University Press, 2005.

Fogel, Cheryl. "The New Polo Park." *Winnipeg Free Press,* 9 August 1986, p. 9.

Ford, Tom. "City Slums Take Huge Toll in Dollars and Bad Health." *Winnipeg Tribune*, 5 January 1957.

Forseth, Gerald, et al. *Lethbridge Modern*. Lethbridge: Southern Alberta Art Gallery, 2002.

Fraser, Graham. *Fighting Back: Urban Renewal in Trefann Court*. Toronto: Hakkert, 1972.

Freedman, Adele. "Modern Life." *Elm Street* (September 1998): 117–120.

_____. "West Coast Modernism and Points East." In *The New Spirit: Modern Architecture in Vancouver, 1938–1963*. Ed. Rhodri Windsor-Liscombe. Montreal: Canadian Centre for Architecture/Vancouver: Douglas and McIntyre, 1997.

Friesen, Gerald. *The Canadian Prairie: A History*. Toronto: University of Toronto Press, 1984.

Froehlich, George. " Plaza Expansion Nears Completion." *Winnipeg Tribune*, 13 August 1969.

Fromson, R.D. "Planning in a Metropolitan Area—The Experiment in Greater Winnipeg." MCP thesis, University of Manitoba, 1970.

Gaboury, Étienne. "Design for Worship." *Canadian Architect* 13 (March 1968): 33–41.

_____. "Gaboury Residence, St. Vital, Manitoba." *Canadian Architect* 14 (March 1969): 41–47.

_____. "Métaphores et métamorphoses en architecture." *Cahiers franco-canadiens de l'ouest* 3, 2 (Automne 1991): 179–215.

_____. "Towards a Prairie Architecture." *Prairie Forum* 5, 2 (1980).

_____. "Wood." *Canadian Architect* 10 (November 1965): 38–44.

Gerson, Wolfgang. "Housing as a Community Art." *The Journal (Royal Architectural Institute of Canada)* 33 (October 1956): 383–387.

_____. *Patterns of Urban Living*. Toronto: University of Toronto Press, 1970.

_____. *An Urban Renewal Study for the City of Winnipeg: The C.P.R.-Notre Dame Area*. Winnipeg: CMHC, 1957.

_____. "Viewpoint." *The Journal (Royal Architectural Institute of Canada)* 32 (August 1955): 306.

_____. and J. Russell, eds. *Community Centres*. Winnipeg: Prairies Rural Housing Committee, 1948.

_____, Allan H. Waisman, and Jack Ross. "Triangle Gardens Housing Project Elwood [sic], Winnipeg, Manitoba." *The Journal (Royal Architectural Institute of Canada)* 35 (July 1958): 275–277.

Gibbons, Lillian. "It's Wildwood Park." *Winnipeg Tribune*, 7 August 1948.

Giedion, Siegfried. *Befreites Wohnen*. Zürich und Leipzig: Forell Füssli Verlag 1929.

_____. *Mechanization Takes Command: A Contribution to Anonymous History*. New York: W.W. Norton & Company: New York, 1969.

_____. *Space, Time and Architecture*. Cambridge: Harvard University Press, 1941.

Gillmor, Alison. "Around Here." *Western Living* (March 2001): 26–30.

Gillmor, D.R. "Architectural Design." *The Journal (Royal Architectural Institute of Canada)* 31 (March 1954): 66–69.

_____. "A City Hall for Winnipeg." *The Journal (Royal Architectural Institute of Canada)* 31 (March 1954): 71–73.

_____. "Good Theatre: Bad Stagecraft." *Canadian Architect* 18 (April 1973): 74.

_____, A.J. Donahue, W. Gerson, W.J. Spotowski, A.M. Nixon, R.F. Ackerman, B.H. Green, M.R. Johnson, D.A. McQuaig, and K.R. Webber in consultation with H.A. Elarth. "Architectural Education at the University of Manitoba." *The Journal (Royal Architectural Institute of Canada)* 31 (March 1954): 63–86.

Goldhagen, Sarah Williams. "Something to Talk about: Modernism, Discourse, Style." *Journal of the Society of Architectural Historians* 64, 2 (June 2005): 144–167.

_____, and Réjean Legault, eds, "Coda: Reconceptualizing the Modern." In *Anxious Modernisms: Experimentation in Postwar Architectural Culture*. Cambridge: MIT Press, 2001.

Gotleib, Rachel, and Cora Golden. *Design in Canada: Fifty Years from Teakettles to Task Chairs*. Toronto: Knopf Canada, 2001.

Graham, John, W. *Winnipeg Architecture: The Red River Settlement 1831–1960*. Winnipeg: University of Manitoba Press, 1960.

Green, Lawrence J. "Obituary: Ralph Carl Ham." *The Journal (Royal Architectural Institute of Canada)* 19 (October 1942): 211.

Habermas, Jurgen. *The Philosophical Discourse of Modernity: Twelve Lectures.* Trans. Frederick G. Lawrence. Cambridge: MIT Press, 1990.

Hainstock, Bob. "Industry Heads Agree." *Winnipeg Tribune*, June 1969 [1778]. University of Manitoba, Archives & Special Collections, Winnipeg Tribune Clipping Files.

Hanna, Pat. "Dennis Carter—Architect: He Always Knew What He Wanted." *Manitoba Business Journal* (April 1970): 31, 79.

Harland, Joan. "Department of Interior Design 1966–67 University of Manitoba." *Architecture Canada* 44 (February 1967): 63–64.

_____. *St. George's Church, Crescentwood, Architectural Design*. [Available on-line www.stgeorges.mb.ca/downloads/History. pdf accessed 1 April 2006]

Harris, Richard. *Creeping Conformity: How Canada Became Suburban, 1900–1960*. Toronto: University of Toronto Press, 2004.

Harvey, David. *The Condition of Postmodernity: An Inquiry in the Origins of Cultural Change*. London: Blackwell, 1989.

Hayes, Jim. "Ald. Tennant Doesn't Know Owner Names." *Winnipeg Tribune*, 21 October 1959.

_____. "City Funds Helped Draw this Portrait of a Slum." *Winnipeg Tribune*, 17 October 1959.

_____. "Cost $4 Million for One Section." *Winnipeg Tribune*, 2 February 1957.

_____. "Mother of Seven Finds a New Life." *Winnipeg Tribune*, 24 October 1959.

_____. "Park Strips to Divide Housing and Industry." *Winnipeg Tribune*, August 1956, [file 3581]. University of Manitoba, Archives & Special Collections, Winnipeg Tribune Clipping Files.

_____. "Rules Halt Cure of Slum Cancer." *Winnipeg Tribune*, 15 October 1959.

Hellner, Faye, ed. *Étienne Gaboury*. Winnipeg: Éditions du Ble, 2005.

Hiscocks, C.R. "An Art Centre for Winnipeg?" *The Journal (Royal Architectural Institute of Canada)* 32 (June 1955): 222–233.

Hills, Nick. "Slum Clearance Three-Way Job." *Winnipeg Tribune*, 2 April 1962.

_____. "We Need Overall Program to Clear Slums—Director." *Winnipeg Tribune*, 30 May 1962.

Horkheimer, Max, and Theodor Adorno. *The Dialectic of Enlightenment*. Trans. John Cumming. London: Allen Lane, 1973.

Horsman, Maureen. "Housing Cooperation Sought." *Winnipeg Tribune*, 24 November 1972.

Hurley, Kent. *Contemporary Architects*. New York: St. Martin's Press, 1980.

Hutton, Jack. "It's All Politics Juba Tells Wolfe." *Winnipeg Tribune*, 21 June 1968.

Jacobs, Jane. *The Death and Life of Great American Cities*. New York: Vintage Books, 1961.

J.M. [James A. Murphy]. "Without Grounds: University of Winnipeg." *Progressive Architecture* (March 1973): 80–85.

Janz, Susan. "Own Practice Long, Hard Pull Local Woman Architect Feels." *Winnipeg Tribune*, 16 April 1971.

Jones, Frank. "Point Douglas Is the Scene of Slums and Fear of Them." *Winnipeg Tribune*, 11 July 1959.

Jones, Mel. "$30–Million Plan Being Considered for Downtown Core." *Winnipeg Tribune*, 21 August 1969.

Kahn, Eve M. "The Modest Architect." *House Beautiful* 137, 11 (November 1995).

Kalman, Harold. *A Concise History of Canadian Architecture*. Don Mills: Oxford University Press, 2000.

_____. *A History of Canadian Architecture*. Toronto: Oxford University Press, 1994.

Kamienski, Jan. "Winnipeg's Old Architecture Is Valuable Heritage." *Winnipeg Tribune*, 1 March 1975.

Kaplan, Harold. *Reform, Planning, and City Politics: Montreal, Winnipeg, Toronto*. Toronto: University of Toronto Press, 1982.

Kostka, V.J. "Manitoba." *The Journal (Royal Architectural Institute of Canada)* 35 (October 1958): 395.

Kroetsch, Robert. *Seed Catalogue*. Winnipeg: Turnstone Press, 1986.

Lahoda, Garry. "Redevelopment—A Beginning Not a Miracle." *Winnipeg Tribune*, 7 June 1963.

_____. "What This City Needs Is a Good Facelifting." *Winnipeg Tribune*, 1966 [file 7128]. University of Manitoba, Archives & Special
      Collections, Winnipeg Tribune Clipping Files.

Lambert, Phyllis, ed. *Mies in America*. Montreal: Canadian Centre for Architecture, 2001.

Lasker, David. "Mr. Church" [Gaboury]. *Western Living* (September 1985): 25–34.

Lauxerois, Jean. *L'Utopie Beaubourg, Vingt Ans Après*. Paris: Centre Georges Pompidou, 1996.

Ledger, Bronwen. "The Ageing Modern 3: Prairie Phoenix." *Canadian Architect* 40, 5 (May 1995): 35.

_____. "John C. Parkin: A Man and an Era." *Canadian Architect* 34 (May 1989): 43–46.

Lehrman, Jonas. "Centennial Hall, University of Winnipeg." *Canadian Architect* 18 (March 1973): 32–41.

_____. "Close, But No Cigar." *Winnipeg Free Press*, 19 September 1987.

_____. "Concert Hall Needs Environment Change?" *Winnipeg Free Press,* 13 April 1973, p. 19.

_____. "Downtown Winnipeg: Need for New Goals." *Canadian Architect* 20 (June 1975): 45–54.

_____. "MTC Building Lives Up to Expectations." *Winnipeg Free Press*, 18 January 1974.

_____. "Precious Blood." *Canadian Architect* 14 (October 1969): 38–47.

_____. "A Retreat for the Initiated?" *Canadian Architect* 17 (July 1972): 32–34.

_____. "Wildwood Park: The Ideal Place to Live." *Winnipeg Tribune*, 8 June 1973, p. 19.

_____. and Luke Rombout. "Winnipeg Art Gallery." *Canadian Architect* 17 (July 1972).

LeTourneau, Michele. "Architectural Drive–by." *Winnipeg Free Press*, 14 June 1998.

_____. "They Left Their Mark." *Winnipeg Free Press*, 11 January 1998.

Lev, Roy, Allan McKay, Vayden McMorris, W. Spotowski, and Jim Varro. "University of Manitoba." *The Journal (Royal Architectural
      Institute of Canada)* 27 (April 1950): 138–143.

Levin, Earl A. "City History and City Planning: The Local Historical Roots of the City Planning Function in Three Cities of the
      Canadian Prairies." PhD thesis, University of Manitoba, 1993.

Lisoway, Bob. "Winnipeg Downtown Development Plan." *Winnipeg Tribune*, 21 October 1972.

Little, Bruce. "Now It's Storefront Architects." *Winnipeg Tribune*, 19 April 1973.

Livesey, Graham, et al. *Twelve Modern Homes, 1945–1985*. Calgary: Aris Press, University of Calgary Press, 1995.

Lortie, Andre, ed. *The 60s: Montreal Thinks Big*. Montreal: Canadian Centre for Architecture, Douglas and McIntyre, 2004.

Lount, Frank R. "Report on 24 Unit Apartment Block, Winnipeg, Man." *The Journal (Royal Architectural Institute of Canada)*
      29 (June 1952): 163.

Lowe, Frank. "Art in the New Airports Gives Canada a Sophisticated Image." *Canadian Art* 21 (1964): 144–145.

Lucas, P. "On Wings of Commerce." *Fortune* 149, 6 (22 March 2004): 109–120.

Lum, Ken. "Canadian Cultural Policy." *Canadian Art* 16, 3 (Fall 1999): 76.

Lyon, D.M. "Recent Past Inventory Project: List of References re Architects." Winnipeg: Winnipeg Architecture Foundation,
      Historical Buildings Committee, City of Winnipeg, 2001.

Macdonald, Sir John A. "Debates of the House of Commons, Canada, 1883." In *Dominion Lands Policy*. Ed. Thomas H. Lewis. Toronto: McClelland and Stewart Ltd., 1973.

Manitoba Culture, Heritage and Citizenship. *Identifying Architectural Style in Manitoba*. Winnipeg: The Author, 1992.

Manitoba Hydro: History and Timeline. 1942–49; 1951–59; 1960–69; 1970–79.

<http://www.hydro.mb.ca/about_us/history/hep_1942.html>

<http://www.hydro.mb.ca/about_us/history/hep_1951.html>

<http://www.hydro.mb.ca/about_us/history/hep_1960.html>

<http://www.hydro.mb.ca/about_us/history/hep_1970.html>

[Accessed 11 August 2005]

Marcoe, Leonard. "Splendid Past Is Antidote." *Winnipeg Tribune*, 26 February 1978.

Mardon, Harry L. "Building Boom Shows Revival of City Spirit." *Winnipeg Tribune*, 21 June 1969.

Martin, Michael David. "The Landscape of Winnipeg's Wildwood Park." *Urban History Review/Revue d'histoire urbaine* 30 (October 2001): 22–39.

Massey, Vincent. *Royal Commission on National Development in the Arts*. Letters and Sciences Report. Ottawa: King's Printer, 1951.

Mata, Robert. "Winnipeg Becoming Planner's Dream." *Winnipeg Tribune*, 28 March 1974.

Matoff, Theodore. "City Hall: Prudence in Tyndall Stone Porridge." *Winnipeg Tribune*, 1965 [file 7128]. University of Manitoba, Archives & Special Collections, Winnipeg Tribune Clipping Files.

_____. "The Sorry State of Our Suburbia." *Winnipeg Tribune*, May 1965 [file 7128]. University of Manitoba, Archives & Special Collections, Winnipeg Tribune Clipping Files.

_____. "A Stimulating, Imaginative Space for People to Gather." *Winnipeg Tribune*, 1965 [file 7128]. University of Manitoba, Archives & Special Collections, Winnipeg Tribune Clipping Files.

Mayne, Alan. *The Imagined Slum: Newspaper Representation in Three Cities*. London: Leicester University Press, 1993.

McClintock, Harry. "The Big Rock Candy Mountain." Folk Song, Public Domain. In *Folk Song America*, Vol. 1 (1991, Smithsonian Collection 461), Track 5, performed by Harry McClintock (2:16).

McGarry, Michael. "A Visiting Architect Looks at Winnipeg." *Winnipeg Tribune*, 1968 [file 7128]. University of Manitoba, Archives & Special Collections, Winnipeg Tribune Clipping Files.

_____. "Shining Housing Project Rises from a City Slum." *Winnipeg Tribune*, 14 December 1967.

_____. "20–year Scheme Would Cost Millions." *Winnipeg Tribune*, 24 January 1968.

McGrath, T.M. *History of Canadian Airports*. Toronto: Lugus Publications, 1991.

McKaskell, Robert, ed. *Achieving the Modern: Canadian Abstract Painting and Design in the 1950s*. Winnipeg: Winnipeg Art Gallery, 1993.

Metcalfe, Bob. "Elmwood to Get 30 Pilot Homes." *Winnipeg Tribune*, 14 February 1956.

Metropolitan Corporation of Greater Winnipeg. *Metropolitan Urban Renewal Study: Final Report*. Winnipeg: The Author, 1967.

Metropolitan Corporation of Greater Winnipeg Planning Division. *Downtown Winnipeg Report*. Winnipeg: The Author, 1969.

Michener, Mel. "Manitoba." *The Journal (Royal Architectural Institute of Canada)* 33 (July 1956): 273.

Moodie, Susanna. *Roughing it in the Bush*. London: Richard Bentley, 1852.

Moody, H.H.G. "Branch Bank Interiors." *The Journal (Royal Architectural Institute of Canada)* 27 (October 1950): 354–355.

_____. "Comment on New Federal DPW Fee Schedule." *The Journal (Royal Architectural Institute of Canada)* 37 (September 1960): 402.

_____. "Criticism of Buildings Called Superficial." *Winnipeg Tribune*, 1965 [file 7128]. University of Manitoba, Archives & Special Collections, Winnipeg Tribune Clipping Files.

_____. "Editorial." *The Journal (Royal Architectural Institute of Canada)* 39 (July 1962): 29.

_____. "The Hudson's Bay Company, Edmonton, Alberta." *The Journal (Royal Architectural Institute of Canada)* 17 (February 1940): 22–24.

_____. "Manitoba." *The Journal (Royal Architectural Institute of Canada)* 34 (July 1957): 276.

_____. "The Profession—Registration and Codes of Conduct." *The Journal (Royal Architectural Institute of Canada)* 37 (July 1960): 306.

_____. "Provincial Page—Manitoba." *The Journal (Royal Architectural Institute of Canada)* 14 (September 1937): 196.

_____. "Viewpoint." *The Journal (Royal Architectural Institute of Canada)* 32 (January 1955): 26–27.

Moore, Robert E. "The Winnipeg Foundation Problem." *The Journal (Royal Architectural Institute of Canada)* 20 (November 1943): 198–199.

_____. "Provincial Page—Manitoba." *The Journal (Royal Architectural Institute of Canada)* 19 (November 1942): 226.

_____. "Provincial Page—Manitoba." *The Journal (Royal Architectural Institute of Canada)* 20 (June 1943): 95.

Mumford, Eric. *The CIAM Discourse on Urbanism: 1928–1960*. Cambridge, London: The MIT Press, 2000.

Munn, Fritz E. "Manitoba." *The Journal (Royal Architectural Institute of Canada)* 19 (July 1942): 154–155.

_____. "Provincial Page—Manitoba." *The Journal (Royal Architectural Institute of Canada)* 18 (March 1941): 52.

_____. "Provincial Page—Manitoba." *The Journal (Royal Architectural Institute of Canada)* 20 (February 1943): 25–26.

_____. "Provincial Page—Manitoba." *The Journal (Royal Architectural Institute of Canada)* 21 (March 1944): 61.

_____. "Provincial Page—Manitoba." *The Journal (Royal Architectural Institute of Canada)* 22 (March 1945): 64.

Nelson Jr., Carl R. "An Indoor Environment." *Canadian Architect* 17 (January 1972): 26–29.

_____, and Donald G. Crockett. *Wildwood Park Study*. Winnipeg: Carl R. Nelson, Jr., 1984.

New, William Herbert. *Land Sliding: Imagining Space, Presence, and Power in Canadian Writing*. Toronto: University of Toronto Press, 1997.

Newman, Roger. "A Silent Spring." *Winnipeg Tribune*, 28 April 1970.

_____. "Three Projects Hint Highrise Building Slump Over." *Winnipeg Tribune*, 4 May 1971.

Nixon, A.M. "Interiors in Architecture." *The Journal (Royal Architectural Institute of Canada)* 31 (March 1954): 80.

Norrie, Kenneth, and Douglas Owram. *A History of the Canadian Economy*. Toronto: Harcourt Brace Jovanovich Canada, 1991.

Organization for Economic Co-operation and Development. *The Teacher and Educational Change: A New Role*. Paris: The Author, 1974.

Osborne, Milton S. "Architecture and the Student." *The Journal (Royal Architectural Institute of Canada)* IX (December 1932): 259–260.

_____. "The Course in Architecture at the University of Manitoba." *The Journal (Royal Architectural Institute of Canada)* 22 (April 1945): 78–80.

_____. "Provincial Page—Manitoba." *The Journal (Royal Architectural Institute of Canada)* 14 (July 1937): 140.

_____. "Provincial Page—Manitoba." *The Journal (Royal Architectural Institute of Canada)* 14 (November 1937): 242.

_____. "Provincial Page—Manitoba." *The Journal (Royal Architectural Institute of Canada)* 15 (January 1938): 294.

_____. "Provincial Page—Manitoba." *The Journal (Royal Architectural Institute of Canada)* 15 (February 1938): 46.

_____. "Provincial Page—Manitoba." *The Journal (Royal Architectural Institute of Canada)* 15 (March 1938): 70.

_____. "Provincial Page—Manitoba." *The Journal (Royal Architectural Institute of Canada)* 15 (April 1938): 101.

_____. "Provincial Page—Manitoba." *The Journal (Royal Architectural Institute of Canada)* 16 (January 1939): 20–21.

_____. "Provincial Page—Manitoba." *The Journal (Royal Architectural Institute of Canada)* 16 (March 1939): 68–69.

_____. "Provincial Page—Manitoba." *The Journal (Royal Architectural Institute of Canada)* 17 (February 1940): 28.

_____. "Provincial Page—Manitoba." *The Journal (Royal Architectural Institute of Canada)* 17 (April 1940): 66–67.

_____. "School of Architecture, University of Manitoba." *The Journal (Royal Architectural Institute of Canada)* 19 (February 1941): 20–22.

Overy, Paul. *De Stijl*. London: Thames and Hudson, 1991.

Page, John E. "Farewell." *Architecture Canada* 44 (April 1967): 59–60.

Pape, Gordon. "Changed Housing Policy." *Winnipeg Tribune*, 18 August 1969.

Parfitt, Gilbert. "News from the Institute—Manitoba." *The Journal (Royal Architectural Institute of Canada)* 29 (April 1952): 121–122.

Parkin, John C. "Architecture in Canada since 1945: An Appraisal." *The Journal (Royal Architectural Institute of Canada)* 39 (January 1962): 33–40.

Parkinson, E. "Provincial Page—Manitoba." *The Journal (Royal Architectural Institute of Canada)* 20 (December 1943): 221.

Parr, Joy. *Domestic Goods: The Material, the Moral, and the Economic in the Postwar Years*. Toronto: University of Toronto Press, 1999.

Pope John XXIII. "Constitution of the Sacred Liturgy" of the Second Vatican Council. 4 December 1963. Documents of the Vatican II.

Pevsner, Nicholas. *Pioneers of the Modern Movement*. London: Faber and Faber, 1936.

_____. *Pioneers of Modern Design*. New York: Museum of Modern Art, 1949.

Porozny, Chris. "In Celebration." *Architecture Canada* 33 (September 1988): 43–44.

Powers, Alan. *Serge Chermayeff: Designer, Architect, Teacher*. London: RIBA, 2001.

Pratt, K.R.D. "Manitoba." *The Journal (Royal Architectural Institute of Canada)* 33 (March 1956): 104.

Price, Fred W. "From the Institute Headquarters." *The Journal (Royal Architectural Institute of Canada)* 43 (June 1966): 9.

Purdy, Sean. "From Place of Hope to Outcast Space: Territorial Regulation and Tenant Resistance in Regent Park Housing Project, 1949–2001." PhD thesis, Queen's University, 2003.

Raeside, Peter. "Govt. Approves Preliminary Plans for Main St. Changes." *Winnipeg Tribune*, 29 September 1965.

Raines, Edwin. "Manitoba." *The Journal (Royal Architectural Institute of Canada)* 34 (April 1957): 143.

Rasky, Frank. "The Agony and Ecstasy of Our Airport Art." *Canadian Weekly* (9–15 May 1964): 10.

_____. "Canada's New Temples of Travel." *Canadian Weekly* (2–8 May 1964): 12.

Reimer, Mavis. *Wildwood Park through the Years*. Winnipeg: Wildwood History Book Committee, 1989.

Rich, S. George. "Metropolitan Winnipeg, 1943–1961." In *Cities in the West: Papers of the Western Canada Urban History Conference, University of Winnipeg, October 1974*. Ed. A.R. McCormack and Ian MacPherson. Ottawa: National Museums of Canada, 1975.

Riley, Terence, and Barry Bergdoll. *Mies in Berlin*. New York: Museum of Modern Art, 2001.

Robertson, Heather. "Urban Renewal Not the Answer for the 'Really Poor.'" *Winnipeg Tribune*, 22 October 1966.

Rochon, Lisa. *Up North: Where Canada's Architecture Meets the Land*. Toronto: Key Porter Books Limited, 2005.

Rombout, Luke. "A Shape Both Startling and Unique." *Canadian Architect* 17 (July 1972): 31–32.

Ross, R. Bryan. "News from the Institute—Manitoba." *The Journal (Royal Architectural Institute of Canada)* 26 (February 1949): 59–60.

Roving Reporter. "Opening of the New School of Architecture and Convocation—University of Manitoba." *The Journal (Royal Architectural Institute of Canada)* 36 (December 1959): 420.

_____. "The Roving Reporter at the Assembly." *The Journal (Royal Architectural Institute of Canada)* 37 (July 1960): 281–285.

_____. "University of Manitoba." *The Journal (Royal Architectural Institute of Canada)* 36 (December 1959): 420–423.

Royal Architectural Institute of Canada. *Committee of Inquiry into the Design of the Residential Environment*. Report. Ottawa: The Author, 1960.

Russell, Frances. "Slums—A City's Cancer." *Winnipeg Tribune*, 8 October 1966..

Russell, G. Leslie. "Manitoba." *The Journal (Royal Architectural Institute of Canada)* 35 (August 1958): 318.

_____. "Viewpoint." *The Journal (Royal Architectural Institute of Canada)* 36 (August 1959): 291.

Russell, John A. "Annual Meeting of the Manitoba Association of Architects." *The Journal (Royal Architectural Institute of Canada)* 30 (May 1953): 130–131.

_____. "An Appreciation: Milton S. Osborne." *The Journal (Royal Architectural Institute of Canada)* 23 (August 1946): 193.

_____. "The Architect and Education." *The Journal (Royal Architectural Institute of Canada)* 36 (July 1959): 233–234

_____. "Architecture Education at the University of Manitoba." *The Journal (Royal Architectural Institute of Canada)* 31 (March 1954): 63.

_____. "Architecture for Canadians." *Winnipeg Tribune*, 9 January 1956.

_____. "Canadian Architecture." *The Journal (Royal Architectural Institute of Canada)* 33 (May 1956): 154–156.

_____. *The Concept of the New Winnipeg Art Gallery Building*. Winnipeg: Winnipeg Art Gallery, 1967.

_____. "Design for Acting." *The Journal (Royal Architectural Institute of Canada)* 18 (May 1941): 79–82.

_____. "Life Begins at Forty." In *Perspective*. University of Manitoba: Students Architectural Society, 1953.

_____. "Light and Colour in Design." *The Journal (Royal Architectural Institute of Canada)* 30 (July 1953): 183–186.

_____. "Manitoba." *The Journal (Royal Architectural Institute of Canada)* 19 (October 1942): 212–213.

_____. "Manitoba." *The Journal (Royal Architectural Institute of Canada)* 24 (July 1947): 256–257.

_____. "Manitoba." *The Journal (Royal Architectural Institute of Canada)* 24 (November 1947): 416–417.

_____. "Manitoba." *The Journal (Royal Architectural Institute of Canada)* 25 (February 1948): 63–64.

_____. "Manitoba." *The Journal (Royal Architectural Institute of Canada)* 33 (December 1956): 483.

_____. "The Mid–Continent Mosaic." *The Journal (Royal Architectural Institute of Canada)* 37 (April 1960): 133.

_____. "A Modern City Hall." *The Saturday Review* 23 (30 December 1933).

_____. "Our Lively Arts." *Queen's Quarterly* LXII, 2 (Summer 1955): 233–242.

_____. "Planning for the Future." *The Journal (Royal Architectural Institute of Canada)* 32 (June 1955): 193–196.

_____. "Programming a School of Architecture Building." *The Journal (Royal Architectural Institute of Canada)* 37 (August 1960): 325–328.

_____. "The Saga of City Hall." *The Journal (Royal Architectural Institute of Canada)* 37 (January 1960): 35–38.

_____. "The University and Architecture." *The Journal (Royal Architectural Institute of Canada)* 32 (October 1955): 361–364.

_____. "The University of Manitoba." *The Journal (Royal Architectural Institute of Canada)* 36 (June 1959): 191–197.

_____. "University of Manitoba, School of Architecture." *The Journal (Royal Architectural Institute of Canada)* 36 (March 1959): 64.

_____. "Viewpoint." *The Journal (Royal Architectural Institute of Canada)* 32 (October 1955): 400.

_____. "Viewpoint." *The Journal (Royal Architectural Institute of Canada)* 36 (May 1959): 170–171.

_____. "Vocational Opportunities for the Architectural Graduate: Manitoba." *The Journal (Royal Architectural Institute of Canada)* 25 (May 1948): 139.

_____. "Winnipeg City Hall Competition." *The Journal (Royal Architectural Institute of Canada)* 35 (May 1958): 196.

_____. "The Winnipeg Show." *The Journal (Royal Architectural Institute of Canada)* 33 (July 1956): 274.

_____, et al. *Ten Farm Houses*. Winnipeg: Planning Research Centre, School of Architecture, University of Manitoba, 1948.

Russell, N.C.H. "Manitoba." *The Journal (Royal Architectural Institute of Canada)* 34 (November 1957): 454–455.

_____. "Manitoba." *The Journal (Royal Architectural Institute of Canada)* 36 (July 1959): 254.

Schachter, Harry. "Major City Construction on Schedule." *Winnipeg Tribune*, 10 August 1967.

Schugurensky, Daniel. "1971: UK Open University Opens its Doors." In *History of Education: Selected Moments of the 20th Century*. [Available on-line <http://fcis.oise.utoronto.ca/-dschugurensky/assignment1/1971ukou.html>. Accessed October 2005]

Searle, James E. "Editorial: Invitation to Winnipeg." *The Journal (Royal Architectural Institute of Canada)* 37 (April 1960): 129–155.

Secter, Marcia E. "Centennial Hall Interiors." *Canadian Architect* 18 (March 1973): 37–45.

_____. "A Tribute to Planners." *Canadian Architect* 17 (January 1972): 34–37.

Seeley, J.R., R.A. Sime, and E.W. Loosley. *Crescentwood Heights: A Study of the Culture of Suburban Life*. New York: Wiley, 1956.

Sembach, Klaus Jurgen. *Modern Furniture Designs 1950–80*. Pennsylvania: Schiffer Books, 1997.

Sewell, John. *The Shape of the City: Toronto Struggles with Modern Planning*. Toronto: University of Toronto Press, 1993.

Shave, Gordon. "Trail of Empty Office Space in Wake of City Building Spree." *Winnipeg Tribune*, 17 September 1963.

Shear, John Knox. "Competition for U.S. Chancery Building, London." *Architectural Record* 118 (April 1956).

Sheffield, Edward T. *University Development: The Past Five Years and the Next Ten*. Ottawa: Canadian University Foundation, 1961.

Shields, Carol. *The Republic of Love*. London: Fourth Estate, 2003.

Siemens, J. "John A. Russell." *Warehouse 14* (2005): 45–74.

Silver, Nathan. *The Making of the Beaubourg: A Building Biography of the Centre Pompidou Paris*. Cambridge: MIT Press, 1994.

Simmins, Geoffrey. *Calgary Modern: 1947–1967*. Calgary: The Nickle Arts Museum, 2000.

_____, ed. *Documents in Canadian Architecture*. Peterborough: Broadview, 1992.

Simpson, E.G., and W.T. Haxby. "City of Winnipeg." *The Journal (Royal Architectural Institute of Canada)* 38 (October 1961): 66–68.

Smith, Ernest J. "Manitoba." *The Journal (Royal Architectural Journal of Canada)* 25 (April 1948): 135.

_____. "School of Architecture." *The Journal (Royal Architectural Institute of Canada)*, 37 (August 1960): 317–324.

_____. "Viewpoint." *The Journal (Royal Architectural Journal of Canada)* 32 (June 1955): 226.

_____. "Viewpoint." *The Journal (Royal Architectural Institute of Canada)* 33 (March 1956): 103.

_____. "Whither the Practice of Architecture?" *Canadian Architect* 23 (July 1976): 8.

Smith, C. Ray. *Supermannerism: New Attitudes in Post Modern Architecture*. New York: E.P. Dutton, 1977.

Smith, P., and B. Toulier. *Airport Architecture of the Thirties*. Paris: Caisse nationale des monuments historiques et des sites, Editions du patrimoine, 2000.

Southern Alberta Art Gallery, Gerald Forseth, and Victoria Baster. *Lethbridge Modern*. Lethbridge: Southern Alberta Art Gallery, 2002.

Steer, Carol, ed. "Culture Recreation Sports and Exhibition Buildings in Manitoba 1990." Winnipeg: Province of Manitoba, 1992.

Stegner, Wallace. "A Geography of Hope." In *A Society to Match Our Scenery*. Boulder: University of Colorado Press, 1991.

_____. "Thoughts in a Dry Land." In *Where the Bluebird Sings to the Lemonade Springs: Living and Writing in the West*. New York: Penguin Books, 1992.

Stewart, George A. "Manitoba." *The Journal (Royal Architectural Institute of Canada)* 36 (February 1959): 61.

Stewart, Ian A. "Global Transformation and Economic Policy." In *Towards a Just Society: The Trudeau Years*. Ed. Thomas S. Axworthy and Pierre Elliott Trudeau. Toronto: Viking, 1990.

Stewart, Lindsay. "Architecture of a City." *Where Winnipeg* (May/June 2002): 14–15.

Students Architectural Society. *Newsletter 1* (Nov. 1964). Students Architectural Society University of Manitoba. Winnipeg: The Author, 1964.

Sudjic, Deyan. *The 100 Mile City*. London: HarperCollins, 1992.

Tallon, Doris M. "Winnipeg City Halls." *Winnipeg Real Estate News* (24 November 1989).

Taylor, Robin. "Unique Arrowhead a Winner." *Winnipeg Tribune*, 19 December 1967, pp. 1–2.

Thomas, Christopher, and Kim Reinhardt. "Victoria Moderna (1945–1975): Of Civic Myth and Difference in Modern Architecture." *Journal of the Society for the Study of Architecture in Canada* 26, 3–4 (2001): 3–14.

Thomas, Lewis H., ed. *Dominion Lands Policy*. Toronto: McClelland and Stewart Limited, 1973.

Thompson, R.L. "MAA Annual Meeting." *The Journal (Royal Architectural Institute of Canada)* 34 (May 1957): 188.

Thompson, William P. *The Architecture of Manitoba: An Exhibit*. Winnipeg: The Author, 1970.

_____. "Green, Blankstein, Russell." In *The Canadian Encyclopedia II*. Ed. James H. Marsh. Edmonton: Hurtig Publishers, 1988.

_____. "Smith, Ernest John." In *The Canadian Encyclopedia III*. Ed. James H. Marsh. Edmonton: Hurtig Publishers, 1988.

_____. *Winnipeg Architecture*. Winnipeg: Queenston House, 1975.

Thrift, Eric W. "Greater Winnipeg, Manitoba." *The Journal (Royal Architectural Institute of Canada)* 23 (November 1946): 272–275.

_____. "Manitoba." *The Journal (Royal Architectural Institute of Canada)* 35 (September 1958): 354.

_____. Foreword from "Metropolitan Plan—Greater Winnipeg." *The Journal (Royal Architectural Institute of Canada)* 25 (July 1948): 219.

Tolstoy, Leo. "How Much Land Does a Man Need." *Leo Tolstoy: Stories and Legends*. Trans. Louise and Aylmer Maude. New York: Pantheon Books, 1946.

Underwood, McLellan and Associates, Ltd. *Proposed Northern Freeway across Canadian Pacific Railway Yards: Cost Estimates of Alternatives, October 10th, 1968*. Winnipeg: Metropolitan Corporation of Greater Winnipeg, Streets and Transit Division, 1968.

UNESCO. *50 Years of Education*. www.unesco.org. [Accessed 19 December 2005]

WINNIPEG MODERN
Architecture: 1945-1975

University of Manitoba. "Annual Report of the School of Architecture and Fine Arts 1946–47." *University of Manitoba Calendar*. Winnipeg: The Author, 1946–47; 1947–48; 1948–49; 1949–50; 1950–51; 1951–52; 1952–53.

University of Manitoba, Faculty of Architecture, Planning Research Centre. *Low Cost Housing Study of Winnipeg: Interim Report*. Winnipeg: The Author, 1955.

University of Manitoba. *From Rural Parkland to Urban Centre: One Hundred Years of Growth at the University of Manitoba, 1877–1977*. Winnipeg: Hyperion Press, 1978.

Veilleux, Michele. "Da Roza Suggests Stucco All Around and Some Expression." *Winnipeg Free Press*, April 17, 1968, p. 17.

Venne, Gerard. "College of Fellows." *The Journal (Royal Architectural Institute of Canada)* 42 (April 1965): 6–R7.

Walker, David. *The Great Winnipeg Dream: The Re-development of Portage and Main*. Oakville: Mosaic, 1979.

Ward, David, and Olivier Zunz. "Between Rationalism and Pluralism: Creating the Modern City." In *The Landscape of Modernity: New York City, 1900–1940*. Ed. David Ward and Olivier Zunz. Baltimore: Johns Hopkins University Press, 1992.

Ward, J.T.L. "Manitoba." *The Journal (Royal Architectural Institute of Canada)* 35 (February 1958): 67.

Ward, Peter. *A History of Domestic Space: Privacy and the Canadian Home*. Vancouver: University of British Columbia Press, 1999.

Welfare Council of Greater Winnipeg, *Housing Committee Report*. Winnipeg: The Author, 1955.

Werier, Val. "About Winnipeg's No. 1 Corner." *Winnipeg Tribune*, 4 March 1971.

_____. "An Arts Centre Needs People." *Winnipeg Tribune*, 8 Feb 1968.

_____. "Ban the Cars, Not the People." *Winnipeg Tribune*, 6 February 1971.

_____. "A City Is Not a Packaged Product." *Winnipeg Tribune*, 19 May 1970.

_____. "For the City's 100th Birthday." *Winnipeg Tribune*, 2 April 1971.

_____. "Getting around Portage and Main." *Winnipeg Tribune*, 20 December 1972.

_____. "Great Chance at No. 1 Corner." *Winnipeg Tribune*, 16 March 1971.

_____. "A Home Can Be Just as Cheap." *Winnipeg Tribune*, 19 December 1969.

_____. "A Horrible Example for Architecture Students." *Winnipeg Free Press*, 16 February 1985.

_____. "Mall On Market Street." *Winnipeg Tribune*, 10 June 1967.

_____. "Most Exciting Building in Town." *Winnipeg Tribune*, 1964 [file 1485]. University of Manitoba, Archives & Special Collections, Winnipeg Tribune Clipping Files.

_____. "Mr. Richardson and No. 1 Corner." *Winnipeg Tribune*, 11 December 1971.

_____. "Old Buildings Can Be Beautiful." *Winnipeg Tribune*, 22 May 1971.

_____. "Our Latest Building for Culture." *Winnipeg Tribune*, 10 August 1971.

_____. "Spark Needed at Portage and Main." *Winnipeg Tribune*, 1970 [file 7128]. University of Manitoba, Archives & Special Collections, Winnipeg Tribune Clipping Files.

_____. "Sun and Gadgets: Musts for the Modern Home," *Winnipeg Tribune*, 8 November 1952.

_____. "Support for the Portage Plaza." *Winnipeg Tribune*, 11 March 1971.

_____. "Support Grows for No. 1 Corner." *Winnipeg Tribune*, 11 May 1971.

_____. "We Have Princess, Vintage 1882," *Winnipeg Tribune*, 25 August 1972.

Wiebe, Rudy. *Playing Dead: A Contemplation Concerning the Arctic*. Edmonton: NeWest Publishers, 1989.

Whitcomb, Edward A. *A Short History of Manitoba*. Stittsville, Ontario: Canada's Wings, 1982.

Whiteson, Leon. *Modern Canadian Architecture*. Edmonton: Hurtig Publishers, 1983.

Wilbur Smith and Associates. *Report on Traffic, Transit, Parking, Metropolitan Winnipeg*. Connecticut: Metropolitan Planning Commission of Greater Winnipeg, 1957.

Williams, Raymond. "When Was Modernism?" *New Left Review* 175 (May-June 1989): 48–52.

Willis, Carol. "Form Follows Finance: The Empire State Building." In *The Landscape of Modernity: New York City, 1900–1940*. Ed. David Ward and Olivier Zunz. Baltimore: Johns Hopkins University Press, 1992.

Windsor-Liscombe, Rhodri, ed. *The New Spirit: Modern Architecture in Vancouver, 1938–1963*. Montreal: Centre for Architecture/ Vancouver: Douglas and McIntyre, 1997.

_____. "The Female Spaces of Modernism: A Western Canadian Perspective." *Prospects* 26 (2001): 667–700.

_____. "Grounding the New Perspectives of Modernism: Canadian Airports and the Reconfiguration of the Cultural and Political Territory." *Journal of the Society for the Study of Architecture in Canada* 28, 1–2 (2003).

Winnipeg Art Gallery Competition. Report of the Jury. *Architecture Canada* 45 (February 1968): 43–48.

Winnipeg Council of Social Agencies, Committee on Housing. *Report: Housing in Winnipeg*. Winnipeg: The Author, 1943.

Winnipeg Emergency Housing Department. *Report: Housing Survey of Central Area of Winnipeg. Bounded by Main St., Sherbrook St., Notre Dame Ave., Canadian Pacific Railway Yards*. Winnipeg: The Author, 1955.

Winnipeg Urban Renewal and Rehabilitation Board. *A Proposal for the Renewal of an Area of Central Winnipeg Bounded by Selkirk Avenue, CPR Yards, Salter Street, Main Street, Based on Urban Renewal Study no. 5*. Winnipeg: The Author, 1961.

Wright, Virginia. *Modern Furniture in Canada, 1920 to 1970*. Toronto: University of Toronto Press, 1997.

Queen's Printer and Controller of Stationery. *Treaties 1 and 2 Between Her Majesty the Queen and the Cheppewa and Cree Indians of Manitoba and Country Adjacent with Adhesions*. Transcribed Edmond Cloutier. Ottawa: The Author, 1957.

Interviews

Blankstein, Morley. Interview by Serena Keshavjee. Summer 2002. Winnipeg.

Bornstein, Eli. Interview by Kelly Crossman. January 1999. Saskatoon.

Brown, Bernard. Interview by Bernard Flaman. February 2000. Winnipeg.

Burns, Gae. Interview by Serena Keshavjee. Summer 2004. Winnipeg.

Christie, James. Interview by Serena Keshavjee. Summer 2002. Calgary.

Da Roza, Gustavo. Interview by Terri Fuglem. May 2003, Winnipeg, and December 2003, Vancouver.

Gaboury, Étienne. Interview by Faye Hellner. 2004 and 2005. Winnipeg.

Gillmor, Douglas. Interview by Serena Keshavjee. Summer 2002. Winnipeg.

Michener, Mel. Interview by Serena Keshavjee. Summer 2002. Winnipeg.

Morse, Lewis. Interview by Aldona Dziedziejko. 28 April 2003. Vancouver.

_____. Interview by Peter McCormack. 13 April 2004. Winnipeg.

_____. Interview by Serena Keshavjee. 08 March 2005, 19 January 2006. Winnipeg.

Stechesen, Leslie. Interview by Serena Keshavjee. Summer 2004. Winnipeg.

_____. Interview by Faye Hellner. 2005. Winnipeg.

Thordarson, David. Interview by Kelly Crossman. December 1998. Winnipeg.

CONTRIBUTORS

David Burley is a Professor of History at the University of Winnipeg. His research has been in the area of urban social history and he is currently engaged in a study of the spatial dimensions of inequality and class formation in Winnipeg. He has written articles and essays for books and journals, and is an editorial board member of *Urban History Review/Revue d'histoire urbaine.*

Kelly Crossman is an Associate Professor, in the School of Architecture, at Carleton University. His primary areas of interest are Canadian architecture, and the history and theory of contemporary architecture and planning. He is the author of several articles and books, including *Architecture in Transition: From Art to Practice.*

Herbert Enns is a Professor of Architecture and Director of the New Media Program at the University of Manitoba. He is Chair of *MOSAIC: The Journal of Interdisciplinary Studies in Literature* and Contributing Editor to *Canadian Architect.* He is one of three partners in the multi-disciplinary design practice, *OS 1 Design Inc.*, and actively engaged in numerous product, graphic, and architectural design commissions. His *Experimental Buildings at Shoal Lake* have been published in Canada and internationally.

Bernard Flaman is a registered architect who has worked in Germany, Toronto, Vancouver, and Saskatoon, and is currently Heritage Architect for the Province of Saskatchewan. He has presented papers on the development of Canadian airports in the 1960s, and participated in UNESCO's policy development on modern heritage.

Terri Fuglem is an Assistant Professor in the Department of Architecture at the University of Manitoba. She has practised in Ottawa, Montreal, and London, England, where she worked for Lorenzo Apicella and Associates (now Pentagram). She is Co-Editor of Design for the *Journal of Architectural Education.*

Faye Hellner is a retired Professor in the Faculty of Architecture at the University of Manitoba, and holds a University of Manitoba Award for Excellence in Teaching. She was also Executive Director of the Faculty of Architecture's Partner's Program. She is the editor and concept designer of the book *Étienne Gaboury*, winner of the "Brave New Words" Manitoba Writing and Publishing Award for best-illustrated book in 2005.

Serena Keshavjee is an Assistant Professor in the Department of History at the University of Winnipeg, where she teaches Modern Western art and architecture courses. Her primary area of research is French Symbolist art, and nineteenth-century transcendental philosophies. She is currently editing a special issue on science and spirituality for RACAR, the *Canadian Art History Review.*

Martin Tessler is a photographer whose architectural and landscape photographs have appeared on the covers and interiors of numerous Canadian and American magazines, such as *Architectural Review*, *Canadian Architect*, *Metropolitan Home*, *Elle Décor*, and *Bauwelt* (Germany). He recently produced a series of photographs in a collaboration with author Douglas Coupland for the book *Souvenir of Canada 2.*